# BOXCAR POLITICS

# BOXCAR POLITICS

## The Hobo in U.S. Culture and Literature, 1869–1956

JOHN LENNON

UNIVERSITY OF MASSACHUSETTS PRESS
Amherst and Boston

Printed in the United States of America

ISBN 978-1-62534-120-4 (alk. pbk); 119-8 (alk. hardbk)

Designed by Sally Nichols
Set in Monotype Bell
Printed and bound by Maple-Vail, Inc.

Library of Congress Cataloging-in-Publication Data

Lennon, John., 1975–
Boxcar politics : the hobo in U.S. culture and literature, 1869/1956 / John Lennon.
pages cm
Includes bibliographical references and index.
ISBN 978-1-62534-120-4 (pbk. : alk. paper) — ISBN 978-1-62534-119-8
(hardcover : alk. paper)
1. American literature—19th century—History and criticism. 2. American literature—20th century—History and criticism. 3. Tramps in literature. 4. Homelessness in literature. 5. Marginality, Social, in literature. 6. Social values—United States—History. 7. Political culture—United States—History. 8. Tramps—United States—History. I. Title. II. Title: Hobo in U.S. culture and literature, 1869/1956.
PS217.T67L46 2014
810.9'3526942—dc23
2014019932

British Library Cataloguing-in-Publication Data
A catalogue record for this book is available from the British Library.

# CONTENTS

# ACKNOWLEDGMENTS

Although the romantic view of a scholar is of a solitary figure typing furiously away in a book-lined darkened office, the truth is that this manuscript was formed through myriad interactions and conversations with numerous people who all contributed to its creation: librarians who tracked down citations, conference participants who came up to me after my talks and told me stories of relatives hopping trains, colleagues at my various academic institutions who encouraged me, friends and family who listened to me go on and on about trains. This manuscript was a long time coming, and there is no way to thank everyone—or even close to everyone—who helped me along throughout the years. So here's the deal: if you picked up this book and thought to yourself, "I remember talking to John about hobos," then next time we meet, I'm buying.

There are, though, a few people that I want to acknowledge for their sustained support and help. Seth Moglen and Dawn Keetley, my key mentors at Lehigh University, offered me both guidance and friendship as I worked through the early stages of my ideas. Chris Robé and Tony Bleach, also present at this project's naissance, have been consistent sounding boards for my wild conjectures—I am lucky to call them friends. Norman Yetman gave a naive graduate student a chance by accepting my article in *American Studies*. Eric Lott, Cindi Katz, and Donald Pease—along with everyone I interacted with at the Futures of American Studies conference—helped me believe in this project (and myself as a scholar). I also owe a heartfelt note of thanks to my external readers who offered wonderful revision advice and to Brian Halley, my editor at University of Massachusetts Press, who has helped shepherd this manuscript to print. Finally, the University of South Florida has provided me a wonderful opportunity to complete this project, and I want to thank my colleagues for their encouragement.

Finally, I would like to thank my family for their unfailing love and encouragement. My parents, John and Helen, and my sisters, Mary Ellen and Kathleen, have been constant sources of strength and love. My daughters, Ellie and Abby, who were born during the years of writing this book and have listened to many a bedtime story about hobos, have allowed my heart to grow exponentially. And finally, to my wife, Liz, my steadfast partner and friend from the first word of the very first draft, I dedicate this book to you.

# BOXCAR POLITICS

# INTRODUCTION

The hobo is a perennial figure ensconced in the cultural fabric of the United States. From the *Chicago Tribune* op-ed piece at the end of the nineteenth century calling for housewives to poison unsuspecting train riders to a recurring comic figure on *The Simpsons* in the nascent years of the twenty-first century, the hobo figure has been on the periphery of public debate and popular cultural sensibilities for over a century. How we remember this figure, however, has drastically changed. Once categorized as members of a homeless army who needed to be jailed or killed, in the present day hobos are punch lines on late-night television or celebrated grandfatherly figures in hobo conventions throughout the United States. No longer feared, the hobo has evolved into a safe image of Americana. *Boxcar Politics: The Hobo in U.S. Culture and Literature, 1869–1956* reestablishes the hobo's political thorns. This study maps the political arc of the hobo from the introduction of the transcontinental railroad to the Federal Aid Highway Act of 1956.

As workers struggled with their alienation from capitalism that decimated the inherited social structures of modern society, naturalist and modernist writers detailed the personal and collective trauma inflicted by these national transformations. But although numerous labor historians and literary critics have focused on the inherent losses felt by the working class, detailing the various political movements formed to combat these injuries, few studies have focused exclusively on hobos marginalized *within* this social bracket. Seen, at best, as weights that slowed the labor movement down or, at worst, enemies of the working class and pawns to the capitalists, the hobo has been understood as a selfish, apolitical figure. Complicating this view, I contend that hoboing was not just a mode of travel; rather, in varying degrees, it was a distinct form of resistive politics.

I am not interested in exploring the issue of resistance solely in terms of organized political movements; in *Boxcar Politics* I analyze hobos' physical movements, locating within these practical travels a wide array of micropolitical tactics and subversions. Some of these movements led to temporary individual gains, while others led to overt communal protest. Resistance, therefore, is examined not only in the documented radical unionized politics that formed among a subgroup of hobos in the early twentieth century but also in the isolated movements of desperate men and women jumping into passing boxcars, heading in the general direction of a long-sought-after job. *Boxcar Politics* rereads the hobo figure in U.S. culture and literature by bridging the lived and theoretical expressions of hobos, locating resistance in their transient bodies and negotiations of invisibility. The hobo's site of resistance was found in the very act of hopping a train, the space created when individuals detached themselves from recognized and organized places and attempted to construct spaces that reflected their social and political identity.

Our knowledge of the hobo spaces formed within the rolling boxcars throughout the United States is fragmented; hiding in the shadows of train cars, hobos were mostly hidden from view. Hobo spaces, however, were articulated in a variety of textual forms, revealing a vibrant transient subculture that helps expand and complicate static, traditional depictions of the working class. If, as Laura Hapke explains in *Labor's Text*, representations of workers throughout U.S. literary history have mostly "remained married to the ideology of American exceptionalism" and selected upward mobility, concentrated examinations of the hobo figure allow for an open marriage by focusing the discussion on transient laborers who did not travel vertically on figurative ladders of success, but horizontally, along well-worn rail lines.[1]

To analyze the hobo, then, is to examine the material relationship between a transient worker and a train. The railroad, from its vital importance to the Northern victory in the Civil War until its eventual decline by the middle of the twentieth century, was promoted by politicians and business leaders as a technological wonder that compressed space and standardized time. Helping to underwrite a self-serving national identity, the railroad was deemed a continuation of the American exceptionalist character. The transcontinentals, as railroad scholars repeatedly state, helped create the modern corporate world, and, with it, these steam-blowing goliaths have become the premier symbol for U.S.-based capitalism in the late nineteenth and early twentieth centuries that institutionalized a form of corporate welfare.[2] That the railroads transformed American identity and culture is undisputed; it is within the margins of this narrative, though, where one can find hidden challenges to this nationalizing narrative. *Boxcar Politics* examines the complicated interrelationship whereby a subculture created by this emerging finance capitalism also created—in a variety of ways—its own spaces of resistance. In stark contrast to the progressiveness that the railroad supposedly offered stood the maligned hobo, a self-identified itinerant worker who survived by illegally hopping trains.

These itinerant workers and their resistive acts can and have been read as solely individualistic; hobos, regardless of their political motivations, hopped trains so they could get somewhere else. This underlying practical motivation led Nels Anderson, author of *The Hobo*, one of the first book-length studies of the train rider, to conclude that the hobo was an apolitical being whose individualistic nature and favored mobility "unfits him for organized group life." Hobos, however, have always been a part of group life as members of the working class. As Frank Tobias Higbie recounts in *Indispensable Outcasts*, hobos were integral laborers in the communities that they briefly inhabited during the Progressive Era and thus an important, albeit mostly misrepresented, subject for labor historians. This misrepresentation of hobos as outside of the working class, underwritten by federal laws and enacted in physical incarceration and abuse, has been one reason why, even though hobos have been essential players in the political economy of the nation, they have been mostly disparaged. Tim Creswell's *The Tramp in America* specifically examines the ways hobos were alienated, tracing the moral panic caused by these shunned transients and detailing the draconian laws passed through legislative bodies that attempted to delimit the hobo's mobility. Todd DePastino's *Citizen Hobo* also focuses on the disempowerment of the traveling worker. In a number of wide-ranging examples, he shows how the hobo was a relational figure in understanding the changing socioeconomic dynamics of the country after the Civil War, pinpointing their homelessness as systemically disenfranchising them from being recognized social citizens in the United States. Mark Wyman's monograph, *Hoboes*, offers an important alternative ethnic and racial labor history of the development of the West, focusing on migrant workers from the 1870s to the 1920s and detailing how their transit labor was an important component to the agribusiness of the United States.[3]

These four histories have added significantly to the study of hobos, uncovering critical documents and marking the hobo as an important figure of study. *Boxcar Politics* builds on this rich and complex history of the hobo as worker while offering a new lens to view this figure. This study analyzes the hobo's journey in distinctly political terms. By hopping trains, hobos, both symbolically and practically, offered their bodies as resistance to the progress of an expanding capitalist society that the transcontinental railroad promised in its billowing smoke and roaring wheels. While previous studies have analyzed the connections of the hobo with radical and reactionary political organizations, this study presses the interpretation of the boxcar ride further by examining how poor individuals desiring to hop trains became influential in the body politic of modern American society and culture. Granted, hobos did not start a revolution, nor did they mount a rigorous political platform with a concentrated message; one will not, after all, find a separate entry on the hobo in the thorough *Encyclopedia of the American Left*.[4] But by hopping trains and disappearing into boxcars in one locale and entering a new geographic area the next day, hobos offered subcultural resistance to the "progress" of a nation newly underwritten by monopoly interests and embodied by the train. By taking on the railroad in physical ways for practical reasons, the jetsam of American society—poor, homeless, mobile laborers—were asserting themselves within the U.S. political economy of the nineteenth and early twentieth centuries.

In turn, from both inside and outside the working class, hobos were seen as pariahs, divested of their identifying attributes as laborers and disregarded as homeless deviants. Although the idea of the worker has been a privileged analytical concept, with traditional lines rigidly dividing the proletariat from the lumpen proletariat, this study dispenses with this foundationalist epistemology that marginalizes the itinerant laborer. Instead, my interpretation of the hobo, itself a concept that emerged from a contradictory ideological discursive universe, forms a hermeneutic that highlights the intertwining relationships between hobos, their subculture, and the train. Examining the hobo as a relationally derived concept allows us to unpack this idea of resistance, oftentimes expressed by hobos in the hidden, dark recesses of boxcars, and illuminate the ways marginalized transient workers exerted a political voice both singularly and collectively.[5]

It is this amorphousness of resistance—the way that it was enacted by participants trying to render themselves invisible from those who wished to stop them from riding—that requires an analytical framework that conceptualizes a boxcar politics of a subculture that was diverse, fragmented, and consistently adapting to its social and physical environment. Narrowly examining the hobo exclusively in terms of the historical record will not allow for an exhaustive discussion of the complexity of hobo resistance, as these renderings tend to recognize and privilege the mobilizations of people in terms of *organized* mass protest. But what about the movements of those individuals—the mobile poor on the fringes of the working class—who were physically slammed together as they shared a bouncing ride in a boxcar, all the while tactically sharing stories and resources to find sustenance and employment? These shared rides happened away from the police, social scientists, welfare organizations, and religious groups documenting the hobos' movements.

Relying solely on historical documents does not help us conceptualize the journey of the poor out-of-work hobo who, alone, hopped a train in Conception Junction, Missouri; rode with radical union organizers through the wheat fields of Great Bend, Kansas; learned which "unfriendly" local towns to avoid from a rail worker in a train yard in Cedar Rapids, Iowa; and, after hearing about a job from a fellow hobo in a jungle outside of Butte, Montana, ended up working for a winter in a Chicago slaughterhouse. By hopping a train, the individual hobo entered into fluid heterogeneous groupings of other working-class members who shared an illegal status and whose subsistence-level survival tactics—let alone organized, aggressive unionizing activities—placed them in a complex relationship to the specific modernity that the railroads helped create. The hobos relied on the train to get them where they needed to go, but these trains also became potential politicized spaces of resistance where members of the subculture would meet, talk, scheme, and help one another.

While there have been excellent histories of the hobo published, these approaches rely on, as cultural critic Alberto Melucci states, a "myopia of the visible" and do not allow for a critical reflection on the invisible movements of hobos who were only successful if they could disappear from the policing agents searching for them.[6] To create an analytical framework that accounts for these "invisible" rides and that considers resistance in expansive, rather than narrowly defined, terms, an integrated approach that intertwines a historical account of the hobo with a theoretical articulation of these rides is needed. To this end, *Boxcar Politics* frames its analysis of the hobo in terms of two types of circulation: actual historical bodies traveling throughout the United States in the late nineteenth and early twentieth centuries and the hobo figure as a cultural body created and used by various entities to promote particular ideological narratives. In Creswell's analysis of the tramp, he discovers that this transient figure was "made up." In other words, this newly formed category of homeless in the nineteenth century was brought into being by the slippery interrelationship between scientific and artistic renderings of the hobo, where "knowing" and "representing" the poor, mobile, marginalized body often were seen as the same. This novel categorization of the homeless was created and made a focus of study by such disparate fields as sociology, eugenics, vaudeville commentary, literary studies, and documentary photography; all these fields helped birth this particular figure.[7] To read the hobo in political terms, then, it is important to build on Creswell's thesis, crossing disciplinary boundaries and following the hobo along the wide-ranging tracks that take us through a diverse hermeneutic landscape.

The analytical framework of this book, ensconced in an American studies tradition, allows for a range of disciplinary conversations (criminology, literary, film, cultural, and Marxist studies) to dialogue with one another when interpreting the hobo. There are, though, two main analytical supports for my framework. The first is a historical analysis of the hobo as a transient worker whose mobility is dependent on hopping trains. The hobo often has been excluded from conversations of the working class, and this project reveals the ideological underpinnings that helped uncouple itinerant laborers from the stationary members of the working class while also highlighting particular bonds that remained intact. Interrelating the rise of the railroad with the formation of the hobo figure, the floating proletariat emerges as a distinct political player in working-class politics in the late nineteenth and early twentieth centuries. In my first chapter's introduction as well as in each subsequent chapter's case study, therefore, a class-based historical record forms the bedrock for my cultural and literary analysis.

The second main analytical support of this study is a theoretical examination of the hobo as a subcultural resistive figure. Through this lens the hobo's invisible moments can be visualized and articulated. Although the term *subculture* was not used widely until the 1940s, the itinerant as a resistive figure of normalizing culture has been around, as subcultural historian Ken Gelder states, since at least the 1560s, when *The Fraternity of Vagabonds* documented the stratified classification of marginalized individuals in Elizabethan England.[8] The study of subcultures, however, popularized by the Chicago School in the 1920s, became a recognized academic field in the late 1960s, when Richard Hoggart founded the Centre for Contemporary Cultural Studies (CCCS). The Birmingham school's foundation (under the stewardship of Stuart Hall) was a modified Marxist interpretation, moving from examining political resistance in traditional forms of union activity in factories to understanding resistance in the realm of popular culture. Using a semiotic approach that applied the works of Roland Barthes and Claude Levi-Strauss, these cultural Marxists located resistance within the quotidian lives of working-class youth from the 1950s through the 1970s. While numerous significant texts have emerged from this scholarly collective, revaluing the class-based experiences of resistance among loosely grouped individuals, the CCCS has been criticized for creating romantic, grand narratives of a homogenous (white, male) working class. In later subculture scholarship, however, the pendulum has swung widely in the other direction, with post-subcultural theorists understanding individuals as reveling in consumerist-based singular choices no longer centrally grounded in the structures of class, gender, or ethnicity.

In contrast to these two modal points of subcultural scholarship, this study, which focuses on the two shared circulations of the hobo, evolves from the grand narratives of the CCCS while avoiding the blindness of many post-subcultural theorists who imagine free consumer-individuals participating in depoliticized play. When imagining boxcar politics, theories and histories of class play a central role in understanding the circulation of the hobo both along the iron rods throughout the United States and their representations in novels, poems, films, advertisements, and legal documents. Hoboing was not a mere consumerist style but an expression of a particular class position informed by the individual's race and gender. The hobo's physical circulation was wedded to the circulation of railroad tracks, with its consequential (oftentimes violent) penetration of capitalism. In this sense, the hobo's resistance was much more than just symbolic abstraction; indeed, it was a lived experience with life-and-death ramifications, fought in the everyday realm of train yards, jungle fires, and squats in towns and cities throughout the United States. When a flesh-and-blood hobo hopped one train in Seattle and emerged from a different train in New Orleans two weeks later, a circulation of socioeconomic knowledges, along with the obfuscations of inequality embodied by the itinerant worker, traveled as well. In a similar vein, when novelists and journalists imagined the boxcar journeys of hobos hopping trains from Seattle to New Orleans, they were—consciously or not—also employing representations of class in their texts. Building off the historical record while theorizing the fluid connections between hobos and trains allows for this project to uncover an instantiation of capitalism's powerful saturation within a misunderstood subculture. This dual framework also allows for an analysis of the ways those hobos both visibly and invisibly circulated tactics of resistance that used the object of capitalism's reach for their own ideological and need-based purposes.

The hobo's resistance was not a monolithic voice, and the various ways that resistance was articulated forms the narrative for what I term *boxcar politics*. I use this label neither to convey an exhaustive ethnographic hobo history or literary examination nor to suggest a purely theoretical concept. Rather, it is an explanatory term intended to reconceptualize a marginalized subculture through a political framework. Hobos were an unintended byproduct of nineteenth-century finance capitalism, and their mobility allowed them to be unique agents in the shifting dynamics of labor within a newly industrialized modern nation.[9] With one foot in the environments where they labored and the other in the machines that brought them to these jobs, they were precariously positioned along the fault lines of the new realities of post–Civil War America. How riders and writers created and manipulated hobo spaces is the subject of *Boxcar Politics*.

This text-centered project interrelates cultural and literary works about the hobo subculture within a historically rooted analysis of the material and symbolic value of the train in the late nineteenth and early twentieth centuries. In a similar vein to the multidisciplinary "border-crossings" that Sherry Lee Linkon and John Russo describe as "flexible, transferable ways of readings" in their approach to new working-class studies and the ways Michel de Certeau's negotiates between the historical "real" and the literary "gaze" in what he described as "textual historicity," this project pivots discussions of the hobo away from a strict labor history of the itinerant subculture, creating an aperture for a literary and cultural studies reinterpretation.[10] Instead of examining hobos as either doctrinally individualistic on the one hand or part of a radical political movement on the other, *Boxcar Politics* is intended to create new scholarly conversations that examine the wide spectrum of political expressions conceived by and about hobos. Some descriptions of hobos are highly individualized, some are romantically tinged, and others lead to radical ways that solidarity among society's marginalized can be conceived and enacted within a moving boxcar. By analyzing these various political understandings of hobos, a complex network of knowledge about this working-class subculture emerges.

The first chapter formulates the framework for my interpretation of the hobo. In the first section I historicize the early relationship among the hobo, the railroad, and American capitalism. By exploring this mutually dependent tripartite relationship, I establish hobos' connection to the working class by dissecting the ways that the railroad created this disenfranchised class of itinerant workers who, consequently, empowered themselves by stealing rides from these same corporate entities. In the second part I theorize hobos' unique relationship with the material object that defined them: the boxcar. Sneaking into the belly of the train, hobos symbolically became parasites to the body of the railroad, forming a transient subculture that offered a counterhegemonic human narrative to the supposed progress that the railroad celebrated in its promotional materials.

From this concentrated history and theoretical base, the other chapters form an overarching chronological literary narrative arc that uses specific texts and close readings to reveal the manifestations of boxcar politics. In chapter 2 I begin with Jack London's *The Road* and his individualistic competitive ideology as he travels with Charles T. Kelly's homeless regiment, participating in the Industrial Army's march on Washington in 1894. This chapter discusses the hobo's reliance on invisibility and the tensions created when oppressed subcultures with different goals attempt to share the same space. In chapter 3, moving away from London's individualism, I examine hobos who desire a subcultural communality with its own evolved traditions, group awareness, and multifarious solidarity. Rereading Jim Tully's *Beggars of Life*, both in terms of its subject matter and its literary form, I explore how an individual and group can beneficially coexist within the same political hobo space of the boxcar.

Chapter 4 examines radical hobos who attempt to connect their individual politics to larger organized activist organizations. While London imagined the hobo in strictly individualistic terms and Tully envisioned the hobo as part of a subculture that communally shared marginalized spaces, John Dos Passos's hobos explore the potential for a working-class anticapitalist vanguard. In my reinterpretation of *U.S.A.*, grounded in a historical contextualization of a range of hobo unions and organizations, I show that although Dos Passos romanticizes these characters, his faith in a sustained anticapitalist fight that intertwines speech and movement rests squarely with the politically aware hobo.

Moving from Dos Passos's literary interpretation of radical hobos to journalistic accounts by radical organizations and activists who used the hobo to project political arguments, in chapter 5 I reexamine ways the Communist Party USA and radical presses framed the Scottsboro case. Specifically, I examine how some radical activists refused a common defensive strategy that examined the case solely in terms of African American men accused of rape. Instead, in their editorials and reports they offered an ideological argument that called attention to the nine young men as itinerant laborers whose means of transportation and livelihood were removed from them. Stopping the train and arresting these hobos revealed not only the racist practices of Depression-era southern justice but also capitalism's insidious attack and long reach into the most hidden of spaces.

My last chapter centers on Jack Kerouac's *On the Road* and the way he detaches his hobo figures from any form of communal activity. In Kerouac's hands the hobo is a ghost, a reminder of a fictionalized past, who acts as a spiritual guide disconnected from a working-class ethos. The result is a political devolution of the hobo in the 1940s and 1950s. Finally, in the afterword, I examine the end of the hobo epoch, symbolically dated with President Eisenhower's much ballyhooed Federal Aid Highway Act of 1956. While train riders continue to be important figures in novels and films, and in reality men and women have continued hopping trains through to the present day, the manifestations of capitalism have drastically changed. Through mapping the rise of the automobile industrial complex and the demise of the train culture in the middle of the twentieth century, the "death" of the hobo is detailed.

*Boxcar Politics* offers an examination of the micromaneuverings of those relegated to the margins of official history, delving into the narrative cracks of a supposedly homogeneous working-class subculture and tracing the varied political expressions of the dispossessed transient worker. In the late nineteenth and early twentieth centuries, men and women held on as boxcars rumbled across the landscape of the United States. Dirty, sore, and tired, they emerged from the darkness of the trains and headed to towns looking for food, shelter, and employment. This book examines these hobo lives—and the literary figures born from these lives—by examining the spaces occupied by these men and women on the train as political spaces.

Chapter One

# VIEWS FROM THE BOXCAR

## A Historical and Theoretical Framing of Boxcar Politics

Two differing accounts of the hobo have calcified this figure in history and literary studies. In the first version, a seemingly pathological one, the hobo is a menacing, selfish individualist who eschews any semblance of community while undermining proletarian solidarity every time he (and it is always a "he") jumps down from a slow-moving train and enters a new town. In the other, exceptionalist version, the hobo is framed as a freedom-loving traveler, epitomizing romanticized white male movement in U.S. society. In both these versions, the hobo is viewed passively; perched perfectly still on the lip of a boxcar, this figure becomes a vessel to transport particular rhetorics of mobility that simplify a subculture that was a vital part of the U.S. economy in the late nineteenth and early twentieth centuries. This project reimagines the political subjectivity—and so the political significance—of the hobo. Examined through this lens, the visuals become out of focus: the hobo is hiding in the darkness of the boxcar, and various additional analytical apparatuses are needed to capture a fleeting glimpse of this fast-moving figure.

## DEFINING THE HOBO

Ben Reitman, hobo, agitator, doctor, anarchist, and confidant of Emma Goldman, echoes many critics, scholars, and other hobos when he categorizes the homeless into three groups: "The hobos who work and wander, the tramps who dream and wander, the bums who drink and wander."[1] While traveling is connected to all three, according to this often-used definition, what separates hobos from the rest of the homeless is their willingness to work. Unlike tramps and bums who avoid work, hobos pride themselves on their ability to find employment by illegally hopping trains to get from job to job.

Scratch the surface of any hobo memoir or history, however, and these terms reveal themselves to be inadequate. Many hobos spent lean times begging for food, many tramps split lumber for their dinner, and bums consistently moved throughout cities and towns working for their meals or bed. The term *hobo* is fluid, and although some might cling to incremental distinctions in the homeless hierarchy, most journalists, politicians, preachers, academics, and hobos themselves used the terms *hobo*, *tramp*, and *bum* somewhat interchangeably.

The term *hobo* therefore has elasticity and bleeds into other homeless classifications; it is not, however, an amorphous category. As Nels Anderson, author of *The Hobo*, one of the first academic texts on the subculture, specifies, "In spite of all that has been said to the contrary, the hobo is a worker."[2] This is a key attribute, and in this monograph's definition, two main aspects make one a hobo: being a self-identified transient worker (even if the individual is without a job for long stretches of time) and traveling by illegally riding trains. The term *hobo*, though, did not gain relevancy until the 1890s. Consequently, I use the terms somewhat interchangeably in this first section as I explore the ways that *tramp* and *hobo* were used inside and outside the working-class community to favorably describe or adamantly discredit a distinctly new form of laborer emerging in the United States after the Civil War.

Although some spiritual hobos, attempting to justify their subcultural lineage, whimsically claim Jesus as the first very first hobo, the hobo or tramp figure originated from a specific set of economic and technological entanglements in the United States in the second half of the nineteenth century. Examining the tramp serial novels that began appearing shortly after the completion of the transcontinental railroad and born from the depressions of the early 1870s that experienced severe labor unrest and numerous railroad strikes, Michael Denning explains that "the tramp is no myth or symbol in the American mind, no eternal archetype of America. . . . Indeed it was an ideological naming of the new phenomenon of unemployment."[3] The cultural anxiety revealed by the new factory-labor system, immigration, and an increasingly vociferous underclass found symbolic embodiment in the tramp figure, revealing a tense nation in the midst of economic hardship that conveniently used this figure, as Christine Photinos writes, to "convert economic uncertainty and social order into a more manageable form of individual villainy."[4] In these tramp narratives, there was an attempt at assuaging the anxieties of the nation by narrowing the labor vision within these stories to a battle between patriotic workers who benefit from the benevolence of their employers and foreign mobile agitators who attempt to destroy the American Dream.

Some of these depictions are like Horatio Alger's *Tony the Tramp*, a stereotypical rags-to-riches story in which white racial identity and observable virtue (combined with a declarative separation from other tramps) lead to a young transient finding a "proper" place in middle-class society through the help of a gentleman benefactor. Others are like Lee Harris's *The Man Who Tramps: A Story of Today*, a bourgeois fiction in which tramps are an itinerant aggressive mob described as "floating populaces, who have no home ties to bind them to society; the vicious who seek to plunder and destroy." As Denning posits, these stories are not allegories of labor and capital but rather sensational tales of tramps implausibly interacting with the rich. When Bret Harte's 1877 short story "My Friend the Tramp," a yarn about a manipulative, gregarious homeless man with no work ethic, found a receptive audience, the vagabond as a popular literary trope was secure.[5]

From the word *tramp*, coined to describe these wandering men who traveled across the United States with "no visible means of support" and no specific working-class ethos, emerged the term *hobo*, which does have a specific class perspective.[6] In western newspapers during the 1880s, the term *hobo* had regional usage, but not until Josiah Flynt's 1891 *Contemporary Review* article, in which he used the word to accentuate the laziness of the "professional tramp" (much in line with the tramp in Harte's story) did it enter into the national lexicon. Western workers, however, quickly readopted the term, revaluing it to imply a positive connotation for a transient worker.[7]

This revaluing by hobos themselves is similar to the way the term *hobo* originated. Most folk histories of the hobo begin with returning veterans from the Civil War who, after finding their homes in ruins and already accustomed to traveling by train during the war, became itinerant agricultural laborers. Some stories suggest that these "hoe boys" did not like the derogatory nature of this term and combined the words, forming *hobo* for a more positive self-identity. Although this origin story is somewhat suspect, this narrative does show the importance of identity politics in defining the term. Placing people within subcultural categories potentially places real and symbolic obstacles in their path, and as seen in the origin myth, hobos were attempting to reframe their mobility in terms that suited their particular needs and lifestyles. By the late 1890s this new mobile working-class subculture had differentiated itself from many other migrants who were part of what Carlos Schwantes describes as the "wageworkers' frontier."[8]

As "indispensable outcasts," hobos were members of a working-class subculture necessary, as David Montgomery writes, "to nearly all forms of manufacturing, transportation, and commerce" in the United States.[9] Not mere vestiges held over from a preindustrial society who had no value in the present day, hobos fulfilled an essential economic requirement. The railroad, steel, and other major industries needed large numbers of laborers; the powerful trains advertised in glossy brochures would not move across the continent if itinerant manual laborers did not arduously strike the rails into the ground. Besides the rail industry, hobos were employed in a variety of jobs; although the popular view of the hobo is of an exclusively western worker following the harvests, hobos worked in both industrial and agricultural environments throughout the country. Oftentimes, laborers would quit their jobs in the steel mills in the East during the summer months and travel west to harvest wheat or beets only to return again as the air turned cold, repeating these cyclical travels the following year.

But while hobos were part of the working class, there were obvious differences between hobos following the spring harvests through Cedar City, Utah, and generational steelworkers in Bethlehem, Pennsylvania. An essential part of this difference was the way hobos defined themselves. Not tied to one job or geographic area, many hobos thought of themselves as workers who picked up various types of employment along the way—as opposed to being defined by a particular job in a specific locale—thus resulting in the "pervasive tendency of laborers and semiskilled workers to quit their jobs at the slightest instigation."[10] In 1,349 interviews conducted by John J. McCook in 1889, Alice Solenberger's data on 1,000 homeless men from 1900 to 1903, and Fredrick Mills's 1914 investigation of seasonal labor in California, all three investigators concluded that a majority of transients articulated their ability to transition from job to job as a way to escape the confines of a stultifying industrial environment.[11] Hobos saw themselves as workers, but their relationship to the workforce was different from those who hitched plows on farms in Ohio or smelt iron in Pittsburg plants. One observer of the working habits of hobos at the turn of the twentieth century stated, "He works for a while in each place, and then moves on. He rubs elbows with home-living men, and they frequently find him a good worker, but they find him a good goer as well."[12]

The working class was not a monolithic entity, and hobos were one subgroup; traveling from job to job in boxcars allowed them a particular labor vision that deviated from other working-class individuals. For example, when one railroad company estimated that they needed 4,593 men to build a section of their lines, they transported fifteen to twenty times that number to finally complete their job.[13] While these numbers reveal that railroad companies had policies in place that were not conducive to keeping men employed (unsafe work conditions, low wages, subpar housing), it also shows that when laborers found these conditions not to their liking, many men simply left out on the next train to find more suitable work.

This ability to move made the hobo an object of much consideration from those who were not hobos. By the turn of the twentieth century, the hobo figure had gained traction, emerging as a staple of popular culture—there even was a National Hobo Convention organized by residents of Britt, Iowa, in 1900.[14] Despite this unique welcome, there generally was a clear divide between the citizens of the town and the hobo traveling through their streets looking for jobs and sustenance. In national news, discussions of the itinerant worker were hyperbolic and often hysterical in nature. As Todd DePastino, author of *Citizen Hobo,* explains, this rhetoric highlighted many deep-rooted socioeconomic issues that had caused tensions in the decades after the Civil War, including the divides between the propertied and homeless over the use of public space, the rising numbers of the floating proletariat, and fears concerning the loss of traditional social control throughout the United States.[15] While previous understandings of homelessness were understood primarily as a result of divine providence, in the nineteenth century, as David Rothman states, "economic failure was due to moral failure."[16] Hobos broke with official conventions of social, economic, and religious life and, like all homeless, were seen as pathologically dangerous, spiritually bankrupt, and harmful to their communities. Their poverty was explained as self-imposed rather than caused by economic or political conditions. Hobos often were viewed as suffering from "wanderlust" or other moral depravities and kept at arm's length; they were ostracized as voluntary dropouts from the working class rather than recognized as a vital subculture within it.[17]

Consequently, hobos' relationship to the working class was consistently underrepresented or completely razed. One way to examine this disenfranchisement is to analyze the stereotypical way most hobos were depicted by those outside the hobo subculture: the comic tramp buffoon or the menacing predator. Tramps were familiar characters in such magazines as *Puck* and *Life* that were popular with European immigrant readers. In these pages hobos were fools; the reader was not meant to identify with these marginalized figures but to laugh at them and, in the case of Wearie Willie especially, to understand that to be lazy in the United States would lead only to failure (and possible physical harm). These tramp figures were not workers but conservative, ideological parables meant to teach "proper" behavior to newly settled immigrants.[18]

If a reader turned from the comics to the front pages of the newspapers, however, a very different figure would appear. These wandering homeless were broadly painted as both a physical and symbolic threat to society who needed to be immediately controlled. As early as August 8, 1875, the front page of the *New York Times* emphatically asked, "What Shall We Do with Tramps?" In this article and in the myriad editorials and commentaries written about this subject, the overwhelming feeling was that the itinerant unemployed were markedly dangerous and the country was ill-prepared to handle this new form of homelessness: "There is perhaps no problem in social science that is just now more pressing, and none, perhaps, more perplexing than what to do with the great and increasing army of mendicants who wander from city to town and from town to city, getting shelter, food, and raiment by public or private charity and their own thieving fingers, and who, from their mode of life, have gained the name of 'tramps.'" These mobile, homeless bodies, dependent on the services of law-abiding citizens, were slipping from "city to town and from town to city" and, as the militaristic term *army* implies, coded as a treacherous, organized force that needed to be defeated. Newspapers from the *New York Times* to small, rural papers wrote of these homeless bodies in oppositional terms; they constituted a resistive subculture, and, as the article states, they must be "snubbed and put down and out" to decrease the numbers of homeless traveling around the United States.[19] While the *New York Times* was somewhat ambiguous about how citizens should enact violence against these itinerants, two years later a *Chicago Tribune* editorial was more explicit in its methodology, calling for housewives to put "a little strychnine or Arsenic in the meat and supplies furnished to tramps" so that the bloated dead bodies of the decaying corpses would serve as a warning sign for anyone looking for a handout.[20]

When itinerant workers jumped down from their boxcars and knocked on the back doors of houses asking for food or wandered along the "main stem" of cities looking for work, they were the visible poor, placing their homelessness and need on the doorsteps of America. While their poverty disenfranchised them, their mobility led to a general fear among the populations they traveled through. In popular representations of these figures, then, they were to be laughed at as lazy buffoons who would never succeed in the United States, where a strong puritan work ethic was a necessity, or as predatory social deviants with animalistic qualities who must be "put down" to protect the nation's women and children.

### *Labor Newspapers and the Spectrum of Working-Class Views of the Hobo*

Despite these caricatures, there was not one monolithic view of what Michael Davis labels the "nomad proletariat"; rather, multiple representations competed against one another.[21] Although these two views—buffoon or criminal—were commonplace, cautiously sympathetic representations of the hobo also existed. For example, metropolitan newspapers were not the only ones to use the term *army* when examining the itinerant unemployed. In the same year that the *New York Times* decried the homeless army as eroding the social fabric of the United States, an editorial in the *National Labor Tribune*, an organ of the Amalgamated Iron and Steel Workers in Pittsburg, Pennsylvania, stated that these able-bodied, out-of-work men *saved* the republic. In one editorial, the writer passionately inverts the logic of tramps as foreign agitators, arguing that these men were veterans of Lincoln's Grand Army and have "hearts as courageous as have ever swept rebellion from a battlefield." Instead of receiving thanks for their service after the Civil War, however, these men found that they were vilified and treated as common criminals. In another editorial from the same paper, a former veteran labeled his fellow tramps "superior men" who had been forced onto the road because of "stock-jobbers and shoddy government contractors." They had fought to unite the nation, but once their service was rendered, this veteran felt they had been victimized by corporate greed and governmental dishonesty.[22]

Labor newspapers of the late nineteenth century featured editorials that formed an ideological link between the precarious position of the employed worker and the out-of-work itinerant, attempting to be inclusive in their view of the proletariat. The *Journal of United Labor*, a Knights of Labor paper that in the 1880s had a circulation of nearly 750,000 readers, attempted to dispel the negative perceptions surrounding itinerant workers by placing the blame for their position squarely on capitalist interests. Recalling the working life of the previous generations in which "no workingman considered himself degraded by being 'on the tramp,'" Jay Gould and other capitalists "have continually persisted in associating the word tramp with words vagabond, idler, and thief. . . . This has been so successfully done by the [mainstream] press that tramp now stands as an incontrovertible term."[23] As described in the journal, the denigration of the term was a calculated move by capitalists to break the solidarity of the working class and to make workers' individualists instead of seeing themselves as members of a larger multifaceted group. By elucidating the etymology of the term *tramp*, the *Journal of United Labor* was attempting to be inclusive and have a wide-angle view of who should be within the auspices of the working class.

The inclusiveness can be seen in Joe Hill's 1913 song, "The Tramp," which uses the terms *tramp* and *'bo* interchangeably within the song but securely impresses upon the listener the working-class ethos of these words. The song, originally printed in the *Industrial Worker*, uses the tune of "Tramp, Tramp, Tramp, the Boys Are Marching," a Civil War song composed by the Union military songwriter George F. Root.[24] Like the Labor editorials previously mentioned, by using this tune, Hill attempted to reclaim these homeless men as vital members of the republic by making connections between the itinerant men looking for work at the opening of the twentieth century with Civil War soldiers marching in the 1860s. In this humorous but biting song, Hill sings about the struggles of an itinerant, homeless man "looking hard for work," but no matter where he went, he was always denied. The Wobbly songwriter takes the listener through the tramp's arduous life and death: he asks a housewife to work for food but is sent away empty-handed; he is willing to "work for Jesus," but the preacher won't allow him; he is arrested for his attempts to find work and labeled a bum by the judge. Even in his death, he is denied refuge as "Santa Peter" refuses his entrance to heaven. Having nowhere else to go, he finally heads to hell, falsely claiming to be "full of sin" to find a resting place. The devil, recognizing him as a worker and not a sinner, will not admit him and sends the hobo away.

In the song the itinerant worker is denied jobs and opportunities; everywhere he goes he is told to "keep on a-tramping" and threatened with jailhouse corporal punishment if he attempts to stay. Charity organizations and government agencies seemingly meant to help the itinerant are merciless scams. The only one to recognize the tramp's worth is the devil, who refuses him entrance into hell, because, "[he's] a 'bo!" The "sin" is revealed as simply being a poor disenfranchised worker looking for a job; although it might make him an outcast in the world, it does not damn him to hell. Rather, he must eternally "keep on a-tramping," fruitlessly searching for work.

While Hill was singing this song in the second decade of the twentieth century, he was tapping into these feelings of disenfranchisement that had been present among hobos for decades. Twenty years prior to Hill's song, the *Journal of the Knights of Labor* was describing an outrageously obvious causal relationship between the involuntary cyclical unemployment among laborers and large numbers of itinerant men looking for work. The derogatory labeling of these men as tramps and the refusal to acknowledge the reasons for their mobility was an abject failure to recognize the volatile status of working people within the United States for nefarious reasons by those making profits from the unstable job market.[25]

Hill and the editorialists emotively examined reasons for the hobo's degraded position, and the journals' letters were zealously written by angry men facing a life of destitution who blamed the government, charity organizations, and Wall Street executives for their dispossession. Others were much more systematic in their evaluation, situating the hobo as a degraded member within the U.S. political economy. In *War of the Classes*, Jack London, who wrote a good deal about his experiences hopping trains (see chapter 2), soberly pinpoints a specific reason for unemployment: a simple case of supply and demand. Because of the number of out-of-work men, the itinerant laborer acted as an anchor, keeping the capitalist system steady and afloat. In this text and others, London also uses the term *army*, writing that, since there are "more men than there is work for men, a surplus army inevitably results. The surplus army is an economic necessity; without it, the present constructions of society would fall to pieces."[26] London does not view itinerant workers as an army of thieves; nor does he romantically connect their lineage to Lincoln's Grand Army. Instead, he uses the term to describe a class of workers who, although vital pieces in keeping the United States economically viable, have become the root cause for their own dispossession.

London's "surplus army" is equivalent to Marx's "floating surplus-population" described in *Capital*, in which members of this reserve group of unemployed were initially groomed in factories as young boys. As they grew older, demanding greater wages and better working conditions, the majority would be fired. New boys would be brought into those vacated positions, and the unemployed would become itinerants, cobbling together subsistence-level jobs. "That the natural increase of the number of labourers does not satisfy the requirements of the accumulation of capital, and yet all the time is in excess of them, is a contradiction inherent to the movement of capital itself. It wants larger numbers of youthful laborers, a smaller number of adults."[27] Thrown out of jobs, these men whom capital discards still must find work. Seen from this Marxist position, they then become complicit in capital's desire to keep profits high and costs low: this army of men is the ready supply of labor if those with jobs begin to agitate.

When examined through this prism, though, these homeless laborers were not "pathologically lazy," as many politicians and charity organizations proclaimed, but victims of capitalism. They potentially were no different from those workers able to precariously hold onto stable employment once they reached adulthood. London lays this fact bare in his book, linking the "sailormen, soldier-men, labor-men" as potential future penniless tramps.[28] The division between the unemployed and employed was a slippery, arbitrary one, and London and the labor presses underline this point, a key aspect of the economic reality that popular presses mostly ignored in their evaluation of the homeless.

The Labor presses highlight in their pages that hobos were products of a new labor economy in the post–Civil War era. The explosion of workers who had to travel to find employment (estimated to be between 10 and 20 percent of the United States population in the late nineteenth century) paralleled the growth of the burgeoning industrial world of the United States. As Eric Monkkonen states, they were "the ordinary working people of the United States on the move between jobs and residences" who were "neither outcasts nor deviants" but part of a diverse population of workers.[29] Through their presses, labor organizations appealed for solidarity among stationary and itinerant workers, vocalizing their opposition to the laws criminalizing travel for would-be workers. Within these groups, they saw, to use the phrase of Richard Oestreicher, a "subculture of opposition" to the corporate dominance of the post–Civil War period.[30] This ideological rhetoric, though, was hard to sustain in the face of harsh realities, and the labor presses show how being an itinerant was not an enviable position—the hobo was seen as a threat who kept many laborers fiercely holding onto unsafe, low-wage jobs. For example, the labor reformer George McNeill bluntly stated in 1887 what was at stake for the men who went out onto the picket lines during the railroad workers' strike on the Baltimore and Ohio lines: "The trainmen were under despotic control. To leave their employ was to become tramps, outlaws." For these men, and for the large majority of laborers throughout the country, to resist the horrendous conditions in their workplace meant possible slippage into the "outlaw" category of the itinerant worker.[31]

In this way, the pressures that caused tension between the working and middle classes along these issues of mobility also created riffs within the working class itself. Many within the stationary working class were uncomfortable with their particular insecure economic position. As mentioned earlier, these workers often faced months of unemployment and were not far removed from being forced to seek work in other towns and cities. Worried that hobos would take their jobs, the working class drew rigid lines of demarcation between themselves and the transient laborer, and the portrayal of the itinerant population into lawless nonlaborers was one method to psychologically, as well as practically, elevate their own place on the slippery rungs of the economy.

As cyclical depressions devastated industries in the last part of the nineteenth century, large numbers of workers found themselves unemployed and on the road searching for work, fiercely competing with one another. Class solidarity was severely tested and often fragmented, as industries used the large numbers of unemployed for their own benefit. For example, western employers, needing their crops harvested but wanting to keep costs low, targeted workers on the East Coast with advertisements promising high wages and bountiful employment if they would travel across the continent. Often when these workers would arrive, tired from their long travels hopping trains from coast to coast, they would find these advertisements false and consequently competed with other unemployed and desperate men for a relatively small number of low-paying jobs.

Labor presses attempted to combat these false advertisements with editorials and columns in their own papers. Creating explicit "Don't Come Here" sections, they pleaded with itinerant workers to avoid their particular areas. Some appealed to working-class solidarity, "begging" fellow workers to stay away from their geographic area out of loyalty to their brother workers, while others logically emphasized the consequences of being on the wrong side of the tramp laws, writing, "The man without capital has no place anymore in the West."[32] Desperate for work, though, the men kept coming. Stresses between rooted and nonrooted workers, itself a crumbling demarcation, was fragmenting solidarity as unemployment swelled.

Michael Davis recounts this narrative of loss and consequential fragmentation of solidarity in the mining village of Bethel, Pennsylvania. In the year before the introduction of the transcontinental railroad, working-class families were enjoying a comfortable economic and social existence with a successful mine at the town's center. Ten years later, when the mine went bust, however, the workers were forced to seek employment in another state. Heading off together, they found that the coalfields of Indiana were no better, and they were forced to disperse, looking for jobs throughout the country. As the *National Labor Tribune* reported, these men were forced to head off alone to "become the dreaded and despised tramps of the day."[33]

### *Law, Gender, and the Policing of the Hobo Body*

Once hobos were categorized as outlaws, their mobility—legally and extralegally—was criminalized. In examining the ways the mobile homeless were read in the nineteenth century, Tim Creswell writes, "Once tramps have been defined, they can be dealt with, argued over, confined, made to work on log piles and disenfranchised."[34] Categorizing the unemployed itinerant populations as tramps had significant repercussions; who defined the large number of homeless workers potentially would then have the ability to control their movements.

The historian Paul Ringenbach points to one particular group with this ability to define and control, detailing how the middle classes "discovered" unemployment at the end of the nineteenth century, interpreting the floating army of workers as an attack on their nostalgic notions of a stable, static workforce.[35] Charity organizations pointed to the men's character as reasons for their unemployment and, while offering some forms of relief, pressed for laws that would place destitute men in jails. They were successful, and the first tramp law was enacted in New Jersey in 1876. By 1886 nineteen states followed with probusiness police forces throughout the country repressing working-class organizers and convicting the homeless in speedy trials. Draconian in nature, this legislation was able to define "legal" and "illegal" travel, thus making it criminal for poor working people to travel in the search of jobs.[36] These reforms, advocated by charity and religious organizations, gained national hegemony in their view of the unemployed as unwilling to work, creating, according to Davis, "a profound gulf between middle-class and working-class opinion in the Gilded Age."[37]

These laws were also responsible for helping gender the figure of the train-hopping unemployed. While state tramp laws outlawed a subsection of the working class by codifying itinerant, poor workers and their mobility illegal, in most states it was legally impossible for a female to be convicted under these laws. The antimobility legislation was meant to delimit the "utterly depraved [and] savage" as Public Charities professor Francis Wayland described the out-of-work homeless man; to place women under this category would be to admit to society's allowance of gendered transgressions.[38] This understanding is articulated in the 1916 study of vagrancy, when Frank Laubach ominously stated, "Society will not tolerate in females the same kind of vagrancy that it will tolerate in men."[39]

This lack of "toleration" of the female hobo has made her somewhat invisible in most public records on the itinerant worker.[40] Lynn Weiner shows in her historical sketch of tramp women from the late nineteenth century until the Great Depression that major studies on vagrancy simply did not count women in their figures; for example, John J. McCook's well-publicized "Tramp Census" of 1893 did not list one female in his whole document.[41] While egregious, this type of absence was typical. From within the subculture, there was also a demarcation along gender lines, with some male hobos dismissing women as unable to deal with the "inconveniences and hazards" of the mobile lifestyle.[42] Others relegated the female train rider as a sexual deviant who was, as one male hobo stated, an "angular-bodied, flint-eyed, masculine-minded travesty upon her sex."[43] While the law rendered the female itinerant body invisible, male members of the hobo subculture also erased the female through either vilification or willful ignorance of women travelers (who often passed as males to ride unhindered). These exclusions are captured in popular representations of the itinerant homeless as well. In a study of Harold Gray's *Little Orphan Annie* comic strip, Joanne Hall illustrates how homeless travelers depicted in those pages not only violate female gender norms but also transgress the masculine space of the hobo subculture. When a text does contain subtle elements of gender subversion, Hall contends that "each woman is eventually re-enfolded into mainstream society."[44]

Complicating this historiography, authentic female voices writing of their own road experiences are noticeably absent. Bertha Thompson penned a Depression-era extended study of female hobos, *Sister of the Road*, recounting her hobo experiences. This ethnographic history, however, has been discovered as a hoax, with Ben Reitman having written the manuscript. Barbara Starke's *Born in Captivity* (published in the United Kingdom as *Touch and Go: The Story of a Girl's Escape*) tells a sensational account of a "rebel hobo girl" in the 1920s. Although fascinating, the narrative interrogates the confining aspects of female domestic space more than it offers insight into the life of a woman in a working-class, train-hopping subculture.[45]

Perhaps the best resource on female train travelers can be found in police blotters. Weiner, in her archival research of police records from Saint Paul, Minnesota, pieces together a short narrative glimpse of Anna Hedstrom, a female transient arrested while hopping trains in 1893. Her arrest was not, however, in violating the tramp laws (which, because of her gender, did not recognize her as a hobo) but in her attire; she was wearing men's clothing, a violation of local laws. Although Hedstrom violated the Gilded Age's gender norms in terms of mobility, she was held in court because of cross-dressing. Much like Ruby Bates and Victoria Price, the two women pulled from the Scottsboro train who were not recognized by the court's ideological gaze as hobos and instead categorized as white southern women (see chapter 5), Hedstrom's deviant mobility likewise could not be officially acknowledged. Although held for a short stay and chastised for her clothing preference, her case was eventually dismissed.[46]

Unlike the sensational accounts in magazines that focused on the supposedly deviant sexuality of female hobos, Hedstrom's case reveals a working-class woman participating in the itinerant trades.[47] As she declared to the court, she was hoboing her way to various lumber camps because she wanted to earn her own money. This case, while difficult to uncover, reveals how women laborers, although rendered invisible by the law and discounted by male hobos, were actively participating within the hobo subculture.

### *Class Consciousness and Transient Mutualism*

There were attempts within the pages of the Labor newspapers to bring divergent members of the working class under one large banner. But the successful tramp legislation passed through the courts criminalizing the bodies of the working-class poor, the economic depressions exasperating the already present anxiety among all workers, and the fractured solidarity within the itinerant populations placed traveling workers in a disadvantaged position when searching for jobs. As their numbers increased, they were often painted with a wide brush as rank-and-file members of a homeless army roaming the land, becoming economic and moral drains on society. As labor historian Alexander Keyssar highlights, in the 1890s between 20 to 25 percent of northern workers spent at least three months of the year jobless, and, as employment became more scarce both inside and outside the working class, many saw the itinerant worker as not only excluded from the working class but counterproductive to the solidarity aims of the proletariat.[48] As Marx indicated, this replaceable, inexpensive "floating surplus population" was advantageous for the growing national industries, allowing wages to be kept low and making unionizing efforts exceedingly difficult. In the eyes of many scholars, therefore, hobos were part of the lumpen proletariat, unable to inhabit class consciousness.

Stephan Thernstrom and Peter Knights, who examined geographic and social mobility among the working class in the nineteenth century, has argued that the "permanently transient" could not form bonds of solidarity among themselves. Being rootless precluded transient workers from establishing connections among fellow workers; unable to get to know one another, they were not invested in a coworker's well-being.[49] This view of the hobo lacking intimate connections to other members of the working class is prevalent in much scholarship.

Class consciousness, though, is more than just a connection to a particular fellow worker; rather, it is an understanding of a mutual shared position within capitalism's economic hierarchy. Experienced itinerant workers, riding together in boxcars along the rolling labor frontier, define themselves in relation to one another. Frank Tobias Higbie uses the term "transient mutualism" to explain this connection among riders and the larger society, in which "a man with money would buy a meal for a hungry man, homemakers and hoboes exchanged chores for food, and jobs could be found through friends, distant relatives, and acquaintances."[50] In this political economy of transient workers existing in the shadows of American capitalism, avenues of solidarity formed along the steel bands of iron. To preclude transient workers from class consciousness, one must rely on static notions of class formations based on personal intimate knowledge existing between individuals. Instead, for some hobos, understandings of class were extremely portable as they participated in seasonal labor occupations alongside fellow transient workers partaking in similar cyclical work and travel patterns; the individuals they met varied, but the forms of labor and travel in which they were participating were analogous.

This reliance on a support system was needed not only for itinerant workers but for all laborers. In the era before the New Deal, most laborers required a network of sustainability, as jobs were often temporary and the search for work constant. This networking was an important survival mechanism that could keep workers in a job or feed their family in the time of need, as they relied on a wide spectrum of people—from the saloon keeper to the priest—for help. As David Montgomery states, "Between jobs they needed to know the techniques for survival in America: which bakeries disposed of stale bread, when overripe fruits and vegetables were cleaned out of the markets, which societies dispensed relief to which nationalities, where a few hours of work might be found distributing circulars or carrying advertisement on sandwich boards, where low tide exposed the least polluted clams and mussels, and which lodging house charged the lowest prices."[51] Just like stationary workers, itinerant laborers required similar networks of sustainability that were equally complex and often shared. The out-of-work cement worker in Chicago who traveled the city looking for work oftentimes would share the same network as a hobo who had just entered town in the middle of the night; they both could find out the schedules of bakeries in town or read the advertisements for cheap food on the main stem. These networks, however, also diverged, as workers with a local knowledge of a city could have an advantageous position in procuring food or jobs (a process requiring careful negotiations along ethnic and religious demarcations). Hobos, who did not have local roots, had to meet in "jungles" by the train tracks to pool their particular knowledges of a city, tactically working together to best exploit opportunities.

Hobos intermingled various forms of class consciousness with a fluid ethos of train hopping, often using the fragile connections of larger working-class solidarity. Just as class consciousness among a city's local working class is a complex network ideologically tangled among ethnic, racial, and neighborhood-specific identities, the hobo network of support was equally saturated with multiplicities and negotiations. For example, Kenneth Kusmer explores the evolving relationship between trainmen and itinerant workers, stating that "after 1900, class solidarity began to play an increasingly important role" as railroad workers began to lose faith in the free-labor ideology when they saw many of their own slip into the hobo's position. While hobos and trainmen often had dramatic and violent confrontations, by the 1890s there also was a shared sense of class allegiance, epitomized by conductor Charles George's 1888 statement, "Many a poor fellow has faithfully worked a railroad during long years, on poor pay, only to be dropped from the roll when old or disabled." When they were dropped from the steady employment of the railroad, many of these men had to take to the road. This sympathy (and potential shared socioeconomic position) toward the itinerant worker led some trainmen, in direct disregard of orders, to allow hobos to ride on their trains. Examining transient workers primarily employed by railroad companies, Shelton Stromquist states, "their perception of class is facilitated by the ease with which they move from community to community, with or without a union traveling card, and find a place for themselves."[52]

To adapt Montgomery's wonderful metaphor, if the house of labor had many rooms, its surrounding grounds were filled with tents, populated by itinerant workers who survived through these shared networks of sustainability. These networks were weblike, sometimes strengthening as laborers on the different rungs of the economic ladder helped one another, sometimes disintegrating as workers in stable jobs separated themselves from the itinerants, but always in a constant state of reform as hobos met in boxcars and jungles throughout the United States.

In their work *Hegemony and Socialist Strategy*, Ernesto Laclau and Chantal Mouffe argue for a revaluing of the idea of a homogenous working class and offer a case for the "autonomization of the spheres of struggle and the multiplicities of political spaces."[53] The focus of this study is on a specific sphere of struggle: the illegal hopping of trains by itinerant workers. But to discuss hobo spaces, the larger multiplicities of the political space of the working class must also be contextualized. The many forms of this intermingling of class consciousness and train hopping are discussed in the chapters that follow, highlighting the nuances of these interrelationships within the hobo subculture that ultimately express what I term *boxcar politics*. To examine the way hobos understood themselves in relationship to the larger working-class culture, though, one must first recognize the material and illegal relationship the hobo had with the railroad, which announced itself, in its full-throated and piercing whistle, as the corporate behemoth of nineteenth-century American capitalism. Railroads spread quickly and haphazardly throughout the United States, and hobos were both a consequence of and impediment to the companies' successes, gaining their resistive subcultural power from manipulating railroad spaces. To understand the hobo, then, one must first understand the train.

## THE RAILROAD AND MODERN AMERICA

President Lincoln, in the midst of the Civil War, said it would be the transcontinental railroad, among all else, that would change the face and future of the United States. He was correct. Even just a cursory examination of literature from the Civil War through the modernist age reveals that the railroad dominates intellectual thought and writing. The train was a technological marvel that, in just a few short decades, completely changed previous centuries' understandings of time and space. Connecting the world together in ways formerly inconceivable, its tracks tattooed on the imagination of U.S. citizens a mythical national identity that they had not possessed prior to the introduction of the transcontinental railroad.

Between the Central Pacific's *Jupiter* and the Union Pacific's *Number 119*, a golden spike was driven into the track at Promontory Point, Utah, on May 10, 1869, allowing for the first time in history a railroad track to span the length of a continent. Four years after the surrender of Lee and the defeat of the South in the Civil War, the golden spike event was hailed as a symbolic moment for a country desperate to be unified and to move forward as both a republic and world power. The Eighth Wonder of the World, deemed by an astonished public as the "most important event of modern times," changed forever the way the United States viewed itself.[54] The transcontinental railroad denoted national progress as the country became ready to move forward at speeds previously unknown; what was a dream in the first half of the nineteenth century now became a reality as the railroad brought mail, capitalists, entertainers, prospectors, and farmers, who, for a grand total of $150, could travel from New York City to San Francisco in fewer than seven days.[55]

As railroad scholarship has shown, railroad corporations transformed the United States by ushering in the modern corporate world. A key tool for westward development, the railroad was the premier symbol of nineteenth-century American capitalism, in which private entities were significantly supported by public funds and favorable political environments.[56] Even in the first half of the century, dreams for tracks spanning the width and length of the continent were ballyhooed from the pub to the White House. Believing that the train would usher in the future, as the country headed for war with itself, the transcontinentals were seen by many as a possible panacea to the nation's ills that could unite a fractured republic.

As early as 1846 a railroad promoter prophesized that the tracks would act "as bands of iron binding us together, a family of states—thus ensuring our greatness and permanence as a nation."[57] These familial relationships were to be economically forged, as the transcontinentals, acting as agents, would conjoin countries, allowing the nation to become a pivotal player in a global market; American railroad companies planned to build across the Isthmus of Panama, Mexico, and Canada, with designs to build tracks in Cuba and South America.[58] From its genesis the railroad was seen as a civic and national duty that would help solidify the United States as a leader in the rapidly changing industrial modern world.

There were many obstacles to this union that concurrently had a direct impact on the creation of the hobo subculture. Prior to the Civil War, southern states refused to connect their lines with the North. Believing that railroads were state issues, they declined corporations the right to control track in more than one state. Consequently, there were hundreds of "short lines" (tracks from approximately ten to one hundred miles long), and the trains running on them had particular local flavors and identities, used mostly by residents to receive mail or to make it—slowly—to other parts of the state. Built with a variety of gauges, the lines were meant to be distinct, rejecting the uniformity of the northern states.[59]

This differing philosophical view of right-of-way for lines is significant when it comes to the creation of the hobo population. The southern view of maintaining short lines within individual states localized the mobility of citizens within states—including the homeless populations. A woman, for example, could not easily get on one train in Tennessee to visit her son in Alabama; she would have to get on and off a variety of rail cars to make her way across state lines. Likewise, an itinerant worker in Georgia, upon hearing of a job in Virginia, would not be able to hop a train and quickly make his way to fill that position. The northern view of the national right-of-way of railroad tracks, however, allowed for individuals to travel across state lines more easily—for those with a ticket and for those without.

For northern speculators, the railroad was a tool that would connect northeastern interests with any place in the country; towns, cities, and factories could spring up wherever tracks were placed. The South, though, resisted the homogenizing effects of the railroad whose interests were clearly favorable to the northern elite. Regardless, whether one lived in the North or the South, railroads made the world "flatter," and both sides wanted to control its physical, economic, and ideological reach.[60] As William Thomas points out in *The Iron Way*, an examination of railroads during the Civil War, the North and the South were hybrids of each other, both building their respective societies by connecting them by rail to the broader transatlantic world. With slave labor bought by southern railroads, the hope was that train tracks would expand slavery throughout the country, promoting a southern philosophical view of localized mobility throughout the West.[61] But while the North and South knew the future was to be found at the end of railway tracks, the North was more advanced in its preparation when the cannonballs began raining down on the battlefield.

After the South's surrender at Appomattox, the railroad was summoned to unite the North and the South with the West. The bloody attempt to dissolve the Union had failed, and as the new nation looked for a unifying symbol that would move them away from the "total war" that claimed the lives of more than six hundred thousand people, the railroad was heralded for its symbolic value for a fractured nation: it was big, powerful, ordered, and mobile. If the nation was a healing body, then rail lines would become its veins pumping life through its wounded extremities. As William Everdell states in his book *The First Moderns*, "we call 'modern' everything that happened to any . . . culture after it had built its first railroad."[62] With the introduction of the transcontinental railroad, the United States, still recovering from its self-inflicted wounds, was staking its future to this technology that would be a vehicle of change, solidifying the nation's standing in the modern world.

This belief in the power of the train as a unifier for the country is championed in John Ford's 1924 film, *The Iron Horse*, a film that, as Lynne Kirby writes, "is suffused throughout, as a text and a narrative, with American national identity and with a great self-consciousness of its fabrication of American mythology." The film is an account of the building of the transcontinental railroad from 1862 until 1869. When Lincoln (Charles Edward Bell) stares at the main character, Dave Brandon (George O'Brien), as he heads west toward the future, the intertitle dramatically states, "the momentum of a great nation pushing westward—he sees the inevitable."[63] By unifying the country after the Civil War, the train would be an embodiment of manifest destiny. As an empire builder, the railroad would have no equals.

But while the Civil War enacted harsh personal sacrifices on individual bodies for a collective goal, as Richard White writes in *Railroaded*, the transcontinentals offered personal gain for projected public purposes. While Ford's film romantically centers on an individual passenger, White examines the individual owners of the railroad corporations—Leland

Stanford, Collis P. Huntington, Jay Gould, Mark Hopkins, among others—showing how their entrepreneurial enterprises "were a Gilded Age extravagance that rent holes in the political, social, and environmental fabric of the nation, creating railroads as mismanaged and corrupt as they were long."[64] Railroads expanded in the nineteenth century due to finance capitalism, where credit built lines and supplied the infrastructure for the trains, allowing individual men to amass enormous wealth, often at an enormous cost to both the public and the republic. These so-called robber barons were entrepreneurs who did not fully understand the technology they possessed, resulting in a seismic shift in the national identity of the United States that caused both excitement and anxiety.

The rapid advancement of lines snaking throughout the United States was dependent on the political environment that favored this large-scale corporate organization. While the Civil War was a response to the tensions created between a free-labor system and a slave-labor economy, in the aftermath of the war new tensions were created between the free-labor system and expanding corporate capitalism. By the turn of the twentieth century, there were a small number of industrial giants, all of whom modeled their corporate lives on the railroad.[65] Charles Francis Adams Jr., a railroad reformer, stated, "Corporate dominance is a new power, for which our language contains no name. We know what aristocracy, autocracy, democracy are; but we have no words to express government by moneyed corporation."[66] While workers might not have known Adams's specific terminology, their labor was being actualized within its framework.

Within a few years after the Civil War, as the ribbons of iron expanded across the United States, there were continual transformations of regions from frontier outposts to settled agricultural societies connected to urban hubs. The four interrelated aspects of political economy—production, distribution, circulation, and consumption—were all represented by the transcontinentals. As Henry Adams famously stated, "The generation between 1865 and 1895 was already mortgaged to the railways, and no one knew it better than the generation itself." Intertwined with the state and federal government, who subsidized their expansion, secured their rights of way, and protected their interests, railroad corporations, as Daniel Headrick, author of *The Tools of Empire,* states, "were the forerunners of a new civilization."[67]

Depending on how one views it, then, the railroad morphs into a symbol of cultural and national advancement or, as Frank Norris describes it, an angry octopus, holding the nonelite in a stranglehold of one of its tentacles. Norris's vitriolic indictment of the railroad, *The Octopus*, is a caustic, unwavering attack on the way corporations were transforming the built environment and ideological infrastructure of the United States. In one particular scene, the author writes of Presley, a poet from the East who experiences firsthand the danger of the railroad as he euphorically walks among the fields. This feeling is ruptured when he approaches the tracks of the new railroad that had been laid in the earth: "He had only time to jump back upon the embankment when, with a quivering of all the earth, a locomotive, single, unattached, shot by him with a roar, filling the air with the reek of hot oil, vomiting smoke and sparks; its enormous eye, cyclopean, red, throwing a glare far in advance, shooting by in a sudden crash of confused thunder; filling the night with the terrific clamour of its iron hoofs."[68]

Presley, who has a potential poem of the glories of the rural West in his head that vanishes upon running into a cyclopean monster steaming past him (Norris is never one to understate a metaphor), is almost killed by the train—a single locomotive that has no apparent practical use. Its power is not being harnessed for anything other than for its own operation; it is not carrying people or crops or animals. Seemingly, almost out of pure malice, the machine causes a quivering to the once-peaceful earth. For Presley, and for many men and women who had become increasingly reliant on trains, the railroad was an oppressive force, an instrument that could cause physical harm or, as Sigmund Freud attests (himself a famous accident victim of railways), a debilitating anxiety that he termed *traumatic neurosis*.[69] While most might not have vocalized their anger at the railroad in Norris-like phrasing such as "the leviathan, with tentacles of steel clutching into the soil, the soulless Force, the iron-hearted Power, the monster, the Colossus, the Octopus," they resisted the overreaching grip the railroad companies had in the political economy of the United States.[70] Hobos were a part of this resistance.

Contrary to the ideologically driven rhetoric of the railroad as a democratic instrument for unification among both people and geographic locations, an alternative history can be found by theorizing hobos' unique relationship with the material object that defined them: the boxcar. Disappearing from view of the "bulls" trained to keep them off railroad property, hobos became "invisible" for the practical reason of socioeconomic mobility. In this process, though, sneaking into the belly of the boxcar, they were offering a lived resistance to the technological wonder of the railroad. These men and women were seen as the detritus left behind the speeding trains crisscrossing the United States. Refusing to stay on the side of the tracks, hobos gained agency by disappearing into boxcars only to emerge suddenly in a different town somewhere down the line—a symbolic and physical resistance to American capitalism.

### *The Railroad and New Frontier Space*

Not only did the railroad affect the ways individuals reacted to their built environment, it also altered the ways individuals conceptually experienced their world. The transcontinental railroad was an achievement that allowed for corn harvested in Mason City, Iowa, to reach street sellers in Queens, New York, encouraging a mixing of culinary regional staples; it also splintered and changed a concept once thought of as whole: time. As technology advanced, units of time became more distinct and regimented. Railroads published schedules; passengers knew the exact moment a train was planned to depart from one station and to arrive at another terminal. Business transactions, family interactions, and board meetings were therefore dependent on the time when a train whistle blew, announcing its presence in a certain locale. Time became more regulated and consistent as technology transformed spatial practices within the United States.[71]

As time became standardized, so did space. What was "wild" and "undiscovered" land transformed into mapped places. Less than a decade after the meeting of the trains on that historic May afternoon in Utah, Frederick Jackson Turner famously proclaimed before the American Historical Association that "the frontier has gone, and with its going has closed the first period of American history."[72] For Turner, the regulation of space led to an end of the initial epoch within the United States.

Technology made progress visible, and the train was a discernible manifestation of the frontier's disappearance. By 1838 there were 2,765 miles of track laid in the United States; by 1869 there were 56,213 miles laid.[73] What was once described as "virgin land" by Henry Nash Smith was now being penetrated by the train in a regulated and precisely timed fashion. The wild, unstable frontier had given way to scheduled time and fixed certainty; this progression led to social and economic interactions of people in expected and unexpected ways, including the itinerant homeless meeting in the recesses of boxcars or among the dying shadows of a jungle fire along the tracks. While Turner's frontier was closing, a new frontier, created by railroads, was just beginning to open.[74] Within this space, hobos found their subcultural power.

As clearly articulated in Richard Slotkin's trilogy analyzing the frontier myth, the frontier—both as a geographic and ideological marker—has been key to the settlement of the United States.[75] The frontier is conceived as a borderland area, a transforming space where the pioneering adventurer adopts savage characteristics to conquer wild areas of nature, making them into civilized, mappable *places.* This liminal space allows an individual to be transformed by adapting to the unfamiliar and exotic, a freedom that one does not have in the regulated, ordered places of civilization. As the spaces become conquered, they are changed into places with established authorities. The freedom to experience the "other" becomes regulated and tempered; the exotic, wild area thus becomes commonplace.

The railroad allowed for places once separated by time and distance—the city and the wilderness—to be joined together; what had once been separate were becoming parts of the same whole.[76] When the *New York Times* in 1875 worried that the army of tramps was too easily moving from rural towns to cities, it was revealing a larger cultural anxiety with the way this technology was radically transforming society. There always has been a psychological as well as a physical distance between these two spheres; one of national myths of the United States has been the embellished narrative of young white males leaving the confines of the city that makes them "soft" and traveling a dangerous, lonely road to the rejuvenating place of nature. With the railroad's rapid growth, the two separate spheres were suddenly no longer so far apart. To combat the anxiety this produced, the railroad was deemed a continuation of the American progressive character. Slotkin explains, "Just as the farm is superior to and replaces the wilderness, so, too, the railroad represents a further development of civilized power which always takes the form of establishing human control over nature, to construct pathways not carved by rivers or the tracks of beasts and hunters."[77] Investment in track and equipment shows this belief in railroads in unambiguous terms: in the 1850s gross investment was $927 million; by the 1870s it reached more than $2 billion; one decade later it was $4 billion. By 1900 the total investment ballooned to over $15 billion.[78] The enterprising businessman who was firmly situated in the (mostly northeastern) places of society replaced the frontiersman who had transformed himself within the spaces of the borderlands. Jay Gould had seemingly supplanted Daniel Boone.

The "annihilation" of space, the controlling of time, and the colonizing mark of civilization on "savage" land that the railroad wrought on the country was debated from one coast to the other, and, as Page Smith summarizes, "all that was best and worst in America seemed caught up in the railroad mania." A Parliamentary report, reprinted in a few widely distributed journals including the *Quarterly Review*, enthusiastically envisioned "the gradual annihilation, approaching almost to the final extinction, of that space and of those distances which have hitherto been supposed unalterably to separate the various nations of the globe."[79] Space was deemed unpredictable and the railroad praised as a technological marvel with egalitarian possibilities unimaginable a few short years before.

The railroads, therefore, transformed spatial practices within the United States, and hobos should be framed within this national, ideological, and physical transformation. One particular way critics have done so is to read the hobo as a modernization of the frontiersman figure. Using Jack London as a premiere example of this type of "industrial cowboy," Christine Photinos examines how the rail rider uses the "extensive railroad system of the industrialized United States as itself a space for preindustrial adventure and physical testing—and for reasserting what was understood as a kind of preindustrial manhood."[80] In this conceptualization of the networked rail system, hopping trains acts as an elixir for the effeminizing effects wrought by the "civilizing" of the nation. The iron rails become extensions of the rejuvenating powers of nature, and hoboing becomes a rite of passage to prove one's manhood.

In this reading the hobo is not a combative member of the exiled working-class subculture but rather a player in the larger narrative of American masculinity, in which one must reject the effeminizing effects of civilized life by learning to survive in an industrialized "nature." Similar to the narrative created around Theodore Roosevelt, who transformed himself into the hypermasculine hero that he is known for today only after he left the (effeminate) East Coast and traveled to the (masculine) West, reemerging as the man who would be president, the hobo could likewise transform himself by hopping trains and outwitting bulls.[81] With the frontier closed, the myth of the masculine hero can be transferred to an industrialized environment; instead of a horse, the train would be a contemporary substitute. Death and rebirth motifs abounded in popular sensational stories of rail riding, as some writers exploited this narrative, selling these adventure stories to literary magazines. Helping solidify rail riding as an exclusively male rite of passage, this masculine narrative also revealed the gendered dynamics of spatial politics as it involved the hobo subculture.

These types of stories celebrate hobos as industrial cowboys playing deadly games of train hopping, reinserting them within acceptable, individualized masculine roles of the American male. What this framing does not do, though, is highlight the fact that hobos were part of a mobile subculture that used the train as a means to procure jobs and sustenance. A greater nuanced understanding of the conceptual space within the railroad car itself—and the way hobos manipulated this space—is needed to understand the communal interactions among the subculture. In his novel *The Iron Tracks*, Aharon Appelfeld writes, "A train is by nature heavy, even clumsy. But in open spaces, when it gains speed, it transforms itself."[82] The hobo, holding onto the train, also transforms within this space. To begin exploring this transformation, let us first explore the differently conceived space of the railroad car when inhabited by a passenger and by a hobo.

### *The Place of the Passenger*

The railroad car represents an invasion of place. Michel de Certeau, in a chapter titled "Railway Navigation and Incarceration" from his influential book *The Practice of Everyday Life*, shows that inside the railroad car is an ordered place. It is "traveling incarceration" in which the "unchanging traveler is pigeonholed, numbered and regulated in the grid of the railway car."[83] Much like a piece of mail that could be found in one of the locked cars, passengers are marked and arraigned in a specific place; as they hand their ticket to the conductor, their movements are controlled and ordered in this closed environment. They have been assigned a place to sit, to order lunch, to smoke a cigarette, to relieve themselves: the price of a ticket allows them to perform certain bodily functions in logically organized, designated places. For the most part, though, they sit, immobile, and look out the glass pane at other immobile objects—cows staring dumbly in fields, mountain peaks covered in snow, streetlamps illuminating the night sky. Like the passengers, these objects are still, silent, and fixed.

Mark Simpson, in his examination of the politics of mobility in the nineteenth century, uses the term *disciplinary pace* to describe the way that technologies of movement under capitalism have allowed for a regulation of velocity by placing inertia at the center of modern speed. In doing so, it has made "bodies in motion the objects, not agents, of their velocity." This inertia is the basis of being a passenger. As Doreen Massey contends, all mobility reflects and reinforces power relations, and as passengers look out the window, they are fulfilling their role as a passive object.[84]

While traveling, neither the passengers nor the objects move; they are immobile, fixed points. The changes in the passengers' vision and the amount they can see, understand, and process the scenery outside their window is dependent on the machine's speed; the faster the train moves, the more the passengers' vision becomes blurred. Inside this module of "panoptic and classifying power," passengers are rational beings traveling within an organized cell, passing recognizable places that have been scouted, mapped, and, after much consideration, time, and money, strategically deemed most appropriate for the building of that particular track. Strategies, as de Certeau explains, are intimately aligned with this issue of place, as they are formed from bases of power used to manage and control objects. By dividing and bordering a particular area, those who are able to use strategies may identify and manipulate objects within their scope of vision.[85] Depending on the situation, the objects under observation do not know (or care) that they are being managed or controlled. Passengers, by paying for a ticket, have entered into a contract, agreeing to be managed by the railroad companies who have both the will and power to own the land that those tracks cover. They rely on corporate operators to take them on their journey, and while they may be unaware of the path the train is taking, they believe in their binding contract (the ticket) that the express from New York will somehow get them to Chicago in time for their meetings.

What once was wild, dangerous frontier *space* suddenly becomes *property* as the iron rails are secured in the ground. These tracks define, categorize, and regulate the environment—something passengers are oblivious to when they sit in their assigned seats. Looking out the glass windowpane that frames the world in a whirl of flying colors, they are part of a controlled environment; the temperature and noise level are regulated and fellow passengers are under surveillance. Immobile, their needs and wants met, passengers, looking out the window, find pleasure (whether consciously or not) in the lack of effort it takes to be a controlled subject in a mobile regulated system. If passengers break their contract, they can be removed from the environment, suffering the penalties. This regulated order is the power of place.

Passengers rely on this order. Traveling through neighborhoods they are afraid to walk through, they feel a sense of safety because the train surrounds them; they are no longer active, worrying about their safety, but passive, feeling sure that order will prevail. Whether it is the fast speed through areas of perceived fear or the feeling of invincibility riding in such a large, powerful machine, there is a comfortable cushion within a train. That is why when that order is disrupted, the anxiety and betrayal passengers feel is of such great magnitude.

### *The Space of the Hobo*

Space, on the other hand, exists when there is a rupture to the stability of the environment, when subjects enter into a "proper" place, using it for their own purposes—purposes not sanctioned by those who own the place. These marginalized individuals assert their oppressed power within a regulated place and, for a time at least, make it their own space. This spatial creation results in an instability, a tear, in the order of things. This practiced place, where subjects use opportunities presented to them, is, however, the power of the weak. Unable to use strategies, they are left in the margins, poaching off the larger powers and taking advantage of the opportunities offered; they must always live in the present, using tactics to play with the oppressive laws. This is the power that subcultures use to exert their space in a hostile, ordered environment.

Hobos are members of an economically mobile and socially unstable subculture, actively carving spaces within the culture's recognized and accepted places. Partially defined by the fact that they ride illegally on trains, hobos, never inside the train's regimented system, are still dependent on it for their movement. Unlike the passive relationship between passengers and the train, the hobos are connected in a more intimate way. There is a physical link between hobos and the machine, a bond that is essential and unique.

De Certeau writes that both the passengers and the objects outside the window are immobile, fixed, and silent objects. At the same time, he observes that the railroad itself is making noise: "There is a beating of the rails, a vibrato of the windowpanes—a sort of rubbing together of spaces at the vanishing points of their frontier. *These junctions have no place.*" The train cuts through the places—towns, valleys, deserts—and at the vanishing point of the frontier, the places disappear at the point of contact.[86] As previously discussed, the railroad's speed and ubiquity have brought places closer together, forcing much of the frontier to disappear. The frontier is still present, though, and when the train is in motion, screaming across the continent, there is a "rubbing together of spaces" indicated by the noisy cries of the machine. Passengers, however, are oblivious as they sit in their seat, cushioned and protected. The only sound they hear is the window's vibrations; they could place their hand on the pane and feel the rhythm or listen to the click-clack, click-clack of the train on the tracks. In these places, there are only sounds. In space, however, there is noise.[87]

Hobos, sitting in the corner of the open boxcar, are physically a part of that noisy borderland where the frontier disappears. Dick Hebdidge writes that "subcultures represent 'noise' (as opposed to sound) interference in the orderly sequence." Although passengers are culturally permitted to raise their voice a bit when ordering pretzels in the bar car, hobos, trying to keep warm in subzero temperatures as the train moves across the country, may yell, stamp their feet, and run around to keep alive.[88] In Jim Tully's hobo memoir, *Beggars of Life*, for example, he writes of a hazardous trip that nearly killed him: "The cold air numbed my muscles until a stupor fought to gain control of my brain. Silently I fought with a primitive lust for life. I pounded the roof of the car to revive the ebbing circulation of my blood. I shook my head violently, as a pugilist does to drive the effect of a grueling smash from his brain. I longed for the train to stop."[89] Unable to control the train, Tully must endure horrific conditions. Since he is not in the railroad car's proper place, Tully is forced to take actions not permitted or warranted by passengers. Unheard above the roar of the engine and unseen in the darkness of the night, hobos can use their voices to yell and hoot; they can laugh or curse; they can rip off some of the thousand-mile paper.[90]

By stealing a ride, hobos are outside history: there is no seat assigned, no money exchanged for a ticket, no knowledge that they are even there on the train. In effect, they do not officially exist. Even though railroad engineers may suspect that illegal riders are there (or, in many cases, turn a blind eye to them), as homeless wanderers participating in an illegal activity, it is as if hobos have become invisible. When discussing everyday train passengers, De Certeau writes that "history exists where there is a price to be paid"; hobos, though, do not pay for their tickets, rendering themselves invisible.[91]

Official history acknowledges only that which can be seen. Space, therefore, is dangerous because the actions taking place are concealed and unregulated. Michel Foucault's classic text, *Discipline and Punish*, shows that there is much advantage in keeping people under the constant, albeit illusionary, gaze of the state rather than plunging subcultures into the dark where they can gather strength in secrecy. But, as Foucault points out, when Jeremy Bentham revolutionized surveillance in the prison system by introducing the Panopticon, he never anticipated that some subjects would resist the gaze, creating spaces not monitored by authorities. Not everyone is passive, and "there would always be ways of slipping through their net."[92]

Hobos slipping into a boxcar are not passive figures, and they resist the gaze by stepping outside of official history. Unlike passengers who are always under the gaze of established authority, when hopping a train, hobos exist in the spatial frontier. And although the time between mapped points has been diminished by the speed of the locomotive, there is still the moment of contact, the "rubbing of spaces" created by the train's movement, that is unobservable. At that moment of contact, hobos, outside of history but within the train car, become part of the train itself. Unlike everyday passengers who are cushioned and protected, hobos, intimately intertwined with the machine, become producers of space. This theoretical concept can best be understood by examining a particular way that hobos hopped trains.

One of the most dangerous ways of stealing a ride, and thus the one that hobo autobiographies often proudly repeated to portray their subjects' hopping skills, was "riding the rods." Kenneth Allsop, author of a history of the hobo, describes this perilous way of traveling: "Beneath the old boxcar . . . the iron frame was underbraced by gunnels, or iron bars, running lengthwise eighteen inches below the belly of the car, leaving a space [where a hobo] could sidle and so be borne, stretched flat on his back like a kipper on a grill, cradled between the thundering wheels and a few inches above the sleepers and spraying cinders." Hobos would find a piece of wood or board and make an improvised bed a few inches above the gravel. If they fell asleep or slipped, or if an angry engineer with a grudge threw a bolt under the car (where it became a lethal weapon used to knock hobos off their perch), certain death was to follow.[93]

Riding the rods was extremely dangerous because the distance between hobos and the train was nonexistent; arms and legs intertwined with rods and steel. Only inches away from the wheels and from the rails just below, their bodies seemingly engulfed by the machine itself, hobos were certainly not passive, and they had no protection from the elements. Any movement—either by him or by the train—that separates the hobo from the machine would mean certain death. As the machine enters the "disappearing frontier," so too enters the hobo into that space.

This image of the hobo riding the rails interrupts rhetorics of progress embodied by the railroad. Instead, this image sutures an alternative body, the poor mobile hobo, into the discourse, illustrating how a subculture physically appropriated the train. De Certeau explains in *The Writing of History* that marginalized figures haunt any attempts at writing histories and that "'resistances,' 'survivals' or delays discreetly perturb the pretty order of a line of 'progress' or a system of interpretation."[94] For this philosopher, history can never fully be grasped and all history is a "heterology"—a discourse on otherness. Although national historiographies attempt to control narratives of the past in particular self-serving ways, it is impossible to close the narrative loop. Disruptions always exist, hauntings by these marginalized others who leave apertures of dissonance in official discourse. When examined through this prism, hobos were not only mere irritants to capitalists, symptomatic of the double binds of economic and mobility dispossessions, but resistive figures, whose bodily actions spoke to alternative illegal ways of using the train that was beneficial in particular, substantive and subversive ways.

Not all scholars read this act of train hopping (or any train hopping) as a type of agency. Mark Simpson, in a reading of Jack London's hobo experiences, describes the act of riding the rods as "sex under naturalism," understanding the anthropomorphic relationship between hobo and machine as to be one ultimately destructive for the rider. Although writers such as London and Tully and numerous hobos stated that they purposely left factory life and sought refuge by hopping trains, according to Simpson, "such coupling can never lead to escape" because the hobo is moving from one machine (factory) to another (train)—both lead to similar forms of dispossession of the worker under capitalism. In this type of reading, the focus is on the train rider's impotency. The speed and repetition that the late nineteenth-century worker experienced in factory life led to what Anson Rabinbach has described as "pathological fatigue"; the hobo, therefore, embodies a "neurasthenia" or an "ethic of resistance to work or activity in all its forms."[95] In other words, the person riding the rails is a "bad worker," unable to "productively" exist inside or outside the factory, which in turn disconnects the hobo from the working class. In these readings, the hobo is a nonresistive body who melds into the phallic train; the hobo intimately intertwined with the machine is viewed more as a rape victim than a person with agency.

Dialoguing with Rabinbach, Mark Seltzer explores the imaginative coupling of machines and bodies whereby the act of train hopping "seems less an alternative to either machine-work or neurasthenia than another way . . . what amounts to an erotics of uncertain agency." Seltzer is interested in the way that riding the rods is not "a demotion of the living body to the machine but [an] intimate correlation," becoming a rivalry between technological and biological bodies.[96] Although seeing more potential in hoboing than Simpson, Seltzer theoretically reads the act of hopping a train as a pseudosexual act ultimately shaped and contained by capitalism's forces.

Like Seltzer, my reading of train hopping amounts to "uncertain agency," although ultimately I do not view its potential as rigidly limited. Instead, hobos' latent resistance ultimately depends on the way that hobos use and experience their rides. While readings by literary scholars are valuable, teasing out the way that capitalism contains workers' movements within tropes of naturalistic sexuality, in my reading of this act I do not see a passive body, nor do I see a "resistance to work." Rather, I see mobile workers risking their lives by stealing a ride. Contrary to the repetitive motions of a worker in a factory who is always under surveillance by policing forces, in riding the rods the actions taking place are invisible. The imaginative melding of flesh and steel is expressive of the tangled networks in which the railway journey celebrated by passengers is paralleled with a circuit of invisible movements by itinerant workers. The result is a hybrid network where these two parallel journeys often simultaneously exist on the same train. But whereas the passenger relies (and is forced) into a mode of passivity, the hobo, to stay alive and make it to the next destination, must remain active. Circulating meanings of hobos—both in terms of actual bodies hopping trains and literary bodies described in memoirs, fictional tales, and newspaper articles—involved negotiations of spatial politics.

My reading of hobos is closer to Michael Denning's view of the outlaw characters in nineteenth-century dime novels, whom he calls, playing with Eric Hobsbawm's terminology, "social bandits." These outlaw figures (such as the western antihero Deadwood Dick) wed "social banditry to capitalism," and they are "less stories of the Wild West than stories of Labor and Capital."[97] Like these western figures, hobos embody a narrative in the larger story of labor and capital but are even more ensconced within its workings; when employed, hobos, unlike their gun-slinging counterparts, were laborers fulfilling an important function in the United States' political economy. They also were homeless, and by stealing rides they too were outlaws whose movements were deemed illegal. Instead of robbing passengers on trains or dynamiting Pullman safes, however, hobos were invisibly stealing spaces on trains, coming into contact and building transient relationships with other members of the subculture doing the same. While riding the rods shows most clearly this physical connection of hobos with the train, through the act of stealing a ride hobos transform train places into hobo spaces. The hobos' labor made them part of the working class, their mobility made them marginalized within it, and their homelessness made their movements illegal. To survive, hobos—like all homeless—needed to control their visibility within places, transforming them into spaces.

### *Hobos' Subcultural Power*

Homeless bodies are illegal bodies that, when seen, are subject to censure. In the contested landscapes between the propertied and transient poor throughout the country, homeless bodies, which exert an "out of placeness," are subject to the controlling gaze of authorities (police, social worker, academic, policymaker, etc.) who compare them in relations to set norms.[98] With the law on their side, these authorities are able to exert a physical and psychological force on the out-of-place bodies. In settings in which homeless bodies are seen sitting on street benches, sleeping in cardboard tents, or pushing shopping carts down streets, they become subjects of study and, both legally and illegally, the object of physical responses.

The homeless do not have any claim to private places; they exist in the public sphere. But it is their very physical presence that anticipates their transformative power. While a park bench may be designed by city planners as a place to sit, talk, and enjoy the parameters of nature in a controlled environment, homeless people may transform that bench into a space to sleep. With no bed or place to rest in the private sphere, they make the public place a private space that is contrary to cultural norms and deemed illegal. By using the park bench in a way that is not intended (and in this case, not legal), they are visibly stating their position in a homeless subculture. By sleeping on the park bench for extremely practical purposes, the homeless enter into a political discourse through their visibility: by being seen, their body is now the focal point of lawmakers' gaze in the ongoing discussion about what should be done with the homeless.

While members of the privileged cultures may gaze on homeless bodies and see only passive subjects, these simple physical actions—such as sleeping on a bench or hopping a train—are, in fact, creative reactions that resistively exert their own subcultural identity. Talmadge Wright, an urban anthropologist, writes, "When the very poor redefine urban space in a manner that meets their needs, their actions are often explained by authorities as 'survival' mechanisms or as creative 'deviant' adaptations, not as resistance or opposition to a bleak situation. . . . The use of the terms *survival* and *adaptation* to describe homeless behaviors fits well with the dominant social imaginary where the urban poor are conceived as passive agents, merely reacting to their immediate situation; the reality is that homeless actions can include both survival and opposition, adaptation and resistance."[99] By understanding the homeless as passive deviant subjects trying only to survive—or gazing on them and interpreting their bodies through romantic, self-serving, bourgeois notions of freedom—these privileged cultures are able to envision and contain the homeless in neutral, passive bodies.

This transformative power to make a public sphere into a private space, as de Certeau notes, is fleeting. Sleeping is an illegal act that forces reactions by those in power who need to reclaim the bench for both symbolic and practical reasons. Given that these subcultural acts of transformation are performed in the public sphere, they subject the homeless to censure because poor bodies are squarely in the gaze of the normative cultures who are able to pass judgment on them.

One way to delimit homeless bodies is to forcibly control their visibility. The punishment for living continuously in public places is to be made invisible in state-sanctioned places—shelters or jails. Active creation of spaces by the homeless is made illegal; their bodies are forced outside the public's gaze (although securely fixed by the state) and are sent to functional, ordered places to contain the inmates. Bodies, therefore, when deemed too visible, are legally made to disappear into places of correction where they are relieved of their individual ability to create personalized spaces.

While all homeless actions contain "survival and opposition, adaptation and resistance," hobos, by hopping a train, are more mobile than traditional homeless and thus treated differently. Only sanctioned forms of mobility are recognized as appropriate, and state discipline limits the mobilities of "shadow citizens" who threaten to undo spatial orders, whether on a micro (local) or a macro (national) level. Citizenship is a precursor for "appropriate" movement and, as previously stated, Creswell's well-documented narrative of the late nineteenth-century tramp laws clearly shows the policy paradigms designed to deny transients the ability to move because doing so unsettled established political and societal orders.[100] Poor mobile people are threatening; consequentially, their movements are degraded and marginalized.

James Scott concludes that modern nations have made it a priority to order and control the movements of poor people. For Scott, these subordinated groups, while never distinctly rebelling openly, still are able to resist "off-stage," away from the gaze of the dominant groups. Instead of the subordinate classes offering one "great refusal" to a dominant culture, Scott shows in a number of studies how the "hidden transcripts" of these subordinate groups helped define their own political and social identity.[101] Similarly, hobos, who attempt to control their visibility, offer their resistance by invisibly hopping trains. They are seen when they need to be seen—knocking on back doors for work, signing up for a job at an employment agency, asking for lodging at a charity organization—but they also can become invisible by crawling into a boxcar and avoiding being caught by a railroad bull. Unlike homeless people arrested for sleeping in public and whose visibility is controlled when they are placed in jail or a shelter, successful hobos control their own visibility by disappearing from view.

In an often-repeated scene throughout the United States in the late nineteenth and early twentieth centuries, a train's whistle sharply blows as smoke emits from the engine and the wheels begin to turn. Hobos, jumping from their hiding spots, grab hold of handlebars and swing themselves onto the train to get somewhere down the line. Through this physical action, hobos locate their source of subcultural power. Although de Certeau's thesis in *The Practice of Everyday Life* is that individuals offer resistance within the constricting environments of society, hobos go one step further, coupling with the machine that is creating spaces at the moment of contact in between places. The hobos' power, therefore, exists when the train is in motion and breaking through the frontier, allowing them to be intimately connected to a force of such magnitude. When hobos are connected to the train by these illegal means—even though death or maiming is a slip away—they have the most subcultural control because they are invisible. The train is thousands of pounds strong, traveling at fast speeds; the hobo, if seen as all, is a blur. Unlike passenger number forty-two on the New York City to Chicago red-eye express, hobos, unseen, have agency because they are invisible and part of the noise of the machine.

Only when the engine dies in the terminal does the hobo's power diminish, as the train embodies "its mute, idol-like inertia, a sort of god-undone."[102] Back in a place that is regimented, ordered, and under surveillance, hobos have to worry about being seen and, more important, about the consequences of being caught without a ticket in the train yard. With the "metal god" no longer spitting smoke and sparks, hobos must untangle themselves from the machine and slink along the tracks until they can find a safe haven in the hidden jungles on the outskirts of town.

The hobos' unique subcultural power, as well as the limits of this power, can be observed in a passage from Charles Chesnutt's *The Marrow of Tradition*, a historical novel about the North Carolina race riot of 1898. One of the main characters, Dr. William Miller, looks out the window of a train and spots Josh Green, a large African American man who has snuck aboard and hidden himself on the train: "As the train came to a standstill, a huge negro, covered thickly with dust, crawled off one of the rear trucks unobserved, and ran round the rear end of the car to a watering-trough by a neighboring well. . . . He threw himself down by the trough, drank long and deep, and plunging his head into the water, shook himself like a wet dog, and crept furtively back to his dangerous perch."[103]

Dr. Miller, an educated man who has received favorable press and prestige for his surgical operations in the North and in Europe, is returning to Wilmington, North Carolina, to open a hospital, when he meets his former mentor, the renowned Dr. Alvin Burns. A few hours into the trip, however, the conductor informs both parties that they will have to separate and that Miller will be forced to move into the "colored" car—for in the ordered environment of the railroad system, only members of certain races can sit in particular cars. When the two object, the conductor warns, "I could simply switch this car off at the next siding, transfer the white passengers to another, and leave you and your friend in possession until you were arrested and fined or imprisoned." The racist law cannot be overtly challenged. Miller submits to the rules and regulations of the railroad company (which are the rules and regulations of the larger state of Virginia) and moves to the designated car.[104]

This scene perfectly represents both the power and the limitations of the hobo. By stealing a ride, Josh Green is not regulated in the same way as Miller, who is forced to surrender to the white conductor his own personal dignity. Although the doctor spots Green from his seat, passing judgment on him by concluding, "Blessed are the meek," Green is, in fact, being more resistive to the oppressive powers than the doctor, who passively follows the racist rules that control his movements. While Miller calls him meek, it is this dusty, parched hobo who, in a race-sensitive place of the railroad car, is able to remain unobserved and uncounted while the train is in motion. Green, therefore, creates a space that allows him to ride in between the law. It is a dangerous space, one that causes him to exclaim, "I kind er 'lowed I was gone a dozen times, ez it wuz," but it also permits him to achieve his goals of getting to where he wants to go.[105] Because of his willingness to travel in between, both literally and symbolically, Green is able to move by creating his particular space on the train.

As Laura Hapke explains, Josh Green represents "a new kind of southern black worker." He is a stevedore, a laborer whose work entails loading goods from ships and interacting with a diverse international working-class community that had led, in port towns such as New Orleans, to a sporadic militarism that both worked with and fought against white trade unionists.[106] Green is a southern black worker at the turn of the century, using his invisibility on the train to get to and from his job. Chesnutt imbues him with fierce strength born from his work on the wharves, a survivalist strength that had protected him against lynching while making him a successful train hopper.

This is the power of subculture. John Fiske states that "there is a power in resisting power, there is a power in maintaining one's social identity in opposition to that proposed by the dominant ideology, there is a power in asserting one's own subcultural values against the dominant ones."[107] It is the power of a subordinated class of people who, because of their (lack of) social position, can be, for a time at least, outside the reaches of the law. It is fleeting, existing mainly when the train is in motion and the hobo is in the act of stealing from the normative cultures, when uncounted and outside of history, when flesh and steel intertwine, and when places turn to spaces. Only then does the subversive power of the hobo manifest itself. It is a power that exerts itself in moments—"what it wins it cannot keep"—and this power continually succumbs to hegemonic forces.[108] Regardless, though, it is a power that shows the cracks—spaces—that can be created by a subordinated subculture.

## POST-SUBCULTURAL HOBO POLITICS

But can the singular act of hopping a train be considered part of a larger hobo subcultural politics? As Chesnutt's Josh Green shows, the hobo's ability to travel in between places helped him achieve his goal of getting to a particular destination, but did it connect him to a political movement? If Green did not hobo his way to Wilmington, then he would not have been an influential part of the violent rebellion that soon would erupt on the town's streets. The militancy present among black dockworkers, connected with Green's ability to control his visibility on the train (unlike Dr. Miller), does begin to tease out the revolutionary potential that some critics have noticed about this character.[109] But Green is no conscious revolutionary, nor does Chesnutt invest him with the characteristics to become a leader of his fellow black workers during the riot; the rebellion for Green becomes a way to settle a score with a white man who injured his father. Green, "suffering from the lingering effects of a white antebellum mindset," thinks he cannot lead the men and instead seeks the help of a man outside the working class to unite the black workers and protect the town.[110]

Despite this reliance, it is Green, a minor character in the novel, who emerges from the margins of the page (and the boxcar) to show the latent capabilities of the black southern worker who refuses to submit to white power. Neither militant revolutionary nor submissive worker, Green's political positioning as both a hobo and a character is complicated. It also raises an overarching question germane to this study: can a hobo's train hopping be read in context of boxcar politics? As stated, this term does not regard revolutionary, overt actions by hobos as the litmus test to consider an action political; rather, the term, as it relates to subcultural mobility, captures a wide swath of resistances, both individual and collective.

Although the term *subculture* is relatively new, originating in the 1940s, marginalized individuals have always congregated outside the spotlight of normative culture. But to what end? In terms of their resistive potential, subcultures often have been seen as not fully evolved in their political stances, and, according to Marx in *The Eighteenth Brumaire of Louis Bonaparte (1851–1852)*, they never were part of the revolutionary proletariat but instead consisted of the reactionary lumpen proletariat. Inherently individualistic and malleable to middle-class interests and ideologies, the lumpen proletariat were not class-conscious (literally they were "beneath" class), and their resistive potential was wholly compromised. Marx's succinct view of the lumpen proletariat (whom he marginalizes in his own texts by infrequently writing about them) had a lasting impression and, as Ken Gelder states, "came to underwrite a logic or way of seeing that continues even today to tie subcultures to non-productivity." From a traditional Marxist perspective, hobos would be seen as potential enemies of the working class and their resistance mere exploitable opportunities for capitalists.[111]

One of the first schools to seriously examine subcultures in general, and hobos in particular, within the academic realm was the Chicago School. Beginning in the 1920s these scholars from various Chicago-area universities approached subcultures in an empiric fashion, quantifying the actions of marginalized men and women and seeking to understand the "deviant" nature of individuals who were not able, or refused, to conform to society. It is no mistake that hobos were examined in much detail by this school, with both former riders Ben Reitman and Nels Anderson (a student of Reitman's) producing book-length studies on the figure. Using pseudo-psychological evidence to examine the "wanderlust" of these individuals, these studies, while striking an appropriate academic tone and remaining overall conservative in nature, clearly were celebratory of the hobo's movement. These academic texts coincided with publications of hobo autobiographies that also were celebratory adventure stories, connecting the hobo to an essential conservative American identity, albeit one with a bit more dirt under its nails. In effect, these scholarly and journalistic treatments did essentially what Marx predicted; most hobos were read not as offering resistance to capitalism, which severely disenfranchised poor workers, but as suffering from a wanderlust "disease" and a misinformed desire for a romanticized, nebulous freedom. Still feared in person when they congregated en masse on the main stem in cities throughout the United States, in print, at least, as Laura Browder writes of the hobos in the early part of the twentieth century, they "became symbols for depoliticized poverty . . . with no political valence."[112]

Subcultural theory, though, changed significantly with the introduction of the Centre for Contemporary Cultural Studies (CCCS). Formed in 1964 by Richard Hoggart but having blossomed under Stuart Hall's leadership from 1969 to 1979, this group of scholars produced numerous studies of working-class youth subcultures, highlighting their radical potential. Whether it was examining pub customers' rooting habits or reading the value of safety pins in a punk outfit, the CCCS saw resistance through (life) style, arguing that subcultures formed as a reaction to dominant political structures and social hierarchies. This was the "heroic phase" of subcultural studies, where, as critics David Muggleton and Rupert Weinzierl state, subcultures often were viewed as rigid and rooted in a coherent group: they were resisting, through their style and practices, what was perceived as a monolithic mainstream.[113] Based on an orthodox Gramscian model of hegemony, the CCCS presumed that subcultures formed in resistance to a dominant culture, signifying their opposition in their practices and style before eventually being co-opted and incorporated by the culture they were resisting.

Although this school was tremendously influential, allowing cultural studies to flourish (and consequently move away from the more pessimistic views of the Frankfurt School), many theorists saw the perceived political rigidness of subculture to be ultimately simplistic. John Irwin, in his 1977 book, *Scenes*, wrote that previous notions of subcultures "suggested too much commitment, determinism, instrumentality, and stability on membership."[114] Rejecting rigidity for fluidity, Irwin saw subcultures as inhabiting "scenes" that were a "social world" whose members had a "shared perspective." This view helped reconceptualize subcultural studies, celebrating the flux and fragmentation of these groups. Moving away from such rigid views of class, Michel Maffesoli builds on this idea of the scene and expands it, preferring the term *tribe* to categorize "an ambience, a state of mind, preferably to be expressed through lifestyles that favour appearance and "form."[115] For Maffesoli, tribe members are more interested in their individual desires (the "emotional community") than in overthrowing particular systems; the individual is elevated above the group. Contemporary, post-subculture theorists Graham St. John, Oliver Marchart, Stephen Duncombe, and David Muggleton also explore the micropractices of individuals within the framework of post-subcultural studies.[116] Examining the hobo through this lens frees this subculture from the rigidness of the CCCS view—hobos hopped trains for a multitude of reasons, and their understandings of class varied. Much of this strand of subcultural theory, however, rejects a macropolitical view of subcultural resistance and marginalizes collectivized efforts, dismissing the centrality of class as identity marker.[117]

The relationship of hobos within their subculture as well as to the larger working class is central to analyzing the manifestations of boxcar politics. While many middle-class reformers and politicians saw hobos as lazy individuals, there was an extensive social network of transient mutuality. This connection among hobos and those outside of their social cast represented a very real community that allowed the hobo to be a hobo. Communities and businesses needed hobos to pick their crops, clear their land, and dig their mines; hobos' lives were distinctly intertwined with the machinations of the larger society. Hopping trains therefore was not simply a "lifestyle choice" but a complex set of desires negotiated through national discourses of mobility, class, and labor.

Both subcultural and post-subcultural studies have derived their theoretical underpinnings from a range of traditions—the former specifically Marxist and the latter postmodern. But the rift between the two, according to Andy Bennett, who had a foot in both camps, is not as great as the volumes of scholarly output proclaim it to be, and important strands tie them together.[118] Most subcultural theorists were not as rigid in their claims of class solidarity as they have been perceived, and most post-subcultural theorists do not believe we live in a class-free society. For Bennett, social structures such as class, race, and gender are always important factors in analyzing subcultures; the way that particular scholars position these structures in their analysis allows different focal narratives to form.

This type of ideological positioning is key in the "mobility turn" in sociology that understands the world as governed by mobile flows. According to this school of thought, to understand society, scholars need to follow these flows—people, money, social structures, popular culture—that, due to their amorphousness, are able to slip through state, federal, and international borders. This mobility turn in the works of John Urry, James Clifford, and Marc Augé is specifically helpful when bridging subcultural and post-subcultural theory and imagining boxcar politics as a type of resistance by hobos.[119]

While post-subcultural theorists imagine identity as being malleable, mobility turn scholars posit that social space also behaves like a fluid in which "boundaries come and go, allow leakage or disappear altogether, while relations transform themselves without fracture."[120] Social structures are not solid but allow for slippage, and people, operating within this space, are able to slide among and through these spaces. For Urry, "the human and the physical worlds are elaborately intertwined and cannot be analyzed separately from each other," and to understand human mobility one must understand both the vehicles for movement and the way people use—or are denied—these options for mobility.[121]

Using the CCCS's view of resistance, the post-subculturalist focus on its members' malleability, and Urry's mobility turn in sociology that weds the flows of people and machines, a theoretical groundwork of boxcar politics begins to come into focus—which then is fleshed out in the individual case studies in the proceeding chapters. In concluding this exploratory chapter that defines hobos as both a historical and a theoretical entity, an examination of Hakim Bey's manifesto, TAZ, a radical view of progressive illegal networking of individuals through the ability to control one's visibility, is a particular arresting way to frame the narrative of boxcar politics.

## *TAZ and Visualizing Boxcar Politics*

Focusing on pirate subcultures in the sixteenth and seventeenth centuries, Hakim Bey uses the lives of these outlaw characters to advocate for practical ways of cultural and political disruption. A proponent of "ontological anarchism," Bey's subcultural politics are on view in his manifesto, *The Temporary Autonomous Zone*, in which he writes that contemporary anarchism has lost its way, and "we are reduced either to nostalgia for the past or nostalgia for the future." Instead of naively wishing for a bloody revolution to take place in the streets (which has led only to martyrdom), Bey challenges those who are not comfortable with the state's control to focus their attention on "uprisings" and "bootstrap operations" that will allow for personal autonomy in a world that is becoming increasingly restricted. Rather than create a movement, Bey instead advocates *moving*. "The TAZ is like an uprising which does not engage directly with the State, a guerilla operation which liberates an area (of land, of time, of imagination) and then dissolves itself to re-form elsewhere/elsewhen, before the State can crush it." The TAZ is a tactic of quick hit-and-run attacks along the fault lines of the state's control. Unlike direct confrontation, it (momentarily) succeeds because it uses invisibility as its means of operation. Therefore, the TAZ is "a perfect tactic for an era in which the State is omnipresent and all-powerful and yet simultaneously riddled with cracks and vacancies." Instead of being visible during a climate of relentless surveillance, "as soon as the TAZ is named (represented, mediated), it must vanish, it will vanish, leaving behind it an empty husk, only to spring up again somewhere else, once again invisible because undefinable in terms of the Spectacle." Using language that seems almost magical—a subcultural community that can "vanish" into thin air at any time—Bey is suggesting that in the modern world, real bodies can render themselves invisible from the apparently omnipresent state's eye by remaining in motion.[122]

Well versed in the philosophy of Baudrillard, Deleuze, and Guattari and their discussions of simulation and spectacle, Bey's debt to the philosophy of Michel de Certeau is apparent. But where de Certeau sees tactics of resistance in seemingly insignificant mundane acts of everyday life, Bey demands an intensification of the everyday. The TAZ that Bey imagines is what he terms "pirate utopias," intentional communities formed outside the reach of the law. Drawing on the firsthand experiences of pirates (and those attempting to bring them to justice), Bey reports the desire of these roving seamen to find spaces where they can meet with other outlaws for both social and economic relations. Here Bey points to a fluid community of outsiders materially linked through an object (the ship) and their resistive actions.

For practical, self-preserving reasons, governments have always made attempts to map and therefore know the area of land under their control. Yet spaces always exist within this environment that can be inhabited without the official powers seeing them. Floating in their ships with stolen booty, pirates would find unknown islands not drawn on parchment paper and locked in a drawer in a government agency, therefore not officially existing. Other ships, also needing to disappear, would sometimes accidentally find these same unknown lands and, if both groups found pleasure (both socially and economically) in the other's company, then they would join together, forming a "band" that productively coexisted for a mutually beneficial time. According to Bey, these formations could be called a TAZ because they were formed off the grid and away from the state's gaze. In other words, they created their own space by existing outside of time and history.

The pirates' collective power existed horizontally among the group and could be disbanded as soon as it needed or wanted to dissolve. For example, if the state's soldiers happened to appear on the horizon, the complexly functioning close band would not stand and fight the overpowering warships. Rather, they would quickly enter their own ships and sail away. The pirates' gains might be fleeting, and the land and friendships they nurtured given up as soon as an enemy's flag appeared on a fast-approaching ship, but, for Bey, this was a type of space that could be continually recreated and cultivated. It is a space that signals a resistance to the Other's control.

This space is similar to the space that hobos create when hopping trains. The hobos' power exists in the ability to control the visibility of their homeless bodies. To be successful, hobos must be able to disappear within the train and exist in the shadows, where they ride with other members of their outlaw community. What the pirate utopia suggests is that a group of individuals gathering together can use their *collective* invisibility to separate themselves from an overtly hierarchal, oppressive state. Whether this is the intended purpose or an unintended consequence, the travelers are still working together to function and survive. Pirate utopias involve more than just individual moments of stealing rides and disappearing; they also can be a resistive expression of group invisibility by existing apart from the gaze of authority.

These fluid, amorphous, shared connections existing between the hobo, the subculture, and the train were a type of boxcar politics that was not vertical but horizontal. One way to visualize boxcar politics is to imagine a single railroad track. Mobility along this single track was limited; one could go only in a particular direction that the train was moving—north or south, east or west. When imagining a hobo grabbing hold of handlebars in the middle of the night and disappearing into the underbelly of a train, this idea of politics associated with hopping a train also can be imagined as an isolated, desolate, and singular action. But viewing this train track from a different vantage point, one sees how this track—and those riding on those tracks—was part of an integrated system.

From a railroad map of the 1890s, what could seem like an isolated hopping of one hobo had the potential to connect that hobo to a large network of other hobos who also were crossing and recrossing the Unites States. Far from being lonely or isolated, hobos were able to meet and share rides through the railways' numerous connecting points. Those solitary tracks, therefore, were part of a web that allowed the hobo to travel throughout the country. Even if a major line was removed from the hobo—by police monitoring the line or a vigilante group tarring and feathering all hobos attempting to disembark in their town (which happened frequently)—the structure did not fall apart. Rather, like the pirates in Bey's articulation of TAZ, new lines were discovered, new routes taken, and new confederations formed. There was agency among the hobos who were constantly creating and recreating their own political identity in real time and real space.

Although this webbed system of tracks was large, with numerous paths to be tried, because many hobos were agricultural laborers, there were well-traveled roads where they were meeting and coming into contact with one another. These meetings were transitory, but jungle fires were shared and conversations initiated. While these talks were practical in nature—"Where are there jobs? Where are the 'hot' towns? Where can one get free food and shelter?"—there were also political discussions of such topics as the economic situation, shark employers, and nefarious police interrogations. Like the image of the isolated track when picturing these conversations, we can imagine secluded, weary hobos talking among themselves around small fires. If we could step back and panoramically examine these fires in one tracking shot, however, we would see thousands of fires all around the country that were just too numerous to put out. Some of these hobo jungle conversations lasted only a night, while others led to the establishing of free hobo colleges throughout the West or to the emergence of radical labor organizers. Still other conversations led to confederacies of hobos working together to find food and employment. These fire conversations were not large explosions but small "starter"

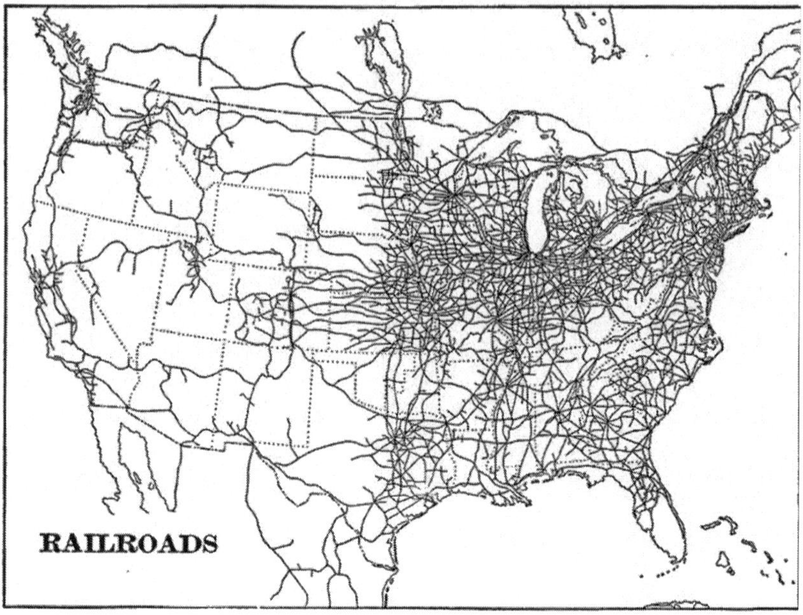


Railroad map of the United States, from Mitchell's New General Atlas (1890). Courtesy David Rumsey Map Collection, www.davidrumsey.com.

fires. And while major fires could be located, isolated, and put out, small fires, while seemingly not as dangerous, were potentially always being rekindled. In essence, the hobo was part of a working-class community in a shadow America. How hobos coexisted within this space runs the gamut from selfishly individualistic to radically communal and is the subject of the remainder of this book.

Chapter Two

# THE CRAMPED BOXCAR

## Jack London and Kelly's Industrial Army

Jack London was a selfish hobo. The man who would become a champion of the Socialist Labor Party of America and tireless advocate for (white) workers' anticapitalism efforts did not like sharing his boxcar with anyone else. London epitomized a specific subset of hobos: the individualistic rider who defined his self-worth by his train-hopping ability. This competitive individualist stance placed him, at times, in competition with all members of society, including those within his hobo subculture. Seemingly indifferent to resisting capitalism's unfair labor practices (of which he was a victim), London instead created a stratified masculine subculture, using his dispossession from mainstream society as the opportunity to prove his "royalty" within his own. This type of hobo, primarily concerned with his personal movement, caused friction when he entered the same railroad space as a political working-class movement advocating for traditional labor reforms.

CHAPTER TWO

# JACK LONDON AND THE HOBO POPULATION

Mostly known for his adventure stories such as *The Call of the Wild*, *White Fang*, and *The Sea-Wolf*, as well as his heavily anthologized short story "To Build a Fire," Jack London was a prolific writer who, when he died at age forty, had published more books than the number of years he had lived. Experimenting with numerous literary forms ranging from proletarian fiction to one-act plays, London's work addressed a wide range of subjects, never shying away from placing himself or his own adventures at the center of his narratives. His willingness to tell and retell his personal struggles with, and conquest over, cultural and economic poverty, along with his penchant for writing stories of man-versus-nature in strong, no-nonsense prose, endeared him to the reading public at the turn of the twentieth century.

From his first success at age seventeen, when the *San Francisco Call* published "Story of a Typhoon off the Coast of Japan" in 1893, to playing a role in a film adaptation of *The Sea-Wolf* in 1913, London was a celebrity superstar who became the first literary millionaire in the United States. A savvy public relations entrepreneur, he closely studied the literary market, learned what techniques and forms were selling and, undeterred by rejection letters, flooded the market with his writings. London's prose and personality were perfectly matched for the last decade of the nineteenth century, when weekly and monthly newspaper and magazine circulations were at never-before-seen highs. Specifically, his adventure stories, filled with hard-living men who both weather and are bested by forces of nature outside of their control, found a substantial readership among many working-class people who saw parallels in their own struggles to survive in a labor market that was significantly and quickly changing. As an autodidact who had an immense larger-than-life personality (he was, for example, one of the first literary celebrities hired to endorse products ranging from fruit juice to designer suits), London, the person, became larger than London, the author, resulting in more than double the number of biographies being written on the man than book-length examinations of his texts.[1]

Biographies of London have created and helped sustain myths that have always shadowed his life and texts—myths concerning his physical adventures, his tempestuous love life, his heavy drinking, and his racialist views. As Jeanne Campbell Reesman has noted, there is a need for a less sensational look at London's biography and a more definitive treatment of the author and his politics.[2] This chapter discusses one of these intersections of his life and ideologies that has been mostly overlooked by scholars: the period from April to September 1894, when Jack London was a hobo. During these turbulent six months, London hopped boxcars across state and country lines, spent time sightseeing on both U.S. coasts, joined Charles T. Kelly's Industrial Army, watched a public whipping of a small boy, befriended socialists and anarchists, worked on a steamer, begged for food, committed petty thievery, and was arrested and sentenced to thirty days for vagrancy in the county penitentiary in Erie, Pennsylvania. As he did with many of his other traveling experiences, he recycled this journey in various periodicals, eventually publishing nine essays in *Cosmopolitan Magazine* that were later collected in 1907 in *The Road*.[3]

But what effect did his hobo travels have on his political understanding? London himself indicated that these six months were a turning point in his life, a juncture that forced him to rethink his lifestyle and turn toward socialism. In two of his most famous essays about why he embraced socialism, London specifically mentions these hobo experiences. In his 1903 essay, "How I Became a Socialist," London describes the road as a place of degradation, where honest, strong men were powerless against the economic forces designed to keep them in a continual state of poverty and subservience. Two years later, in "What Life Means to Me," London again states that the road gave him a "terrible scare," and his experiences convinced him that he needed to get off the road, head back to school, and become a "vender of brains" instead of a directionless wanderer mired in the Social Pit. Scholars have taken London at his word, using these articles and *The Road* to prove that his time as a hobo was clearly a catalyst that changed him from an avowed individualist to a strong believer in socialism.[4]

But Richard Etulain, who collected London's hobo diary entries and stories in *Jack London on the Road*, questions the impact these experiences had on his overall psyche, pointing out that neither *The Road* nor London's travel diary contain much criticism of the social and economic problems of the day. Instead, they are primarily boastful and lively essays about life on the road as a young, single, white male.[5] Seemingly, there are inconsistencies between London's romanticized and witty account of his hobo experiences in *The Road*, his stark analysis of these journeys in his articles about socialism, and most critics' credulous acceptance of the author's analysis of his travels. Some of these disconnects can be erased, however, if instead of looking exclusively at what London *wrote*, we contextualize and analyze what he *did*. In the depths of the depression of the late nineteenth century, when the industrial unemployment rate reached as high as 25 percent and as many as one-fifth of American workers spent at least one night homeless and sleeping in a local police department, Jack London quit his job in a jute mill and spent six months living as a hobo.[6] By focusing on London's time riding the iron road, we can better understand how his individualistic politics were both fostered and sustained by his intimate and illegal intertwining with a premier symbol of capitalist expansion and modernization: the railroad.

One reason London hopped trains was that he felt his vagabond life would be full of adventures and experiences, offering him a respite from the stratified world of capitalism, with its dangerous factories, corrupt managers, and poverty-level wages. In an oft-told story of why he headed for the road, London recounts being tricked and abused by his boss: "I was willing to work, and [my employer] was more than willing that I should work. I thought I was learning a trade. In reality, I had displaced two men. I thought he was making an electrician out of me; as a matter of fact, he was making fifty dollars per month out of me. The two men I had displaced had received forty dollars each per month; I was doing the work of both for thirty dollars per month."[7] Realizing his exploitation, London quit his job. Much like the character Johnny in his 1906 short story "The Apostate," who, after realizing his employers had cruelly used him, quits his job and, smiling, crawls into a boxcar, London, after he abandoned his job, also became a hobo.[8] Both were escaping the confines of factory life for an uncertain life on the road.

Not all scholars, however, view Johnny (or any other hobo) crawling into the boxcar as a form of escape. Mark Simpson understands London's depiction of Johnny lying in a boxcar as a continuation of the automated reality that has broken his body and "refines his spirit as a motionless machine," thereby having the boxcar ride offer no repose from the modern condition. Instead, the boxcar becomes a type of coffin for the undead Johnny. Christine Photinos also gives a compelling reading along similar lines, writing that the character was not a "heroic American wanderer so much as the latest arrival to the Social Pit" that London detailed in his socialist writings.[9] While both readings are persuasive when examining this story through the lens of naturalist fiction, I read Johnny as someone who is finally able to break free from the death grip of his bosses and crawl, undetected, into a boxcar. Instead of reading the train as a substitute coffin, I understand it as a conduit of escape for a young man struggling to break free from the confines of the factory. He is after all, an apostate, no longer blindly following a mechanized, ritualistic life. My reading certainly does not project Johnny's ride as a romantic ideal; the escape might be only momentary, and it would be fraught with many unknowns. I do, however, see this move from the factory to the railroad as resistance to the deadening world of automated life. In reading "The Apostate" through the lens of London's autobiography, a parallel is clear: Johnny realizes his exploitation and escapes; London did the same. Although his young body is damaged and his mind dulled, as Johnny hides in the shadows of the boxcar, he begins to smile. London imbues the boy with agency simply by allowing him to disappear and become a hobo.[10]

Todd DePastino, in his introduction to a reissue of *The Road*, encapsulates London's view of the hobo as a resistive figure. In London's reminisces of his time on the road, it was the middle-class bourgeoisie and the factory foremen who were seen as monstrous and dull-witted, "while the hobo emerges as a self-reliant and full-blooded refugee from a despoiled social order."[11] To stay buried under the harsh automation of factory life or to have absurd Algeresque dreams of rising through the social order was to remain passive and submissive. Contrarily, the hobo was defiant.

For London, though, it was a defiance embodied within the actions of the singular hobo. Johnny's agency is limited because he is an individual, cut off from the rest of the working-class subculture. By leaving the factory, not only was London, like Johnny, separating himself from the bosses callously exploiting his labor, he was also distancing himself from his fellow workers who were likewise being exploited. His sense of superiority to these workers toiling in the same types of jobs that he just left, while he "freely" traveled throughout the country in 1894, is evident throughout *The Road*. It can best be summarized, however, in his romanticized descriptions of his hobo lifestyle as he enjoyed a free meal from two older women who had worked their whole lives at the same job: "Into the sweet scents and narrow confines of their uneventful existence I brought the large airs of the world, freighted with the lusty smells of sweat and strife, and with the tangs and odors of strange lands and soils."[12] By voluntarily giving up his job to travel, London was consequently separating himself from what he viewed as the traditional laborer living a feminized "uneventful existence." Instead, London was creating a mystique around himself as a masculine adventurer whose core identity was centered on his ability to move. Jobs, he felt, could be had when needed, but it was specifically his mobility that undergirded his identity at this moment in his life. As DePastino succinctly states, "London extracts and distills the subcultural elements of the hobo life and leaves behind as an unsavory residue the labor upon which the subculture was based."[13] While London in his later years championed the (white, male) proletariat in his numerous books, plays, and articles, in 1894 he consciously and excitedly separated himself from the other members of the industrial working class.

But what happens when a person whose identity is based on perpetual movement meets a politicized group traveling in order to *stop* moving? Exploring the contact zone of the boxcar where the individualistic hobo, as championed by London, meets Kelly's Industrial Army as they marched toward Washington to demand jobs and security from the federal government not only allows us to flesh out the author's complex political ideologies but also to discover how an itinerant individualist interacts within a collective working-class political movement.

General Kelly's army of unemployed men was a regimented, political labor organization that slowly traveled from Oakland, California, to Washington, D.C., to protest the federal government's indifference to the unemployed while simultaneously demanding jobs to be created for them. By 1894 there was no shortage of people looking for work. As the industrial armies began their marches, more than 150 railroad companies and 30 steel companies had gone bankrupt. A total of 500 banks and 1,600 businesses had failed.[14] The country was experiencing a major depression, and the armies were one of many outbursts of public contempt toward the government. Kelly's army was an offshoot of Jacob Coxey's Commonweal of Christ, the first regiment to walk to Washington to petition Congress for $500 million for a public works program that would give the unemployed jobs building roads. They believed that by being this "petition in boots," their visibility would force the government to act.[15] But while Coxey left his Ohio mansion for the (relatively) short trip to Washington, many other industrial armies formed around the country, making their own pilgrimages to the country's capital. Unlike Coxey's army's overall religious tone, the armies from the West were much more secularly militant. General Kelly headed the largest of these armies, over twelve times greater than Coxey's.[16]

Kelly believed that if Congress would give jobs to men for three years building irrigation ditches in the West, "the people would be on their feet once more. . . . This is the richest country in the world and there is no reason why a single individual should beg for bread." The plan's central goal was to give men jobs so that they could create their own homes; the arid lands irrigated, these unemployed men would then settle this new fertile land and build houses. While some saw this petition as dangerous, because it allowed dependence on the federal government and foreshadowed a modern welfare state, the plan actually had its roots in a Jacksonian belief in the yeoman farmer.[17]

But while the trek was hailed as a "March on Washington," most of the armies of the West commandeered trains to take them to the nation's capitol. The distance was too great for the armies to walk, and, consequently, the various regiments illegally commandeered more than fifty trains.[18] It seems logical, then, that the armies stealing whole trains and hobos stealing individual spots within trains, would make compatible riding partners. But this shared ride, while not completely antagonistic, was a bumpy one. An examination of this time provides a closer investigation of one subsection of the emerging hobo labor class that became a critical part of early twentieth-century revolutionary working-class politics as well as its foil. To understand this contentious contact zone between the individualistic hobo and collective army, the hobo that London idealized and epitomized is closely examined.

## THE INDIVIDUALISTIC HOBO

As discussed in chapter 1, definitions of the term *hobo* were inexact, and in the 1890s, as many found themselves being forced to search for jobs, this categorizing of hobo and nonhobo was difficult. Consequently, the mainstream press painted the homeless with a wide brush, noting little distinction between the different categories. This influx of people traveling by train led many of the seasoned riders from within the subculture to declare the death of the "authentic" hobo almost as soon as the term became widespread during the economic depressions of the last decade of the nineteenth century.[19]

Whether or not they were deemed "authentic" hobos, many men and women were forced from their homes onto the road. If they could not find a job in a particular town, they moved to a place that did have a job available—even if it was only temporary. Boxcars became crowded, as large numbers of the unemployed hopped trains when rumors of jobs gave them hope for a few days of work. Many laborers, therefore, who had deep ties to communities and geographic locations, found themselves rootless. In his examination of hobo labor in the Midwest between 1880 and 1930, Frank Tobias Higbie writes that for many "seasonal work was a way of life," and therefore "very few people held year-round employment," resulting in a somewhat fluid movement of workers traveling between the city and the country.[20]

Reactions to this hobo lifestyle were varied, as some workers saw it as a dangerous, unwelcome component of economic downturns and desperately wished to get off the road.[21] Others, however, embraced their mobility and viewed it as a freedom from the exploitative labor found in the factories. Some hobos, therefore, traveled to find work; others, such as London, worked to keep traveling. This difference is important; the ability to move allowed some men to view work in alternative and resistive ways. Jobs could be seen as continually temporary due to an intense desire on the worker's part to escape the perils of the industrial labor market. In *Down and Out, on the Road*, an examination of homelessness in the United States, Kenneth L. Kusmer specifically reads these workers' mobility in the 1890s as a possible site of resistance to industrialization, resulting in both a real and imagined agency as they traveled around the country taking and leaving jobs. They were men who "declined to adapt quietly to the demands of the new factory production system, or who viewed life on the road as preferable to starvation wages in dead-end jobs. . . . A man who rebelled against being 'cooped up in a factory' found intervals of vagabondage made work more acceptable."[22]

These types of hobos did not define themselves solely in relation to a job, but rather to the mode of transportation that allowed them to stay in motion. Their ability to illegally hop trains and to move whenever they needed or, more important, wanted to gave them an agency that they did not feel when they were connected to factory life. They were redefining the terms *homeless* and *unemployed* as transitional terms; they could find "homes" in the jobsites that relied on transient labor and they could find work when they hopped off trains, walked the main stem of a city, and picked up temporary employment. Although the constant and hazardous traveling was extremely perilous, it did offer an alternative to the exploitation many found in their jobs. "Life on the road was arduous and, at times, dangerous," Kusmer notes. "Nevertheless, it represented a respite from—and often a reaction against—many of the trends that were transforming the American social and economic system in the decades after Reconstruction: the increasing power of technology, the quest for economic efficiency and the growth of organizations and bureaucratic thinking."[23] These particular hobos were finding agency, not in their ability to find jobs, but rather in their train-hopping skills.

One by-product of this agency, however, was competition. Not only were hobos of this type in competition with the police and railroad employees attempting to keep them off the train, they also competed with all other hobos and unemployed transients for space in the boxcar. If hobos (re) defined themselves in terms not of their labor but in their ability to "catch out," then their success would not be in terms of getting a permanent job at the end of their travels, but in riding out on the next train. Jack London was this type of hobo when he found himself riding in the same train car with Kelly's army in 1894, and, consequently, his competitiveness put him at odds with the politics of the Industrial Army. In fact, it was the way he defined himself as a hobo that made him a foil to the ideological underpinnings of Kelly and his men's cause. To pinpoint this hierarchal, individualistic hobo identity, the best example can be found in London's initial train-hopping experience when he was a young man of sixteen.

## JACK LONDON'S COMPETITIVE HOBO BEGINNINGS

Increasingly disillusioned with factory work and feeling that his life as the hard-drinking "Prince of the Oyster Pirates" was not sufficiently rewarding or exciting, London in 1892 found himself fleeing from the law and hiding out along the Sacramento waterfront, where he met some "road-kids" swimming near a railroad bridge.[24] Never having met anyone like them before, he was instantly intrigued. What first captivated London was the way they talked: "It was a new vernacular. They were road-kids, and with every word they uttered the lure of The Road laid hold of me more imperiously." The aspiring writer found their language compelling, but he was mainly attracted by the allure of the train-hopping adventures about which these young hobos talked—adventures "that made [his] oyster-piracy look like thirty cents." His awe, however, did not last long, and he soon dismissed them, writing, "I was just as strong as any of them, just as quick, just as nervy, and my brain was just as good."[25]

No one could accuse London of being modest, but beyond the bombast, his statement suggests that he saw the road as a means of competition with the road kids. Instead of desiring to join them for a communal adventure, he seemed to need to prove that he was better than they were. He set himself up for a test. With the moniker "Sailor Kid," he and another novice, "French Kid," attempted to hop a train that was going "over the hill" (the Sierra Nevada mountain range)—an experience that would initiate them into this subculture and earn them recognition as road kids. It was a tough first journey in which London had to pass undetected not only by the railroad men but also by the approximately forty young hobos who, in an initiation rite, tried to throw him and his companion off the train. But while "all" of the other experienced and inexperienced hobos had been thrown off and "French Kid" had slipped, losing both legs under the wheels of the powerful locomotive, London, "alone, had made the train out."[26]

This was London's initiation to the road: a novice who had never hopped a train before was not only able to survive his first foray into riding the rails but also succeeded where all the experienced hobos had failed. He was a successful, self-professed "natural," whose skill and nerve in his very first trip allowed him to rise rapidly in the hobo hierarchy, evolving from a "road-kid" to a "blowed-in-the-glass profresh" without ever having to be a "gaycat" or a "prushan."[27]

## AVOIDING LAW = CREATING LAW

What is significant about the bravado with which London described his hobo travels is that, unlike some who saw transitory life as a defeat, London's handling of the hobo lifestyle as well as or better than anyone else made him feel victorious. He wanted to be part of the profresh class who were, as he wrote without any sense of irony (and, at the same time, completely misrepresenting the philosopher), "the lords and masters, the aggressive men, the primordial noblemen, the *blond beasts* so beloved by Nietzsche." In the factory, London was earning $1.40 for a ten-hour day with seemingly no way to advance in the company.[28] His experience with the road kids, however, showed him that he could, through his own efforts, rise quickly in the world of the hobo.

While London realized that he had a lot to learn from the road kids in terms of begging and "the strong arm" (a technique for robbing unsuspecting victims) so he could eat on a daily basis, he knew, from the very first trip, that he was one of the special "knights of the road" because he placed himself in a situation where he would either survive or perish—and he had succeeded where the others had failed.[29] While those who did not have London's skills or bravery might, literally, fall to the side of the road, London competed and quickly rose to the top of this subculture.

This immediate success (and his desire to brag about it) is not necessarily the case with other riders who have ridden the rails. Other young travelers who did not have the luxury of a "proper" education usually were not as lucky as London on their first rides. Jim Tully, who received attention for his later books but who is known specifically for his hobo memoir, *Beggars of Life*, which was turned into a 1928 movie of the same name starring Louise Brooks, writes "I made three unsuccessful journeys before I finally became even an amateur hobo. For it may be recorded here that hoboes regard their chosen profession seriously. There is much to learn in the game and more to endure."[30]

Much like Tully, William Bailey did not have the same macho bravado of London and writes in his autobiography, *Bill Bailey Came Home*, of the fear he felt as he waited for his first freight train. Despite being able to get on the train safely enough (unlike London, he hid in a Pullman when the train was stationary and not moving), his first attempt to get off the moving train showed his inexperience: "I jumped straight out the door. I hit on my feet all right but my body kept on going. I made more rolls than are put in a cinnamon roll. How many times I have no idea, till I came to a halt with a well bruised body." After recuperating, he learned from some more experienced hobos "just how to catch a fast-moving train, as well as how to hit the ground when you are leaving it," and in the following three months, he slowly (and painfully) learned the way of hobo life.[31]

Charles P. Barth, in his hobo memoir, *Hobo Trail to Nowhere*, also describes having trouble leaving the boxcar during his first experience: "In getting off, I stumbled and fell rolling over the rock ballast." An older hobo, who saw him take his tumble, helped him up and, cautioning, said, "Lucky you didn't roll the other way—under the wheels," before instructing him on the proper ways to train hop. Archie Lawson writes in his memoir, *Freight Trains West*, that he had no difficulties getting onto his first boxcar in the dark, but a few minutes into the ride he and his friend, not knowing the rules of the road, were attacked by the brakeman and robbed of their money. Jack Black, in his memoir, *You Can't Win*, tells of how he barely survived his first ride when the lumber in his Pullman shifted and fell on top of him; another hobo who was also traveling in the same car was not as fortunate, and, as Black writes in graphic prose, "his body, from the waist up, was flattened between the lumber and the front end of the car. His legs dangled below, down where I was imprisoned, with each movement of the car, like the legs of a scarecrow in the wind."[32]

While these other authors discuss the fear they felt when they hopped their first trains and the communal learning they received from seasoned hobos, London viewed himself as a success, characterizing himself as the hero of a bastardized American Dream story—the "lord and master" of all other illegal train riders who could not reach his stature. When he had "won" and was standing above all other road kids who were ditched and on the side of the tracks, he simply left the trains and the road kids, heading back for the coast. This first trip accentuated his individualistic ideological framework that he would continue to cultivate two years later during his travels with Kelly's army.

Without extensively discussing how London's misreading of Nietzsche undergirded his ideological framework, it is important to note that he conflated Nietzschean philosophy with social Darwinism. This misreading enabled him to believe that his quest to rule over this underworld was a masculine ideal of which both Nietzsche and Darwin would approve. Eight years after he rode with the Industrial Army, London wrote "Rods and Gunnels," in which he clearly defines and adamantly defends the profesh title, lending insight into why this accolade was so important to him: "[Skilled hobos] are . . . *the blond beasts* of Nietzsche, lustfully roving and conquering through sheer superiority and strength. Unwritten is the law they impose. They are the Law, the Law incarnate. And the Underworld looks up to them and obeys. They are not easy of access. They are conscious of their own nobility and treat only with equals."[33] London thought of himself as belonging to the class of nobility that was the Law—a man who had dominion over all in the underworld. There was a strict divide for London in the hobo subculture, and as "the Law" he did not want to unite those within it—he wanted to stratify and hierarchize it.

The profresh were "conquerors," and their "superiority" and "strength" allowed them to decide their own rules. They constituted a reactionary masculine ideal, and for London they established the law that all others of the underworld must obey if they wanted to attain his stature. There was no class solidarity in the boxcar for London; the unemployed men in his boxcar looking for work were competitors, and as a "lord" he strove to impose his own laws on them. There was, however, a practical limit to the superiority of the hobo. Although London received pleasure from being a profresh, rising to nobility within the underworld, he still had to remain invisible from the world of the police and their laws to retain his top hobo position.

The presence of the law is prominent throughout London's massive oeuvre. In what is probably London's most famous novel, *The Call of The Wild*, Buck, the fearless St. Bernard / Scotch Shepherd dog ruled the kind Judge Miller's house in sunny California but then quickly learned in the cold climate of the Klondike that "a man with a club was a lawgiver, a master to be obeyed."[34] Those who had the power to inflict their law on others were to be strictly observed; Buck understood this point after numerous brutal blows by the man in the red sweater. The law, for London, was something that must be learned, not as an abstract concept, but rather felt and experienced in the blood and skin. Buck felt the sting of the club on his back, side, and nose and learned to respect the law; London, who witnessed an actual whipping while he was hoboing across the country, knew that the body always broke under the law, and, cognizant of this, he was mostly able to avoid spilling his own blood: when he saw that the law was bigger than he, London simply headed for the next train and disappeared.[35]

To London, hopping a train was neither merely an escape nor a means to get to another locale. As the example of his first train-hopping experience shows, London defined himself, and consequently all others who could not reach the stature of the profresh, in terms of the very act of riding the rails. This understanding of the hobo lifestyle, however, made him a disagreeable riding partner with Kelly, who was trying to unite out-of-work men into one visible display of working-class solidarity. While London might empathize with Kelly and his men, he was not interested in the politics of the march. He was committed, instead, to his own brand of boxcar politics.

## LONDON'S BOXCAR POLITICS

Like all hobos, London, when "catching out," sought to create a space for himself on the train by staying out of sight and hiding in order to ride. If he was seen and caught, he would not only miss the train but, depending on the moods of the train crew and the police, might find himself in places (jail, for example) that would delimit his future movements. Using tactics that relied on presented opportunities (for example, a moving train with an open boxcar and no police or train employees looking), London needed to stay out of sight, remaining hidden to be successful and safe.

Train riders knew that if they were visible, there was a possibility of sanctions. The transient's labor was sometimes needed, and townspeople actively searched for these men at harvest times. But when men were plentiful and work scarce, the hobo was viewed as, at best, a nuisance and, at worst, a threat to the community. Be it a constable ready to lock up the hobo on vagrancy charges or a vigilante crowd "welcoming" him with bats and guns, hobos found it very difficult to make their way through many towns and cities during the hard times of the 1890s.

Jack London's writings, along with many hobo autobiographies, indicate that there was a real sense of pride resulting from outwitting and tricking the bulls, whose job was specifically to ensure that hobos stayed off the train. Although London put his physical self in much danger when hopping trains, his movements were no longer subject to the same regulations as those who were "riding the cushions." As previously discussed in chapter 1, this disappearing from the panopticon-like eye of the railroad companies' surveillance infrastructure allowed London to move more freely. He had, in a sense, rendered himself invisible.

Being unable to gaze on the hobo was disconcerting for farmers dependent on the labor force of men who appeared, suddenly, in the middle of the night. Ted Grossardt, a social geographer, writes in his article "Harvest(ing) the Hoboes," "When the activities of a mobile group of people are no longer observable and thus cannot be fully known, those people become potentially omnipresent to the fixed observer. The observer suddenly faces the possibility of being the observed." Numerous laws were passed to make the hobo's movements more visible and therefore less threatening.[36] London, however, sneaking alone onto a train in the middle of the night, resisted the authorities' gaze (and swinging batons) by stepping outside of "official" history. While ticketed passengers were placed under the gaze of established authority, London, in an act of resistance, existed in the space of noise and movement. This resistance used invisibility as its tool. If London was able to become invisible and escape those who wished to stop him from riding, he was successful. If he were visible, he would have failed. His resistance was in the individualized spaces that he created when hopping a train. Like the other members of Kelly's army, London was an unemployed worker, but unlike the army faithful, he could define himself as a profresh whose success was determined not by the job he received *after* the journey but rather by the journey itself.

In his 1894 travels London was an individual whose strong sense of self centered on his ability to disappear and move. But how, then, did London deal with the apparent inconsistency of being a "primordial noble man" and yet, at the same time, also be forced to hide and remain invisible? How did he reconcile his lofty position as a hobo with the sneaking around the underbelly of a train?

The answer lies in his particular understanding of being a profresh. Being a part of this elite group of hobos—a group based on individual masculine ideals of fearlessness, strength, and skill—allowed London to place himself as both the dispenser and the very embodiment of the law, thus transcending any feelings of inferiority. He was playing by his own set of rules: that he was invisible to those searching for him was, in fact, *the very thing* that made him part of the nobility of the underworld. He was a success, a "lord and master," only if he perfected his ability to disappear. Those "gay-cats" and inexperienced rail riders that London so despised would eventually be seen and caught by the bulls, but the profresh would remain undetected and ride wherever they wished. Instead of reading his invisibility and hiding as marks of weakness, London wore them as badges of honor.

The professional train rider, as constructed by London, dictated the rules of the game as he manipulated his invisibility to hop a train without being thrown off by bulls or the train crew. For London, it was a competition the hobo, *as personified by him*, could always win. As he writes confidently in *The Road*, "Barring accidents, a good hobo, with youth and agility, can hold a train down despite all the efforts of the train-crew to 'ditch' him—given, of course, night-time as an essential condition. When such a hobo, under such conditions, makes up his mind that he is going to hold her down, either he does hold her down, or chance trips him up. There is no legitimate way, short of murder, whereby the train-crew can ditch him."[37] As long as it was dark and chance did not look unfavorably on the noble train hopper, the hobo would always be able to ride. This success, however, meant isolation and did not come without consequences. There could, after all, be only one "lord" of a particular train.

### *The Isolation of the Hobo*

In his chapter "Holding Her Down" from *The Road*, which details one of his attempts to train hop, London makes clear the competition involved between the individual hobo and the rest of the "world" of the train—including bulls, train crews, and, most tellingly, other hobos. Much like his initial ride when he met the "road kids," London writes that his attempt to hop a train guarded by "two brakemen, a conductor, a fireman, and an engineer" was an individual contest, in which he lacked all feelings of cooperation with the other twenty hobos also trying to ride out.[38] When the train started moving, all headed for it. London, the arch individualist in direct competition with the other hobos, wanted to be the "tramp-royal" who alone succeeded in getting a spot on the train.

The train crew was ready, however, and with clubs in their hands reminiscent of the man in the red sweater from *The Call of the Wild*, they quickly knocked off five of the least experienced. "The weeding-out process had begun nobly, and it continued station by station. Now we were fourteen, now twelve, now eleven, now nine, now eight."[39] As a profresh, London hoped that his fellow riders would be knocked off. And indeed, through daring and skillful moves, he was able to outlast all other hobos and outwit the train crew who, although they knew that he was somewhere on their train, could not see him and were unable to get their hands on him.

In a moment of realization, London, tired and out of breath, suddenly understood the enormity of what he had done, writing, "As I wait in the darkness, I am conscious of a big thrill of pride. The overland has stopped twice for me—for me, a poor hobo on the bum. I alone have twice stopped the overland with its many passengers and coaches, its government mail, and its two thousand steam horses straining in the engine. And I weigh only one hundred and sixty pounds and I haven't a five-cent piece in my pocket!" London, the individualist ("I alone"), was able to disrupt the ordered and regimented world of the train. In this David and Goliath scenario, the boy won—"It is five to one, including the engineer and fireman, and the majesty of the law and the might of a great corporation are behind them, and I am beating them out." Although it was not a knockout shot, London earned the reluctant respect of the crew who, after a consultation among themselves, knew that they were beaten and yelled out into the dark, "Well, I guess you can ride, Bo. There's no use trying to keep you off." London's euphoric feeling perfectly encapsulates his individualistic boxcar politics. The young hobo does not view himself in competition with a capitalist ideology or as consciously resisting the modernization that the train is bringing to the United States. Instead, London is taking on the physical train, trying to best its crew, not the system.[40]

For London, his successful hop was proof that the professional hobo could win. The law, however, was actually never fully defeated; the train crew still *allowed* London to ride. There was a ceiling to the success of the hobo, and London, through his skill and bravery, was hitting his head against it. If they had wanted, the crew could have stopped the train indefinitely and called in additional authorities to capture the young hobo. In other words, London's success as a hobo, as Michel de Certeau would attest, was fleeting, one that he had to relinquish as soon as he had won it.[41] The train moved again, and people and merchandise, even though slightly delayed, made it to their stations; the hobo's resistance forced only a mild inconvenience. London, though, had created a new set of rules for himself, and by remaining invisible he had become the law in the underworld—his actions on this train proved that he was part of the elite of illegal train hoppers. For the hobos left on the side of the road, and for the train crew who could not get their hands on him, London was recognized as a premier hobo who, for a night at least, had bested all others. And for young Jack London, breathing deeply in the dark and swelling with pride, that was enough.

For many of the fifteen hundred jobless laborers who joined Kelly's army, however, stable employment was preferable to an adventure. This hard journey across hundreds of miles was not seen as an enjoyable expedition—for many, their lives as workingmen depended on it. London's celebration of the solitary moments in the dark was not what the army was searching for, and these unemployed men had no interest in creating new invisible subcultural systems or laws. In joining Kelly's army, they were seeking to reestablish many of their communal working-class bonds that had disappeared when they no longer could find jobs in their hometowns or cities. They eschewed individualistic, self-appointed titles such as "profresh" or "comet." Far from desiring to disappear, these dispossessed workers wanted to make themselves seen to force Washington politicians to acknowledge their needs as workers. These men sought visibility, and they refused to sneak or hide on their way to the nation's capital. United in their message of solidarity, there would be no space for individualized addendums.

## THE INDUSTRIAL ARMIES AND THE RAILROAD

With faith in this power of group solidarity, Charles Kelly rose through the ranks of the largest industrial army and assumed leadership of his men in April 1894. In one of his first public acts, he demanded railroad transportation for the initial leg of their journey from Oakland to Sacramento. Knowing that he and his men could not make it to Washington simply by walking, Kelly realized that western railroads would play an important role in the army's crusade and audaciously demanded free transportation from the Southern Pacific Railroad.[42] When he was quickly refused and jailed, he replied that he was going to once again call for transportation the following day. Believing that poor men had rights under the current laws, he was not a revolutionary; rather, he wanted to receive rights that he felt were guaranteed to him as a U.S. citizen. Kelly, therefore, did what London could never do when he was sneaking around trying to avoid the train engineers on the *Overland Express:* after leaving jail, he rallied the men by climbing on the roof of a railroad car, urging them to stay and fight together because public opinion was on their side. Unlike London and other hobos who had to hide in the bowels of the train, Kelly stood proudly on top of the boxcar while being photographed, allowing his face to be a visual representation of the poor man conquering the machine.[43] Here Kelly was symbolically taming the iron horse: refusing to hide in the shadows, he was grabbing its reins and directing it toward Washington.

Kelly's men and the public received him most favorably in California, where antirailroad sentiment was high and there was anger toward the Southern Pacific, which was particularly antagonistic to the army. By the 1890s railroads were crisscrossing across the continent "creating systems that . . . made no rational sense but that could yield vast personal fortunes through construction, speculation, and financial manipulation." Middle and working class alike shared this bitterness against these corporate behemoths; consequently, sympathy for the Industrials grew daily.[44] The mayor of Oakland, feeling pressure from citizens who supported the men as well as from the drain of more than one thousand army regulars (who still needed to eat) on the local economy, finally convinced the railroad to offer free boxcar transportation to the army. But Kelly, after receiving this concession, initially refused the "gift," demanding coaches to take him and his men: "We, the Industrial Army, emphatically refuse to ride in boxcars. We are United States citizens and not hogs. When we are furnished with proper transportation we will then proceed to Sacramento, not otherwise."[45] In other words, although they were unable and unwilling to pay, Kelly was separating his men from the hobos who poached off the railroad and illegally rode trains; the army, he implied, would arrive in Washington with dignity. Again, Kelly was speaking about his men as workers connected to places because of their crafts—the farm, the mill, the mine—and was distancing himself from a transient workforce. While listening to Kelly, men, unemployed and with very few prospects for a job, were able to stand together on tracks and, confident in their numbers, stop trains from moving past them. Unlike London and his profresh ilk, these men were not content to hop a train; they would stop it dead in its tracks.

To have any chance of the march leading to a productive end, Kelly needed to stay visible in both the towns and the media that reported their trek and show that they were collectively united, honest working men in search of relief from their joblessness. Although there was widespread public sympathy for the Industrial Army's search for employment, there were also many pundits who, from their pulpits or their newspapers, denounced their tactics. A Dr. Stetson of Des Moines College, in a chapel talk harshly criticizing the march, stated that "no men with a determination animated by high moral purposes will live like swine." Thorstein Veblen saw the men only as idlers with no clear goal and therefore an unsubstantiated crusade. The dean of Yale Law School denounced them as both morally and physically "dirty." Numerous editorials, especially after trains were hijacked by those sympathetic to the armies, called for a return of whipping posts for vagrants.[46] Kelly clearly tried to disassociate himself by publicly proclaiming that the Industrial Army's cause was just and the army was not a ragtag outfit of mere hobos. The furtive and beggarly image of the itinerant homeless was not what Kelly wanted the general public to conjure up when they thought of his army. He denied that any professional wanderers were in his regiment, and because the army conducted itself in an orderly and disciplined manner, the thousands of men and women who came to gaze at the army throughout their trek generally believed him.[47] To gain public sympathy, Kelly needed to convincingly show that there was an end to their travels—a job building roads that would lead eventually to stable domiciles—and that, unlike London and his hobo brethren, they did not wish to keep traveling and moving.

But London, and it can be assumed other hobos with his individualistic leanings, shared the train with Kelly and his men. Although Kelly was squarely against having any hobos in his regiment, London was not antagonistic to the central idea of Kelly's army; he just defined success differently. Success for him was not based on a possible future homestead somewhere in the arid lands of the West, but rather in his ability to move and remain in motion. In other words, his success was not dependent on how he measured up as a worker but rather how he measured up as a hobo. During his six months on the road, whether he was with the army or traveling alone, Jack London defined his own measure of success by his ability to outwit those who attempted to limit his movements—be it a railroad engineer who did not wish him to ride his train or General Kelly, who wanted him to walk from town to town and refused to allow him to ride in the back of a supply wagon.

## LONDON AND THE INDUSTRIAL ARMY

London's sympathies were with the army; like the out-of-work miner and the landless farmer, London felt he had been exploited and, when he heard about the Industrial Army, decided to join. But, as his daughter and biographer, Joan London, notes, London "was mastered by the determination to be his own boss."[48] Unlike the other members whom he shared a boxcar with on this trek, London identified himself as a profresh who was the law of his own underworld kingdom. During the six months when he traveled across both the United States and Canada, London was convinced that his mobility would keep him from harm; his quick-wittedness, agility, and skill as a train hopper would always allow him to continue unmolested down the line. His loyalty was therefore to himself and not to the army.

London attempted to join Kelly on April 6, but missed him by just a few hours when the army left Oakland, and, consequently, London spent eleven days hoboing his way through Utah and Nevada trying to catch up. Finally, he met up with Kelly near Council Bluffs, Iowa. Unfortunately for him, during this time the army was having trouble moving forward and was stalled, desperately searching for transportation to allow them to continue onto Washington.[49]

As London was hopping trains searching for Kelly, and the Industrial Army was heading out of Sacramento toward Utah, the police, preachers, politicians, and the army itself ardently debated the laws that these unemployed men were breaking when they were traveling on the trains. Could state and local authorities of California transfer large numbers of homeless men to Utah? Could the Southern Pacific railroad company transfer these men to the Union Pacific and the Rio Grande Western? Who was responsible for these men, and who could be held accountable for their actions?[50] For the most part, local and state politicians, fearing riots and also the cost of maintaining these armies in their towns, wanted simply to pass Kelly and his men to the next locale. Even though the Industrials did not consider themselves hobos, authorities attempted to treat them as such, as towns wanted to keep pushing them farther down the line. Kelly's insistence on the army's visibility (as well as the complex logistics of the march), however, made this impossible.

When London was hopping trains on the sly into various hostile towns as he made his way to Iowa, he thought of himself as an individual against all others. If he won, he was able to ride the train. If he lost, he would have to watch the train from the side of the track as it sped past him. Unlike the impotence he felt when he was working in the factory, as a hobo he was dependent on his own skill and determination—and nothing else—to ride. But because of the visibility of hundreds of men on the side of the road, London, when he began riding with Kelly's army, would no longer be able to disappear. The visibility of Industrials caused them to be the subject of debate from the courtroom to the barroom with no clear solutions or strategies emerging for dealing with a stranded army. While the law clearly stated that these men did not have the right to ride on the train, editorialists and street preachers began to question the validity of these laws. The men were stationary and under the gaze of the public, who came out in droves; at one point it was reported that thirty thousand people were witnessing the spectacle. With the large crowds and the excitement surrounding the men, every time the Industrial Army entered a new community it was as if "a big circus had come to town."[51] The army was a public event and the drama was on center stage for all to see. With throngs of people coming to observe and mingle with these men, restlessness abounded.

What the owners of the railroad companies feared most was that the army was operating in the public sphere. They were the subject of too much talk; if citizens of the town did not come out and see it personally, they could read about it in the newspapers, hear about it from the Sunday pulpits, or listen to debates over a glass of beer in a saloon. The carnival-like quality of the "petition in boots" scared the owners and politicians because the visibility of the men made many fear—especially in this time of economic hardships—the threat of collective politics. And so government officials relied on what they knew: the law. Clearly, transporting the Industrial Army across state lines defied existing laws: large numbers of dependents of one state could not just be transferred to another state where they would once again become dependents. Although local officials were quite capable of handling individual transients who attempted to cross their borders, no one was quite sure how legally to handle the armies struggling to get to Washington.

While officials were debating legal ways to deal with the army, others found an illegal way: find a train and steal it.[52] In Council Bluffs, Iowa, local citizens, tired of seeing the army wait for politicians and railroad executives to decide on what would happen to Kelly and his men, "liberated" a train and brought it to the army. But while there was much celebration by those involved, including Jack London, who wrote about it favorably in his diary, after a few hours, the train was returned. Despite the fact that Kelly asked for free transportation whenever he had the chance, he stated that the reason he did not take this particular train was not because of the lack of boxcars (it was insufficient to carry the whole army) but because that act was illegal and he and his men had pledged not to do anything against the law.[53] Kelly believed fully that they were on the right side of the law, and, as good citizens whose only crime was that they were poor and looking for work, they would follow it. Whether Kelly was anticipating that the authorities were looking for an excuse to arrest him and his men or he really believed that they had not violated any laws is debatable. Either way, Kelly was trying to work within the law.

This collective regard for society's law, however, marks a clear distinction between the Industrial Army's mass politics and London's brand of boxcar politics, where he was the dispenser and embodiment of his own law. The Industrials called for a helping hand from the government, and Kelly was beholden to the laws of the states they passed through. London's boxcar politics positioned him to be beholden only to himself. Eventually this ideological difference would form an irreconcilable wedge between the two. While numerous examples show the various manifestations of this difference, it becomes most apparent when the army was finally stopped in Des Moines, Iowa, and all requests for rail transportation were adamantly refused. After realizing there was no way to continue their pilgrimage on foot, Kelly had the army turn into a navy, and they constructed rafts to sail down the Des Moines River. Here the former "Prince Oyster Pirate" found a perfect opportunity to break away from the collective, crystallizing his competitive nature that kept him from embracing the army and its collectivized politics.

On Wednesday, May 9, 1894, London and the rest of the army headed down the river in boats that were each built for ten men. Soon, London's boat manipulated its way to the front of the group and separated itself from the rest of the army. London explains why in his chapter "Two Thousand Stiffs": "There were ten men in my boat, and they were the cream of Company L. Every man was a hustler. . . . The ten of us forgot the remaining forty men of Company L, and by the time we had missed one meal we promptly forgot the commissary. We were independent. We went down the river 'on our own,' hustling our 'chewin's,' beating every boat in the fleet, and, alas that I must say it, sometimes taking possession of the stores the farmer-folk had collected for the Army." Townspeople, fearful that the army would descend on them en masse but also sympathetic to the cause, would leave food, tobacco, and milk on the shores for the men to pick up. London and his crew of "independent" men, however, went first down the river, getting far ahead of the rest of the boats and reporting to whomever they met that they were the emissaries for the army; in the process, they grabbed possession of anything they wanted. In his journal entry for May 11 summarizing his life on the water, London writes simply that he was "Living Fine."[54]

Tellingly, there was hardly any mention of the other men in the army, except when London boasted about how he had outwitted them. Just like the incident in which London hoped other hobos attempting to board "his" train would fail, London here was fulfilling his desire to be the "tramp-royal" whose success came at the cost of his fellow travelers. While he acknowledged that he stole from the men, he also felt it was his right as a strong individualist to get what he could—and the group politics be damned. He explains in greater detail in *The Road*, "While we were ahead, skimming the cream, and while the commissary was lost far behind, the main Army, coming along in the middle, starved. This was hard on the Army, I'll allow; but then, the ten of us were individualists. We had initiative and enterprise. We ardently believed that the grub was to the man who got there first, the pale Vienna [coffee with milk] to the strong."[55]

Here is a concrete example that shows the individualistic hobo lifestyle in conflict with collective action. As a hobo, London survived by hiding and remaining invisible in the bowels of a boxcar. To be brought into the light and made to stand collectively with the army was not directly beneficial to him, so he used the name of the army only to fulfill his individual desires. In his diary London makes constant mention of the soreness of his feet from walking or his attempts to hide on the back of a supply cart; there is no mention of his political affiliation with these men. To be part of the collective body meant to suffer, and to a man who wanted to be his own boss, this was not acceptable. As a profresh, London believed he could board any train that was pulling out and, therefore, to be waiting with other hobos to be *permitted* to ride to Washington was degrading to his sense of self. Priding himself as an individualist, London would not accept subservience to the higher ideals of the group. In other words, his success as a hobo would outshine the eventual failure of the Industrial Army.

For London, unlike many of the out-of-work factory workers who had so much riding on their trip to Washington, the dissolution of the Industrial Army was not the end of his travels. After a few weeks in the national spotlight, London was able to fade back into the dark crevices of the train and once again cloak himself in his invisibility. There would always be another ride. London's daughter later described her father's experience: "He left the army lightheartedly, careless of whether it would reach its destination or not and pushed off alone. He was still lighthearted and believed that [although] he was a member of the lower class, he was different, special."[56] Throughout his travels with Kelly's army, London was ever the individualist, and when opportunities appeared before him, he took them with both hands. Evaluating London's entries in his diary, William McDevitt writes, "What puzzles me is that in all the pages from his diary . . . there is not a *single word* as to the political, sociologic, economic views of the members of the Industrial Army that he contacted or fraternized with, during the month and a third."[57] London's belief in his own brand of boxcar politics afforded him a buffered space from the politics of the Industrial Army.

For the hobo that London both was and admired, success was equated with slipping around unnoticed. During his time on the road, then, London was in a constant state of competition, and his resistance to the laws and regulations of the states that he passed through were comparable to the competition he had with other train riders. For him, the prestige of being a top profresh was more immediately gratifying than the hope for some promised change in the political landscape, and he centered his sights only on the physical landscape on which he traveled. The boxcar might have been lonely, but there was always a ride to be had.

## THE LONELY BOXCAR

Contrary to what London expressed in *The Road*, however, the odds were against the hobo—skilled or not—and eventually even a "tramp-royal" of his stature would become visible at the wrong moment. This happened to London shortly after he deserted the army and was arrested for vagrancy on his way to see Niagara Falls. Standing in court along with sixteen other homeless men who were each sentenced to thirty days in fifteen seconds by a judge more interested in having breakfast than administering justice, London discovered that his profresh standing meant nothing to the courts or to the other men. Lumped together with all the other vagrants who had no money in their pockets, London found out that he was, in fact, not "special, different" from the other disenfranchised members of the working class. Because he had no money or home, London writes, "I had been denied my right of trial by jury; I had been denied my right to plead guilty or not guilty; . . . I had not been allowed to communicate with a lawyer nor anyone. . . . I was forced to toil hard on a diet of bread and water and to march the shameful lock-step with armed guards over me."[58] When he lost his invisibility, London lost his freedom of mobility along with many other freedoms that he thought impossible to relinquish. Even though later in life he would champion the causes of the proletariat, in 1894, when he was a young hobo happily traveling the iron road, whenever he found himself in a boxcar with someone else, he made sure that he was the only one who would be able to successfully "catch out."

This competitive desire to be the best within the boxcar was one way that some hobos found meaning within their lives. But other hobos did not find this gratifying and saw the stratification of the subculture to be making life on the margins increasingly tougher. Attempting to survive on the road was a precarious position, and many hobos relied on a transient mutualism for subsistence. Although not committed to effecting radical change in the larger political sphere, these hobos rejected London's type of monolithic individualist ideology and instead created a materialist politics based on the relationship among the individual hobo, the subculture, and the train. This type of hobo is most exemplified by Jim Tully in his work *Beggars of Life.*

Chapter Three

# THE POLYPHONIC BOXCAR

## The Hobo in Jim Tully's *Beggars of Life*

In 1914, with his hobo travels behind him and having difficulty finding a publisher for his first book, *Emmett Lawler*, Jim Tully found himself working in California as a taxi starter for a cab company. One very late night, when a group of drunken men fell out of a cab and entered a nightclub, Tully recognized one of the inebriates as his literary hero, Jack London. The previous year, after reading *John Barleycorn*, a memoir of London's drinking habits, Tully had written to London, addressing their similarities as former road kids while also soliciting advice for a neophyte writer. Surprisingly, London not only replied but offered Tully a place to stay in his home to write and chat. Tully never visited but, seeing a perfect opportunity to meet his idol, sent a note to London, who agreed to meet the following night in the bar of the Alexandria Hotel. Possibly hungover and looking bored, London was a disappointment for Tully. Instead of listening to writing advice, Tully got drunk.[1]

As a poor boy from St. Marys, a small town in Ohio, who had dreams of being a writer as he hopped his first train in 1901, Tully had always had a great admiration for London. Trying to impress a young woman whom he was falling in love with, he declared that he would someday be as great as the "brilliant tramp writer." When Nellie Dingley, a librarian, compared him to London, it cemented his romantic feelings for her. But name dropping was not just a simplistic way to justify his transient ways as he seduced would-be lovers; Tully placed London on a literary pedestal and, for a time at least, carried a picture of him as he traveled along the iron road.[2]

His desire to emulate London was not a passing fancy. With his sister Virginia's willful encouragement, Tully believed he could become a writer, all the while he was a road kid, dishwasher, cab starter, tree surgeon, chain maker, boxer, railroad laborer, and circus handyman. Well read for an autodidact, he particularly enjoyed, and felt a connection with, writers who had also spent time on the road, later in his life keeping some of his favorites on a wall in his home office.[3] As the former pugilist pounded out numerous plays, poems, stories, novels, memoirs, and articles on his typewriter, these men were his justification that he belonged to the world of writers.

On the surface, then, this meeting over drinks between two former hobos should have gone more smoothly. Both were disowned by their fathers and worked grueling jobs as young boys in factories. Both viewed themselves as writers even as they rebelled against a stultifying labor market by hoboing for a time in their lives. Sitting across from each other in the bar, however, Tully was rankled by London. After leaving the famous author, he reread London's books and found that they lacked "the ring of truth" that Tully was especially adamant about placing within his five books that would eventually be a part of his Underworld Series—*Beggars of Life*, *Circus Parade*, *Shanty Irish*, *Shadows of Men*, and *Blood on the Moon*. These books, published over the course of ten years and detailing his early life and wanderings on the road, showcase Tully's distinct style of short, hard-hitting sketches of poor dispossessed individuals. At their best, these books reveal an underclass of forgotten, wandering men at the beginning of the twentieth century. Brimming with dark humor, an undercurrent of raw violence weaves itself throughout all the stories. Moving away from the naturalist mode of Frank Norris, Tully was a hard-boiled realist writer who seemingly did not have an obvious overt political agenda. Instead, a rumination—a brooding—pulses throughout these texts.

On further reflection of their writings, then, it is not surprising that there was tension between London and Tully, with the older writer feeling bored partaking in the conversation and the younger writer becoming thirsty. Tully's 1924 hobo book *Beggars of Life* is very different from London's book *The Road*, especially in terms of overall tone. Tully was angered that London romanticized his six months hoboing and found his work to be inauthentic; the now famous socialist's bravado annoyed the former road kid who was on and off the road for six years.[4] Tully, who eked out a living and barely survived many harrowing travel experiences, did not feel as though London's competitiveness with other hobos was reflective of his own more seasoned boxcar experiences. An anger simmered within Tully for years after that particular meeting in the hotel bar.

In a caustic article, "A Baffled Greatness," that he wrote six years after London's death, Tully, in a misogynistic harangue, criticizes the character of the former hobo who, as a "famous" writer, "drank tea with the ladies . . . [who] tied his brawny hands with invisible silken cords." He assails London's politics, stating that although he might have criticized capitalism, he was fully gripped within its tentacles, choosing to write one thousand words a day just so he could earn twice the salary of the president. His hunger for wealth was a detriment to himself as a writer: "A great man was Jack London and well he knew that the mine was producing slag."[5]

*The Road* was one of the "slag" pieces, and it particularly irritated Tully. In this article Tully retells a story of a time that he, London, and Hobart Bosworth, an actor and former hobo, were speaking about the book. Bosworth complained to London that he didn't tell the truth and that he wrote about his experiences just to sell articles to magazines. This was, in fact, true. When London wrote the essays that would eventually be printed as *The Road*, he was a popular, accomplished writer—who had numerous debts. Playing different publishers off one another to finance the making of his $30,000 sailboat, *The Snark*, he found himself unable to pay back advances to publishing houses. Admitting that he was "not prepared to return" the $1,610 that *Cosmopolitan* had previously advanced him, London asked if "subject to [their] approval" he could pay off his debt by writing about his "tramp reminisces."[6] London's request, and the way he phrased his offer, disclosed a desire to give to *Cosmopolitan* a series of articles that would comfortably reach the magazine's target audience. Tully, who was seeking realism in his writings, angrily ruminates on why London "sold out" and didn't become an American Dostoyevsky, acerbically arguing that London used his hobo "adventures" to afford his bourgeois lifestyle and did not realistically represent the hobo subculture. London might have written about a particular type of selfish hobo who hopped trains, but he did it with too much flourish; Tully wanted a hobo figure that reflected his own worldview and experiences.[7]

On the one hand, we can see that Tully grabbed the mantle of hobo-writer from London and followed in his footsteps as he crisscrossed the country, avoiding bulls and knocking on back doors, eventually compiling (and oftentimes retelling) his traveling experiences in various memoirs and stories. On the other hand, the way he represents the hobo subculture and his individual political outlook of living on the road is radically different. As discussed in chapter 2, London's boxcar politics is individualistic, wherein as a profresh he is actively engaged in beating other road kids and rising in the hobo hierarchy. Tully's interaction with the hobo subculture, however, is distinctly noncompetitive. He does not attempt to rise sharply in the stratified world of the hobo, nor is he a labor activist attempting to reform society by tearing down the social system. Although he is aware of the inequalities he and his fellow train riders face, Tully never stands on a literary soapbox, attacking capitalists for the hobo's dispossession from society. For the most part, he does not question his lot in life while on the road, nor does he have a nihilistic outlook: like a railroad car that travels in one direction along well-worn tracks, Tully travels down his own road, examining and recording his experiences with men who find themselves in similar circumstances.

This does not mean, however, that Tully's writing about his days as a train hopper is apolitical. Rather, his rejection of a monolithic individualist narrative and adoption of a polyphonic structure in *Beggars of Life* reveals Tully's specific political philosophy. Offering no "truth" or singular narrative focus, Tully situates the reader among the crowd as it rolls down the track. With no one individual grabbing the attention of the reader for longer than a chapter or so, the result is a panoramic view of itinerant poor people. Tully, however, refuses to have the individual become lost within the group narrative. Instead, the author offers a networked view of individuals within this train-riding subculture: these hobos have independent melodies, but when together they form a harmony. This triadic relationship among the individual, the hobo subculture, and the train is the basis for Tully's class-based boxcar politics.

Janet Zandy, a cultural theorist who examines the multiplicities of working-class writing, identifies a text as working class if it is "not so much collective writing but rather communal sensibilities . . . [leading to] a consciousness of connective tissue and multiple histories and lives that comprise the self."[8] *Beggars of Life* is an example of the way that an author can create these communal sensibilities by relying on layered histories of multiple individuals, thereby creating a panoramic working-class narrative from the perch of a boxcar. While London's text shows an exaggerated view of the profresh, Tully details a more sober glimpse of communal living within the margins of society.

## COMMUNITY IN *BEGGARS OF LIFE*

The railroad—the reason for St. Marys' early lumbering growth—was also Jim Tully's means of escape from his Ohio hometown. As he recounts in *Beggars of Life*, he would sit along the tracks in Auglaize County and listen to hobos' travel stories. After being abandoned by his father soon after his mother died and "rescued" from an orphanage by his sister only to be placed in slavery-like conditions as a hired farmhand, Tully imagined the tracks as a way to lead him away from the "horror of the town and of [his] life there."[9] Much like London, who was working in a jute mill for starvation wages, soon after absconding from the farm, Tully found himself working for three dollars a week (two dollars going for board) as an apprentice of an alcoholic chain maker in an oppressive factory. Fed up with his stultified life and feeling that hoboing was a resistance to the crushing drudgery of industrial life, Tully looked toward the tracks, saw an opportunity, and left.

This initial hobo experience, and how Tully subsequently wrote about it, underscores his relationship with this transient subculture. Tully's hoboing begins with the romantic impulse of a young man excitedly leaving the harsh confines of his town, while looking forward to the adventures soon to come his way. During this first trip as a self-described "amateur hobo" depicted in *Beggars of Life*, however, the romance of the road disappears immediately. As a "scared" Tully and old "derelict" hobos warm themselves around a fire while waiting on a train, they are arrested at gunpoint.[10] After being questioned, the group is led to a flophouse, where they are made to stay the night before being forced to catch the first train out of town the next morning.

Through the snores of these bone-weary hobos, Tully hears moans coming from the next bed. Wanting to help, he sees blood trickling down the man's face; soon, other hobos come to the bed and together they try to help the man as best as they can. Not long after they began their vigil, though, the man dies. Soon after, two policemen carry the body out of the dormitory, but not before they rifle his pockets, finding eight cents that they give to the landlady. Quickly and without discussion, the lights are put out and the hobos sleep the few remaining hours before dawn.

This story of his first hobo trip perfectly encapsulates the way Tully views the world.[11] Tully begins his travels with the naivety of a young man entering a subculture he knows little about, and the harsh reality of the situation confronts him quickly and without warning. There is no romantic, false bravado in his retelling. Most significant, as in most of Tully's Underworld cycle, he retreats from the center of the narrative, allowing the other hobos to begin to take over the text en masse. There are memorable individuals throughout *Beggars of Life*—many of the chapters center on one particular rider—but the collective impression presented to the reader is one of a *group of individuals.* In these conjoined scenes introducing Tully to the hobo subculture, a type of forced bonding exists among the men; first as they attempt to stay warm around the stove as a storm rages, and second around the body of the dying hobo. In both scenes a center holds the orbital men in place—the stove, the body—and Tully, with a cinematic eye, writes of the men the way a camera would slowly pan through a crowd scene. Readers are witnesses to these individuals, but after Tully's lens pans across the crowd, we are left with an overall impression of a collective, as the individuals dissolve into the larger hobo subculture.

This collective subcultural view is a significant difference between London's romanticized recounting of hopping his first train through the Sierra Nevada range and Tully's painful recapturing of his first hobo experience. In London's text, while numerous road kids are attempting to secure a boxcar, his attention is on one individual—himself—and the train is an object used to prove his superiority in the subculture. Competition leads to winners and losers, and, for London, there can be only one winner. For Tully, he and all of his traveling companions are losers—part of a disenfranchised class of itinerant men. Unlike London, who closed off the subculture that he was a part of and made himself the "tramp-royal" or Übermensch able to dictate "laws" to all other hobos who could not compete with him, Tully embeds himself within the hobo subculture. No individuals stand apart for long periods; they either never separate themselves from the group in the first place, as is the case in these scenes, or, if they do, they mostly disappear after the chapter is done. The polyphonic form of *Beggars of Life* allows for an impression of a loose communal hobo subculture. Although individual men are described throughout the text and their unique voices are heard, like the unknown man who dies as a light is shown on his face, we see these men for only a short time before the literary light is extinguished and they retreat back into the darkness where Tully narrates from the group's perspective.

The unmistakable difference between the 1928 William A. Wellman film version of *Beggars of Life* and the novel highlights Tully's polyphonic writing style.[12] In the cinematic version, Nancy (Louise Brooks) is a combination of a number of characters from the novel, becoming an embodiment of normative heterosexuality for Jim (Richard Arlen), the character loosely based on Tully. The important homosocial bonding present in Tully's novel is absent, and instead the film follows the two individuals attempting to flee the hobo subculture, thereby "saving" themselves from the hobo gang led by Oklahoma Red (Wallace Beery). As in most Hollywood films, the main characters are the focus of the camera's eye, and Nancy and Jim's "redemption" is accomplished in the particular way that they are able to stand morally and physically apart from the other hobos. The individual characters' moral purity allows them to transcend the mob of degenerate men, even somewhat transforming Oklahoma Red. Jim, although he is a hobo, is not a part of this group. Instead, he risks his life to keep Nancy safe, revealing himself as an outsider and target for the other hobos. His willingness to protect Nancy, who repays his help with quick-witted action that saves them both, rejects base desires and moves them toward a moral righteousness that Wellman celebrates through multiple individual close-ups of the character's faces. Although Wellman utilizes many of the same characters and situations that Tully devises in *Beggars of Life*, the director plays the heroic individuals against the group. In Tully's book, however, individual hobos, although allowed to keep their unique voice, are more fully immersed as members of the hobo subculture.

The result is that in the book version of *Beggars of Life*, the group holds center stage. Readers witness and understand this communality among the men. Due to a lack of an individualistic center, then, the text covertly begs the question about the state of a nation that allows large groups of men to live as communal transients. These Underworld novels, the bulk of which were published in the 1920s, stand in stark contrast to the Jazz Age roaring stories of F. Scott Fitzgerald. Instead of bootleg gin and wild parties featuring flappers under elaborate chandeliers, there are stolen kegs, clusters of worn-out men in boxcars, and the white lights of oncoming trains offering nonstructured, "invisible" mobility. And while writers such as Hemingway wrote stories of middle-class masculine men trying to act brave in a world quickly changing around them, Tully wrote about the underclass in the United States, refusing to single out anyone—himself included—as separate from the group.[13]

In this way Tully's writing style is even significantly different from Jack Black's 1926 autobiographical cautionary tale, *You Can't Win*. Although sharing a similar cast of characters with *Beggars of Life* (Black recounts the evolution of a train-hopping thief who spends his time hiding out in jungles and hopping trains), this autobiography securely anchors the author at the center of the narrative, a move contrary to the way Tully wrote about the hobo subculture. Although his writing style led one of his critics to emphatically announce that Tully "cannot understand the harm done to his art by his voluptuously sympathetic senses," because he makes himself only a minor character in his own novel, this framework is the basis for Tully's boxcar politics.[14] While cunning and strength may place someone in a more strategic position while on the road, the hobo is still ensconced within an unwanted and illegal subculture. Tully is committed to this view; this symbiotic relationship allows for the individual hobo and the larger subculture to survive.

## BEING A PARASITE

*Beggars of Life*, however, is not a clarion call to action to help the poor people of the United States. This lack of a recognizable political agenda allowed Tully's work to be read by contemporary reviewers as distinctly apolitical, a view that has continued through to the present.[15] Negatively comparing Tully to Michael Gold, the left-leaning *New Masses* editor whose autobiography, *Jews without Money*, is one of the most widely read of proletarian fiction, the *New Republic* stated that Tully's hobos are "simple" and "merely garnish his philosophy of weary misanthropy."[16] On the surface of these texts, this may seem to be true, but a more complicated analysis contradicts this view.

In *Beggars of Life* the only scene of overt politics can be found in the chapter "An Election Victory," in which Tully recounts his participation in a rigged election. He describes how he was paid to travel across a particular district, get fitted with a false name in each locale, and vote for a particular candidate. In his retelling Tully does not question the morality or the ramifications of vote fixing; it is simply a way for him and other traveling men to make money. He writes of his communal crime, "This weighty matter [of choosing a false name] settled, neglected future citizens of America, we walked in and voted."[17]

Although the scene is dealing with national politics, Tully, through this sentence, is announcing his own personal politics. As a member of a loose group of traveling men, Tully enters a town and makes a few dollars while having free drinks, exploiting an election scam. Even still, in his rhetorical mode, he moves from thinking individualistically to collectively: from Jim Tully to "neglected future citizens of America." These dispossessed men, who will be ignored by the politicians they illegally helped get elected, are part of the vast hobo subculture who must hide in the recesses of boxcars to remain safe. And because their poor bodies are subjected to the numerous vagrancy laws that could easily place them in jails or work camps, this line shows Tully's view of himself as a noncitizen—citizenship is imagined to be in the future. Just like in *Circus Parade*, where the "carnies" think of themselves as an insular subculture apart from the townsfolk "rubes," Tully, here thinks of himself as part of the imagined community of the hobo subculture, apart from the "citizens."

Tully's cynical view of politics leads him to believe that even citizens are as neglected as hobos. Tully works for the politicians who will rob him and everybody else of their voice because that is the way national politics works, and he understands that when he does become a "citizen" he will be as "neglected" as he is as a hobo. He has no interest in combating the political system head-on or, in his view, ineffectually pointing out its inconsistencies. Unlike London in *The Road*, who creates his own system of law within the hierarchy of homeless travelers for purely individualistic gain, or Mac, from John Dos Passos's *U.S.A.* trilogy, who attempts to use his mobility as a hobo for revolutionary purposes by joining the

Industrial Workers of the World, Tully rides squarely in the ideological middle, knowing that as a member of a mobile hobo subculture, he needs to look for exploitable spaces. This parasitic nature of the hobo is forged to face the daily violence of living a life of a marginalized outcast traveling through a society that considers him a member of an "army of tramps." Tully embraces this parasitic role, manipulating the train to leech off a rigged system.

But unlike some parasites that destroy anything in their path, Tully's hobo palette is more discriminating, complicating the notion that a hobo was purely individualistic. As seen in his first hobo trip, as well as in numerous trips throughout the text, the narrative focus is placed on the communal interactions among the hobo subculture. In fact, toward the end of *Beggars of Life*, Tully pulls back from the narrative to underscore this realistic and parasitic philosophy of life on the road. The hobo's existence is violent; death can at any time come in the form of a train, a bull, or a vigilante mob. Scoffing at idealists who have no "knowledge of life" or sociologists who offer their views on the state of the homeless population, Tully has a great disrespect for those who can think only in the abstract, and their visionary dream "blurs their eyes when they look at the viciousness of it all. . . . They cannot see life around them, their eyes being fastened on the great dream ahead, a few million years after they are rotten." In other words, a dream of "One Big Union" happening in his lifetime or the next is not on Tully's political radar, and, as he states adamantly, he is "no reformer."[18]

Interestingly, this attack on idealists also sketches out his political framework: "Some idealists are selfish as individuals, but lovers of the mob. And who can really love a mob? Evolution helps the mob. One can only help the individual."[19] Tully is neither an individualist caring only about himself nor a believer in the potential for seismic political and social changes in his lifetime—evolutionary change is a prolonged organic transition that takes place over a marked amount of time. But he never loses sight that the individual is part of a fluid subculture. As evolution benefits the mob, Tully offers that it is in the day-to-day exchanges *within* the immediate subculture where the individual can be helped by—and can help—other hobos. This nuanced idea forms the basis of his boxcar politics.

This subtlety is different from London's view of the hobo; it is also different from a popular hobo-turned-writer, Harry Kemp, whose autobiography, *Tramping on Life*, received favorable attention when it was released two years prior to *Beggars of Life*. A quick evaluation throws into relief Tully's differing worldview. In this text Kemp relates his experiences sharing boxcars with other riders, traveling from town to town as he dreams, like Tully, of being a writer (Kemp carried a volume of Shakespeare's plays as he hopped trains).[20] In his patronizing prose, though, there is a revealing moment when he describes the itinerant group functioning as a community, organized in their ability to infiltrate a town: "These tramps were gathered together on a definite plan, and I was invited to join them in it; the plan was to go, *en masse*, from town to town, and systematically exploit it; one day one man would go to the butcher shops, the next, another man would take them, and the first would, let's say, beg at the baker's . . . and each day a different man would take a different section among the houses. Then all the food so procured would be put together and shared in common."[21]

What Kemp describes is an example of a sophisticated form of transient mutualism wherein poor men acknowledge their place on the margins of society, join together to share resources, and tactically create plans to procure food that would benefit them individually and collectively. But unlike Tully, Kemp keeps the subculture at a distance. When he is invited to join, he partakes in eating the communally shared food, but his writing style signals to the reader that he always considers himself separate from these men. While the community interaction was key to the success for the individual hobo, Kemp simply "grew tired of the gang and started on alone."[22] His writing and view of the rail rider is a celebration of vagabondia, of what literary critic Arthur Compton-Rickett described in 1906 as a wandering instinct "with a certain detachment from the majority of men."[23] While Kemp dramatizes issues concerning the life of an artist, his memoir does not offer insight into the hobo subculture because he refuses to place himself within it. He is an individualist whose literary aspirations cloud his vision of the group.[24] Tully, who likewise had literary aspirations when hopping trains, viewed life on the road differently, embedding himself securely among the homeless men.

This slippery interaction between the individual and the group did not just concern Tully; it was also an important ongoing discussion emerging at the beginning of the twentieth century. To specify Tully's boxcar politics, then, it is beneficial to contextualize Tully's hobo politics within the larger macropolitical theoretical discussions involving conceptual interactions between the individual and community.

## THE PEOPLE, THE MOB, AND THE INDIVIDUAL

Although Tully saw the individual as existing independently while simultaneously being a part of a hobo subculture, social scientists studying the behavior of groups and their effect on the body politic of American citizenry at the turn of the twentieth century were not sure this was possible. Walt Whitman's exceptionalist view of "the people" as having "measureless wealth of latent power and capacity" was a beautiful democratic nation-building idea in the aftermath of the Civil War, but as strikes abounded in the Gilded Age and Progressive Era, there was much to fear from a collectivized polarity.[25] The people, as signified by the preamble to the Constitution, defined a normalized idea of American citizenship. But while the people reported to be inclusive, as the threat of miscegenation and "dark" immigrants from Europe evolved, the term was revealed to be always exclusionary: when the white, propertied class came together, the people participated in rational democratic politics; when those on the margins of society, such as the working class, gathered together, they were a mob.

Nicolas Mills, in *The Crowd in American Literature*, shows how these collective purposes had conflicting agendas; while the people "devotes itself to leveling whatever or whomever is exceptional," the mob challenges "the social and economic structure of the country." Individuals are therefore identified with the law, and the mob is identified as an extra-institutional embodiment of irrationality and emotionalism. For the nation to be unified, the body of enfranchised people, as political philosophers Michael Hardt and Antonio Negri state, "synthesizes or reduces these social differences [of a population] into one identity." The mob, on the other hand, represents "man, the animal, left off his leash." Describing how individuals lose their identity when brought into the group, Gustave Le Bon, a prominent social scientist at the turn of the twentieth century, describes rational beings morphing into a "collective mind that makes them feel, think and act in ways that are very different from how each individual would have felt, thought or acted had he been alone."[26]

While the fear of socialism and radical unionization that the "collective mind" represents is apparent, another primary underlining fear of collectivity is a loss of liberal individualism. According to the adherents of this view, the rational individual is subsumed into the group, easily manipulated, and subjected to the ever-present potentiality of (revolutionary) violence. Although Le Bon's work was criticized as being hyperfearful of the collective by some of his contemporaries, there was an overriding view among social scientists and policymakers that "enlightened leaders" embodying the "social intellect" of the cultural elite were needed to control the mob.[27] Mixing a distinctly racialized social Darwinism with an exceptionalist view of American republican virtues as the nation was awkwardly dealing with the consequences wrought by industrialization, a great faith developed in the white, Anglo-Saxon, technocratic elite (such as the owners of railroads) to control the mob and deliver the people to the promised land of American democracy. As members of an illegal subculture slipping into the recesses of train cars to avoid the law, Tully's hobos, looking upward from the substrate position, did not fit into a normalized view of the people. But while it seems obvious that Tully would distrust the people and all this term symbolically represents, in his texts, he consistently holds up contempt for the mob.

Although this may seem inconsistent on Tully's part, when looked at from the position of the hobo subculture, it fits with his political philosophy. At the beginning of the twentieth century, the mob is coded as working class. Although he took jobs whenever he could find them, if considered along strict Marxist lines that make a distinction between "productive" and "unproductive" labor, Tully, as he chronicles in *Beggars of Life*, is not working class. As discussed in chapter 1, the hobo's mobility, habitual unemployment, and cultural differences resulted in a split between this subculture and most working-class organizing efforts. Seen as part of the lumpen proletariat that was the "industrial reserve army," a reactionary group of would-be strikebreakers who kept labor tied to its slave wages, hobos were mostly excluded from the social and imagined working-class community, including full participation in union life.

Unlike his connection to the hobo subculture, Tully had a haphazard relationship with organized labor. He did receive a union card from the chain makers' union, whom he describes as "the gypsies of manual labor," after he left the road, and he even found himself ghostwriting for his brother's union's journal, but he was never a dynamic force in union politics. The most vocal he seems to have been was when he published in the *Kent Currier* a poem titled "Samuel Gompers," where he (unironically) compares the leader of the American Federation of Labor to both Jesus and George Washington. This praise seems to be self-serving, as he mailed the piece to Gompers himself in the hopes of receiving a job.[28]

Tully was more enthusiastic about radical unionization and the Industrial Workers of the World, who were the most accommodating to itinerant workers, even having a specific recruiting wing dedicated to its organizing efforts. But while his heart went out to the "head-battered and bloody" Wobblies, he "would join no lodge or anything else" because they were a mob. He stated succinctly, "I do not like the mob," and he had "contempt for them" when on the road.[29] Tully, too, feared a loss of liberal individualism. As someone who, when he was employed as a boxer or carnie, worked on the societal margins beyond the reach of most unionization efforts, his distrust of the mob shows the tensions that existed along the fault lines of the hobo subculture and the normative working class. Tully's boxcar politics were therefore shaped not in these radical proletariat organizations but through his relationship with the hobo subculture. Tully's politics reject the connotations associated with the mob and instead advocate for a fluidity of identity that allows him to keep his individuality as he shares boxcars with fellow hobos.

## THE MULTITUDE AND THE HOBO SUBCULTURE

While Tully's rejection of the people and the mob helps us know what his boxcar politics are not, Hardt and Negri's term *multitude* is a good initial place to begin to define what they are. As opposed to the terms *people* and *mob*, *multitude* is plural and "composed of a set of *singularities*—and by singularity here we mean a social subject whose difference cannot be reduced to sameness, a difference that remains different. . . . The plural singularities of the multitude thus stand in contrast to the undifferentiated unity of the people." According to their definition, the multitude does not just consist of passive subjects led by ruling parties (or the "technocratic elite"), nor have they formed into one singular homogenous identity. Contrasting the views of political philosophers who state that there needs to be a singular head (be it monarch, president, party, or dictator) to the political body of the polity, Hardt and Negri believe that the multitude is "the living flesh that rules itself," rejecting "the organic unity of the body." The key to understanding their term is that the multitude is "singularities that act in common" where "there is no conceptual or actual contradiction between singularity and commonality."[30]

As part of their radical project examining potential global responses to empire, Hardt and Negri see the multitude as "the becoming common of labor in all its generality—economically, politically, and socially"; it is not exclusionary, delimited by rigid Marxist distinctions, but inherently inclusive and celebratory of differences, including "the poor, the unemployed and the underemployed." This expansive view of labor (which would include members of the floating proletariat) is a significant change from, for example, the "golden days" of subculture studies as exemplified by the Centre for Contemporary Cultural Studies (CCCS) model that viewed the working class as a (mostly) monolithic identity. Hardt and Negri's idea of the multitude is also significantly different from some post-subcultural models that have removed "class" as an essential defining component and that see subcultural practitioners as embodying a unique "choice" that individuals freely create for themselves. Contrary to the traditional Marxist-influenced CCCS and the hybridity of other subculture theorists, Hardt and Negri's philosophical treatise celebrates the polymorphous nature of multitude while clearly categorizing the multitude as "a class concept."[31]

The fluid term *hobo* is equally a "class concept." In *Beggars of Life*, Tully's description of hobos is composed of the singularities (individual hobos) that cannot be reduced to a sameness (a generic, traditional group). As they warm themselves by the fire, hobos are part of a loose subculture of networked individuals that share similar socioeconomic positions—their mobility as a transient workforce and their relationship to the train are the connecting tissues among the subculture.

Do Tully's hobos, then, anticipate Hardt and Negri's multitude? Does Tully's boxcar politics perform a twenty-first-century radical political philosophy? In a word, no. While similar, Tully's hobos lack a key ingredient. "The multitude needs a political project to bring it into existence."[32] Tully and his fellow riders, while they are singular subjects riding in a shared existence, never share a cohesive, *acknowledged* political project. Although each act of train hopping offers a physical, parasitic resistance to the capitalist system embodied by the train, they do not attempt to gather these resistances together. While they are collectivized within a boxcar or around a jungle fire and work together in small moments, they cannot see the shared political project and therefore, at times, are splintered, fractured, and at odds with one another.

For example, as Tully and a companion, Bill, are riding together in a boxcar, an officer boards and handcuffs the two together, informing them that they are heading to jail for a long stretch of time. Instead, as the train gained speed, "Bill held tightly to the rung of the iron ladder with his free hand, and kicked the majesty of railroad law in the south as he looked north." Although they are able to get away, as a result the town of Clinton, where they were traveling through, becomes "hostile" to other hobos. When Tully expresses remorse for his fellow hobos who would get caught, Bill says, "It's all'n the game, Red. When you're on the bum long enough someone'll stick you up for somethin' some other guy done. The big trick's don't let 'em ketch you."[33]

The result of being successful in "the game" and not being caught—this time—is that other unlucky hobos traveling unawares through the town of Clinton are made to "run the ga'ntlet," subjected to a terrible beating by a vigilante mob.[34] The communality of the hobo group, it is apparent, does have its limits. While large, the hobo subculture did not have a political platform and dues-paying members. This was a free-flowing, amorphous group in which the personal body often was placed in greater importance to that of the group body. And although Tully expresses remorse that others would pay through broken bones and bloody lips the check that he and his companion wrote, he does not believe in any greater political movement that could alleviate the suffering of these traveling men.

## A MATERIALIST POLITICS

If Tully's boxcar politics does not fit into the term *mob,* nor does it fit neatly with Hardt and Negri's view of the multitude, how do we define it? Tully's boxcar politics is a materialist politics based on the relationship among the individual hobo, the subculture, and the train. This subcultural connection is literal and symbolic. Expanding on the view of cultural theorist Ginette Verstraete, who states, "systems of transportation and communication have been the site of fierce struggles for power among the nation-builders," the awesome technology that the train represents is also a site of struggle among those excluded from true citizenship.[35]

By hopping a train, hobos materially offered their bodies as resistance to the progress of an expanding capitalist society that the transcontinental railroad promised in its curling smoke and screeching wheels. The train is a powerful symbol and example of late nineteenth- and early twentieth-century American capitalism, and by physically stealing a ride hobos were parasitic as they attempted to get to the next town, state, or nation. This materiality of resistance—of living the body politic—is crucial to understanding the hobo subculture and Tully's boxcar politics. By hopping trains and disappearing into boxcars in one place and entering a new one the next day, hobos were offering resistance, literally and symbolically, to the "progress" of the country underwritten by finance capitalism and embodied by the train. By stealing rides, hobos were parasitic to the life force of the train (and to the profit margins of the owner of these railroads), and like parasites circulating within blood, they sometimes went unnoticed, often caused minor ailments, and frequently had the potential to inflict serious illness.

Tully's hobos were not mere individualists like London and his profresh ilk, but relied, for their survival, on a complicated political economy of transient mutualism in which the passing interactions among the group (and with the larger culture) allowed them to remain clothed, fed, and (occasionally) housed. Tully's hobos are what Frederic M. Thrasher, a sociologist and Tully's contemporary, calls "interstitial groups," or a subculture situated within, but not restricted to, the culture that it borders.[36] In the jungles, boxcars, or non-places purposely forgotten or ignored, hobos met and gathered. As Nels Anderson writes in *The Hobo*, released one year before *Beggars of Life*, hobos were marginalized to areas around the railroad tracks and cut off from normalized social networks, including members of the rooted working class. Within these cracks in society, the subculture formed a collective behavior that evolved its own traditions, group awareness, and loosely based solidarity. The boxcar was the conduit that allowed for the singularity of the individual riders to coexist with the commonality of the hobo subculture.[37]

Tully's hobos meet in particular places, and they share stories, food, and information. Within these jungles and boxcars, there are rules to follow. These lessons are taught in physical locations reinforced in the daily contacts among themselves as they ride across the United States. The rules are somewhat fluid, but an imagined hobo community forms. As Anderson states, "absolute democracy reigns in the jungle. . . . The hobo enters into this life as he does no other. Here he turns his back on the world and faces his fellows, and is at ease." Ken Gelder in *Subcultures* accurately points out that Anderson's view of "Hobohemia" is utopian-tinged and that Tully's own retelling of his experiences in *Beggars of Life* show how racially abhorrent the subculture could be.[38] But while the sites of the hobos' gathering spaces are fraught with inconsistencies, Tully's hobos are a part of an imagined community of riders. Their mobility and their identity are intertwined with their ability to co-inhabit a space on the train, harnessing its power to get them where they want to go. This is outside the intended functionality of the train, but hobos expropriate it for their own purposes.

A compelling example of the way these multiple voices are joined together through the train itself is found in a compact scene toward the end of *Beggars of Life*. Once again, Tully finds himself in a boxcar with other men. Noticing a hobo carving his moniker into the train, Tully writes, "When he had finished, he stood up and admired it like an artist. An arrow was cut through the letters of his name. It pointed west, and denoted the direction in which he was traveling. The month and the year of the trip were cut beneath the name . . . form[ing] a crude directory for other tramps who might be interested in the itinerary of their comrades."[39] Here we see a symbolic communication system that uses the actual train itself to send and receive messages. Only those who are within the subculture can read—or even think to look at—these systems embodied within the train. Learning to read graffiti is taught from one hobo to another as new riders become acquainted with more seasoned riders. This learning process is not a formal education, but like any language system, it takes practice and time to learn. In this way, graffiti is a way to link individuals, even though these people have no prior knowledge of one another and may not have even met. Reflecting on the individuality of the person, these markings or monikers are part of the shared language that helps suture the geographically disperse hobo subculture together.

The system of hobo graffiti has a rich, mostly hidden, subcultural tradition. Hobo graffiti began within the realm of rail workers who chalked railroad cars for utilitarian purposes, writing instructions to other trainmen about which cars needed to be sided or rebuilt. While doing so, some trainmen also began placing their monikers on the cars as well, sending their messages and symbols throughout the country. Hobos, who physically shared the same geographic spaces as the rail workers (and were sometimes former railroad workers themselves), also created a similar set of discursive emblems that were (as the Tully quote shows) both practical and artistic. This freight train graffiti, made with chalk or scratched with knives, rocks, or other sharp instruments, was used to convey sentiments to other hobos who, as members of this discursive community, could read the signs. While sometimes crudely drawn, as semiotician Jules Wanderer concludes, hobo graffiti was a complicated language system using signs that fell into three categories: ideographs, metonymies, and metaphors.[40] Ranging from practical pictorial signs (supplying important information such as the location of sympathetic doctors in a particular town) to imagistic philosophy (abstract detailing of a particular hobo's moods and thoughts), these hobos were actively using the train to conduct conversations, reinforce friendships, or relay requests for help and information. This chalking or carving aesthetically and physically altered the train, underlining the subcultural bonds.[41]

These markings on the train represent a physical reminder of the illegal relationship that the individuals shared with the subculture through their contact with the train. The railroad, as Verstraete states, is much more than a technology of transportation; it is also a technology of representation "about figuratively emplacing a specific citizenry" at the cost of others.[42] But what this graffiti shows is that the displacement is never fully complete and individual hobos are (literally) leaving their marks on the train to be read by other members of a subculture who are parasitically appropriating the train. This functional tripartite relationship is the source of Tully's boxcar politics.

## THE RADICALIZED BOXCAR?

Tully, at the end of *Beggars of Life*, recounts, "The road writes with heavy hand its lines of degeneracy, brutality, and all-around wretchedness on their faces and bodies."[43] His Underworld Series shows these lines in great detail. Perhaps this is why the *New Republic* described his work as "weary misanthropy" and apolitical. But Tully is fiercely interested in writing about the individual among a maligned subculture, and this fluidity between the singular and the community does, in fact, produce a political framework: Tully illustrates how the individual and the group share the same political space on the train whose connection is real and viable.

But while Tully, as opposed to London, believed in working together with other riders in the boxcar, when the train's engine died and the hobos were forced to sneak into the bushes of the train yards, the communality was, for the most part, lost. Tully himself did not believe in hobos (or anyone else for that matter) changing the political paradigm of the United States; he was more interested in surviving by traveling along the rails. There were others, however, who did believe that the hobo population could be radicalized and effect revolutionary change within the United States. With no secure place in society, they felt they had little to lose except, as the Wobbly mantra states, their chains. John Dos Passos, in his *U.S.A.* trilogy, created characters that detail the excitement as well as the frustration of hobos radicalized by their time on the road. Contextualizing these books within a radical hobo history allows us to unravel another significant strand of boxcar politics.

Chapter Four

# THE RADICALIZED BOXCAR

## Hobos, the "Speech of the People," and John Dos Passos's *U.S.A.*

John Dos Passos's trilogy, *U.S.A.*, an epic and cautionary modernist text that spans the years from 1900 to the Great Depression, was born from the author's stated desire to write "so fiery and accurate" in response to the U.S. government's execution in 1927 of the anarchists Ferdinando Nicola Sacco and Bartolomeo Vanzetti.[1] Principally concerning itself with the systematic suppression of the anticapitalist movement within the United States, these novels recount the political loss felt by the Left in the first third of the twentieth century. Taking approximately a decade from conception to completion, the first novel, *The 42nd Parallel*, was published in 1930, followed by *Nineteen Nineteen* in 1932 and *The Big Money* in 1936. The trilogy was published as one volume in 1938, with Dos Passos adding the prologue "U.S.A." and a short final section titled "Vag," a vignette of an enervated vagrant hitchhiking along a nameless highway.

Critics have generally praised these novels for their experimental achievements and cinematic scope, with some, such as Jean Paul Sartre in 1947, hailing Dos Passos as "the greatest writer of our time." There is, however, almost universal agreement that these novels are foremost about political despair, and critics from the 1930s onward have been troubled with the overwhelming pessimism that seemingly entombs these novels. Malcolm Cowley, in a tepid review of the trilogy, states that the work is too politically cynical, lamenting that the author included no expression of "the will to struggle ahead, the comradeship in struggle, the consciousness of the new men, and the new forces rising." Cowley's contemporary T. K. Whipple is even harsher, finding that the characters have "no strength of resistance. They are weak at the very core of personality, the power to choose." While Lionel Trilling specifically calls both of these critics to task and praises *U.S.A.*, he too focuses on the misery in the trilogy, writing, "I can think of no more useful political job for the literary man today than, by the representation of despair, to cauterize the exposed soft tissue of too-easy hope."[2]

Even though Trilling, unlike Cowley and Whipple, found these novels to have a constructive political purpose in representing despair, he also found no affirmations of a radical political movement in the trilogy. While these reviews show the initial reactions immediately after publication, subsequent critical responses followed in this vein; Alfred Kazin in the 1940s called *U.S.A.* "one of the saddest books ever written by an American," and John William Ward in 1969 decried it as "the coldest, most mercilessly despairing book in our literature." A decade later, Ian Colley titled his book-length study of the author and his works, *Dos Passos and the Fiction of Despair*.[3]

In the past twenty years, there has been a welcome reexamination of *U.S.A.*, with critics Barbara Foley, Michael Denning, and Seth Moglen, among others, offering astute textual and cultural analysis, carefully relating the author's complex relationship with the Left to the trilogy's multifaceted experimental prose, enriching our understanding of the nuances of the anticapitalist movement in the early twentieth century. Although these critics have made immensely valuable contributions to Dos Passos scholarship specifically, and to reinterpreting radical movements of the twentieth century generally, they reject what I find to be a basic, hopeful message found within this text: the interrelatedness of Dos Passos's hobos' movements and speech indicate the endurance of a strand of radical political dissidence that, unlike revolutionary organizations, are neither stopped nor silenced.

There are certainly limits to the power of the hobo to effect change; as Moglen points out in his book *Mourning Modernity*, Dos Passos is capturing a bleak political moment when the anticapitalist and radical movements within the United States were being razed by governmental forces and policies. Ideologically and physically attacked, labor organizations and their leaders were being jailed or exiled, and the darkness that Dos Passos weaves throughout the text is appropriately oppressive. Contrary to Whipple's belief that the characters have "no strength of resistance," however, the hobo characters, although battered, do not succumb to defeatism. Instead, through words and actions, they continue the radical political tradition in the United States. Although by the close of the trilogy political organizations that directly confront the machinations of capitalism are decimated, *U.S.A.* clings to the hobo as one figure who, marginalized from regimented political organizations, can keep the radical tradition alive.

Hobos' conjoined acts of speech and movement should be read as a hopeful belief in the continuation of the radical tradition in the United States. Dos Passos, at one point, suggests that the hobo, much like the revolutionary, is a figure who can no longer exist in the modern world, correlating the hobo's "death" with the decline of anticapitalist radicalism in the United States. But, just as important, at the very end of the trilogy, when he is seemingly at his most pessimistic, Dos Passos revives the hobo and exalts him as one of the few radicals who can continue to spread the anticapitalist message. In Dos Passos's divided America of two nations, wherein capitalism is victorious and the revolution stands defeated, the hobo is, in fact, not only sentient but entrusted by the author with both the history of the radical cause and, because of his physical movement, its future as well.[4] In this hopeful glimpse, *U.S.A.* places its (bruised) faith not in a particular organized political movement, such as the Industrial Workers of the World (IWW), but in the independent movements of radicalized hobos traveling across the country.

In his hobo scenes throughout the trilogy, Dos Passos highlights the conjoined ideological transitional space of the radical boxcar: in one end we witness the early moments of radicalization of some hobos as they travel their perilous journeys throughout the United States, and in the other end we see organizations using these radicalized hobos for direct action. While there is a logical progression from hobo to radical activist, it is not necessarily a smooth transition as an individual moves from one end of the boxcar to the other. By juxtaposing the hobo figures in *U.S.A.* alongside firsthand accounts of radical hobos who traveled the country in the early decades of the twentieth century, this chapter complicates previously held notions of *U.S.A.*'s abject pessimism while concurrently identifying and exploring boxcar politics' radical expressions.

Lisa Nanney, in her examination of *U.S.A.*, articulates the principal question of the trilogy as "How can the common individual prevail against the massive systems of industrial capitalism that have turned the promises of the American Dream into a lie?"[5] In my reevaluation of the trilogy, I suggest that after over a thousand-page ride, *U.S.A.* is pointing to the hobo as one possible answer. If *U.S.A.* is about finding the "speech of the people," as Dos Passos asserts in the prologue to the trilogy, the hobo is speaking a democratic American idiom: he speaks the language of the boxcar.[6] And although this language has a different accent from that of labor organizations such as the Wobblies, its peculiarity allows it to be one of the few radical languages to continue to be spoken. To highlight the interrelationship of hoboing and the nascence of radicalization, let us first turn to an extended examination of Mac, the hobo-cum-Wobbly-cum-bookstore owner.

## MAC, THE TRAIN, AND HIS INTRODUCTION TO BOXCAR POLITICS

As the first volume of the trilogy opens with "Noise," "Labor," "Churches," and the "Nation" greeting the new century, the reader is introduced to Fainy "Mac" McCreary, who, not so joyously, is choking on the smell of "whaleoil soap . . . cabbage and babies" that pervades the decrepit four-family frame house where he was born. But the young Mac must soon leave his home that faced Chadwick Mills. His mother dies from overwork, and his father, after becoming lame and consequently fired from his job as night watchman, must steal away from under the hospital and funeral bills. Feeling like a "whipped cur," his father leads the family west to make a new start in Chicago. Only six pages into the narrative, young Mac soon finds himself in a train yard, where "with an enormous, shattering rumble, sludgepuff sludge . . . the train came into the station."[7] It is a scary and bewildering introduction to the train, and within seconds Mac and his sister Milly are scooped up and placed inside the train car, anxiously looking out the window. Watching states fly past their window in a blur as they are shuttled across the country, the young boy loses all sense of time, geography, and reality.

Mac's narrative opens with defeat; his mother is dead and his father reduced to an insignificant mumbling figure. The McCrearys are absconding from their town, and Mac, frightened and disoriented, has no control over the train—a train that Dos Passos imbues with monstrous qualities. This startling introduction occurring in the first pages of the trilogy, however, will be the last time that Mac is intimidated by the railroad. Trains will continue to play a vital role in Mac's narrative (as well as for other characters in the trilogy), and he will soon learn how to manipulate the railroad car for his own ends. By learning the ways of the hobo, Mac discovers a powerful tool that helps sustain his political action.

Shortly after arriving in Chicago, his father dies and Mac is placed under the tutelage of his left-leaning, alcoholic uncle, who gives his young nephew a trade as a printer while planting the seeds of his future radicalism. After a few years, however, Mac's uncle, refusing to buckle under the pressure of the capitalist interests, has his business shut down and, defeated like his brother-in-law, spends the rest of his days in front of a half-empty glass in a local saloon. Both of Mac's father figures have been defeated by capitalism's long and intrusive reach. In a final meeting before Mac is forced to find his own way, his uncle gives him one last message: "Don't ever sell out to the sons of bitches."[8] Mac, here, sees quite plainly the result of his uncle's idealism, and while certainly taking his message to heart, the soon-to-be hobo will find it advantageous to express his politics in his movements and conversations rather than standing toe to toe with capital.

Needing to support himself, Mac takes a job with "Doc" Bingham, head (and only member) of Truthseeker. Bingham, a comic figure, quickly gets in trouble with a married woman and leaves Mac in the middle of the night.[9] The young apprentice, escaping the buckshot from the cuckolded husband's shotgun, abruptly finds himself with little money and "nobody following him." He is drifting, jobless, and completely alone—or so he believes. Mac falls asleep on a deserted bench and wakes to find himself part of a "brotherhood" of transient workers when George "Ike" Hall calls out to him, "Hey, bo, you better not let the station agent find you."[10] Although Mac might think he is completely alone, he soon recognizes himself as part of a migrant, hobo subculture.

Willing to split his last dollar with Ike, Mac learns they have the same fledgling political bent as they spend the afternoon lying in the sun talking politics and books. The relationship between the two is clearly an example of transient mutualism where strangers, recognizing their shared socioeconomic position, financially and emotionally help one another. Undaunted by their lack of funds, they are able to enjoy the afternoon. They want to read, talk, and travel; as hobos, they will be able to live this lifestyle. This form of homosocial bonding that interrelates traveling and talking is clearly contrary to Jack London's subcultural competitiveness as recounted in *The Road.* While London was interested in the road kids' vernacular, he was not interested in sharing any rides (or anything else) with the other young hobos. This bonding is also different from the strand of boxcar politics found in Jim Tully's writing: while numerous examples of transient mutualism were found in his texts, Tully's hobos traveled to survive and did not have faith in, nor particular interest in discussing, national politics. Contrary to these authors, Dos Passos celebrates these young men who are both figuratively and physically on the road to becoming radicalized.

Creating an idyllic scene as the two young men talk, Dos Passos captures the way that life on the road could become a space for political engagement:

> They went out with a roll of newspapers and sat under a big pine a little way out of town. The sun had come out warm; big white marble clouds sailed throughout the sky. They lay on their backs with their heads on a piece of pinkish root with bark like an alligator. In spite of last night's rain the pine needles were warm and dry under them. In front of them stretched the singletrack line through thickets and clearings of wrecked woodland where fireweed was beginning to thrust up here and there a palegreen spike of leaves. They read sheets of the weekold paper turn and turn about and talked.[11]

Here, a few feet away from the single tracks that will take them, as cultural critic and train rider William Vollman states, "riding toward everywhere," they sit and talk politics.[12] It is a fraternal bond that, like their lives, is transitory, but they are happy to connect among the warm pine needles. With this relationship Mac gains agency and strength. Standing up by the track with his "blood . . . like fire," he stares at an approaching handcar that has a group of rail workers on its back. The machine that roared into the station while he was a frightened child has been undressed, and the smoke-blowing monster has been reconstituted as the self-propelling tool of ordinary workingmen like him. Through his conversation with a member of the hobo brotherhood and this discovery of the railroad track that will lead to education, work, and companionship, Mac, who felt alone a few hours earlier, now feels confident as they decide to hobo their way to Seattle to find jobs and study.

Mac embraces this type of mobility, and Dos Passos romanticizes the young hobo's experiences. The deafening "roar" and chaotic clatter that describes the train on Mac's terrifying first journey as a child is now transformed into "singing" as the train makes its way into the station.[13] What was noise to him when he was younger is now music to his ears, as the train that had been overpowering to him as a passenger he subdues as a hobo. Although the trip is loud and bumpy, Mac and Ike are far from powerless as they create a warm space for themselves in the boxcar. The two young men continue to hop trains, taking jobs and leaving them, consistently moving through various states, as well as slipping past the U.S.-Canadian border.

As hobos, they participate in an "in-between" hobo subculture, floating between the respectable and dangerous classes. Their itinerancy mirrors countless flesh-and-blood hobos who found themselves on the road during the first part of the twentieth century. Kingsley Widmer, author of *The Literary Rebel*, evocatively summarizes the dual life of the hobo: "In a society where 'the job' ('What do you do?') provides the major way of identity, the hobo had one but frequently shifted and violated it. Thus, imaginatively, the hobo well represented American uncertainty about self-definition since he is neither fully a pariah to the social order nor fitted into a fixed place. His justifications to others was his work; his justification to himself was his flight. The image of the American hobo becomes representative in being both unfixed and righteous."[14]

As Widmer explains, it is a lifestyle filled with paradoxes. The very nature of their marginalized lives allows hobos to float in between cultures. Mac and Ike's transient lifestyle connects them to a number of social scenes that are, like the scenery outside their boxcars, consistently changing; they meet and talk about life, politics, and the issues of the day with the other travelers and workers they meet. Not restricted to one geographic place or job, their travels inform their practical political ideology. For Mac, this particular form of traveling within a "shadow America" leads to radicalization. Although Mac's hobo narrative evolves once he joins the IWW, it is this period of homosocial bonding, and his naive, earnest belief in the potentiality for radical change, that *U.S.A.* endorses.

Mac's road to radicalization was relatively smooth; in reality, the search for jobs, the accruing of money for the often-jobless winters, and the dangers of the road were significant facets of the hobo's life. Ralph Chaplin, who became radicalized by his travels as a hobo and who in 1948 wrote a compelling autobiography, *Wobbly,* concluded that hobos "were indeed a sad lot of unskilled, unorganized, overworked, and underpaid undesirables. . . . We were expected to keep moving yet we couldn't move at all without breaking the law. And every time we broke the law, the law tried to break us." Another hobo-turned-Wobbly, Charles Ashleigh, who emigrated from England in 1910 and wrote a semi-autobiographical novel titled *The Rambling Kid,* and who frequently wrote for the *Hobo News,* examines in "The Floater" why many were forced to live on the road, concluding that "the wholesale firing of men by foremen, the arduous nature of the work, and the temporary nature of the employment, keep the worker constantly in motion."[15] For Chaplin and Ashleigh, being a hobo crystallized for them the substrate position of the transient worker in the hierarchy of American capitalism that chained them to poor wages and dangerous jobs. The romanticizing of the hobo lifestyle by Dos Passos is completely nonexistent for them; the harsh hobo life led both men to seek political action.

Mac's travels also led him to join a radical organization, but this radicalization moves him, for a time, away from the hobo subculture. After a drunken evening during which Mac and Ike are robbed by two prostitutes, Mac wakes up with a headache and comes to a sudden realization: "I wanta study an' work for things; you know what I mean, not to get to be a goddamn slavedriver but for socialism and the revolution an' like that, not work an' go on a bat an work an' go on a bat like those damn yaps on the railroad." Mac, now, wants neither to be part of a "slave-driving" class nor one of the "damn yaps" who followed the make-money / lose-money cycle that many hobos found inescapable.[16] He is ready to become a party man.

It is a significant moment for Mac, and shortly after he makes this decision, he is accidentally deserted by Ike. Soon after, Mac finds himself working for an Italian anarchist named Bonello, and together they head to socialist picnics and libertarian meetings on their days off from work. Eventually Mac finds himself in an audience inspired by a speech by Upton Sinclair. This signals the organizational period of Mac's politics, and soon after he meets Fred Hoff, who introduces him to the Wobblies. Immediately, he feels connected to them, and when he fills out the registration card, Mac thinks to himself, "I was just on the point of selling out to the sons of bitches," before heading to Goldfield, Nevada, to help print leaflets for the large IWW-led general strike.[17]

Interestingly, Dos Passos has Mac listening to Upton Sinclair, who in 1919 wrote about a political hobo figure in his novel *Jimmie Higgins*, a novel that also uncovers the challenges facing American leftists. Jimmie's and Mac's attitudes, however, are significantly different and can best be epitomized by the divergent ways that they use the hobo lifestyle. Sinclair writes, "[Higgins] was no longer a blind and helpless victim of a false economic system, but a revolutionist, fully class-conscious, trained in a grim school. The country was going to war, and Jimmie was going to war on the country. The two agitators got off the train at a mining-village, and got a job as 'surface-men,' and proceeded to preach their gospel of revolt to the workers in a lousy company boarding-house. When they were found out, they 'jumped' another freight, and repeated the performance in another part of the district."[18] Sinclair's character is a radicalized man who uses his train-hopping skills the way that the IWW advocated. This is not the way Dos Passos frames the Mac narrative. In *U.S.A.*, the world of the hobo who is becoming radicalized and that of the party man working for the revolution are separated. Mac does not hop a train on his way to Goldfield; rather, he heads to the station and pays his own way. Immediately after Mac has his revelation and knows that he wants to fight for the revolution, Dos Passos undercuts any romanticizing in his prose connected to the hobo: no longer does he include lyrical passages describing the beauty of nature when looking out a boxcar, nor does he show the fraternal bonds formed in the hobo subculture. Unlike Jimmie Higgins, when Mac is a party man, he no longer hobos. Mac has seemingly given up the hobo lifestyle for the organized revolutionary one.

This separation is notable and can be read in line with the author's own restlessness with regimented, organized politics. In the summer of 1932, when John Dos Passos was at the height of his connection with the Communist Party, V. F. Calverton, editor of *Modern Monthly*, asked him and other prominent writers a straightforward question, "Should a writer join the Communist Party?" Dos Passos's reply was acerbic and illuminating: "It's his own goddamn business. Some people are naturally party men and others are naturally scavengers and camp followers. Matter of temperament. I personally belong to the scavenger and camp follower section."[19] While this explains one possible reason why Dos Passos was never an official member of the Communist Party USA, it also illuminates the division between organized politics of the IWW and the hobo lifestyle. Dos Passos clearly respects the scavenger, the one who is forever on the edge of the official party. Perhaps he is romanticizing the outsider, but it also significantly highlights tensions that exist when a diverse group of individuals coalesce under a banner of a particular political party.

Regardless of his well-documented fluctuation in his political leanings, as John Trombold explains, Dos Passos always had a strong anarchist thread running through his political thoughts.[20] He clearly had deep respect for Wobbly idealism, basing Mac on Gladwin Bland, a hobo and former Wobbly, whom he met while traveling in Mexico in 1927. As he announced in a letter to his friend Edmund Wilson in 1934, "I can't make up my mind to swallow political methods. Most of the time I think the IWW theory was right—Build a new society out of the shell of the old."[21] Dos Passos is, of course, writing a bit wistfully here. As is shown later in this chapter, the Wobblies employed a concentrated methodology to further their union that used the hobo for their propaganda purposes more effectively than any other radical organization.

Even though the author felt "more in common with the Wobbly line of talk than any other," his faith in the scavenger, which becomes more apparent when we examine Camera Eye (50), allows us to read the divided world between the hobo and the party man as two separate politicized spheres that sometimes shared the same space in the radicalized boxcar but were not always compatible.[22] A quick sketch of this complicated relationship between the IWW and the hobo allows us to explore this radical geography of the boxcar, shedding light on a possible reason why Dos Passos, despite his admiration for the Wobblies, allows the hobo, unencumbered from the IWW or any other political group, to continue the radical tradition in the United States.

## THE HOBO AND THE INDUSTRIAL WORKERS OF THE WORLD

Melvyn Dubofsky's influential history of the IWW, *We Shall Be All*, explains why the organization placed such great importance on politicizing the hobo to achieve its overall revolutionary goals, stating, "No workers were more mistreated by their employers, and none so lacked the elementary amenities of a decent life: a home, a family, an adequate diet."[23] What made hobos outcasts (no family, no roots) made them advantageous to the Wobblies. Embittered from being on the frontline of the class war, and without any place to root them, hobos could be used as "scouts" and "advance guards," slipping into towns undetected, using guerilla-style tactics to spread party propaganda.[24] Train hopping was an important tool to propagandize the organization, and, consequently, as William Foster, whose political life follows many of the same patterns as Mac's, writes in his autobiography, *Pages from a Worker's Life*, "Many I.W.W. militants were skilled hoboes."[25] To hobo their way across the country saved money, helped them avoid detection, and connected them intimately to the very people they were hoping to convert.

The hobo and the IWW were seemingly a good match. For many years, though, organizers were unable to get a significant number of hobos to be their frontline soldiers. They often were unemployed, and they rarely could pay dues to maintain good standing in their memberships; making inroads with these transient workers seemed impossible.[26] Discounted and seen only as strikebreakers or unskilled scabs by other unions, in 1915 (ten years after the IWW's naissance) Wobbly leaders finally found an effective way to organize the migrant workers. For their April convention Wobblies from all over the West hoboed their way to Kansas City to found an affiliate organization, the Agricultural Workers Organization (AWO), specifically aimed at organizing the harvest workers. Deciding that speaking on soapboxes and in the street were not proving effective in persuading the everyday worker to join their organization, they decided to concentrate their efforts on producing immediate improvements in workers' lives (advocating for the ten-hour workday, minimum wage, overtime pay, and sanitary boarding). They wanted to have hobos thinking of themselves as participants in the same struggle by illustrating that Wobbly-organized successes would effect concrete changes in their day-to-day lives.

Frank Tobias Higbie notes that, "like their adversaries and allies, the Wobblies wanted 'community' and 'stable labor markets' in order to solidify their base."[27] To this end W. I. Fischer wrote in *Solidarity*, the official newspaper of the IWW, that Wobblies must work and organize side by side with laborers instead of having delegates in far-off cities. Using militaristic language Fischer states that the IWW would have to infiltrate the places where hobos gathered: "The union must 'colonize' camps and mills, and where possible hold local business and propaganda meetings and where not possible hold meetings of secret job groups."[28] Changing strategies, delegates of the union no longer waited for the workers to come to them; instead, "one hundred delegates [went] out into the field, who brought in at least one hundred new members a week."[29] These new strategies worked almost immediately. One of the delegates, Henry McGuckin, author of *Memoirs of a Wobbly* and whose radicalization also mirrors Mac's, proudly states, "We began with nine members and reached more than one hundred thousand!"[30]

McGuckin was a part of a group of five or six delegates who traveled around the country, staying for a week in one place and organizing and selling literature before leaving in a boxcar for the next town. For him, there was a fraternal bond that formed with his fellow train riders coalescing within the auspices of the IWW. For example, in one particular instance, a large group of Wobblies tried to catch out on the same freight train. Immediately there was trouble; the conductor expelled them from the train two different times with a threat that if he saw them again, "someone was going to get hurt."[31]

This scene is very reminiscent of the incident from London's *The Road*, albeit with a substantial difference. When London found himself one among many trying to jump the same freight, he enjoyed the battle between the crew as well as other hobos. Giddy over the fact that his fellow train hoppers were getting knocked off by the train crew, London relished his superiority over all other hobos and guarded his title of "profresh" with fierce pride. Although London was aware that the power of making a train purposely stop for him was a fleeting one, he was still overjoyed with the fact that he was able to make it out, alone, on the train.

McGuckin, however, was not ready to leave behind any of his fellow travelers. It was not a competition among the hobos but political action. When the trainman came into the boxcar with a .45 in his hand, the "boys" stuck together. Even though the train was in motion, they decided that since they were not *all* going to be able to stay on, they would *all* jump off. After distracting the pistol-waving crew member, every one of the Wobbly agitators jumped out of the slowly moving boxcar, reformed on the side of the tracks, and, as McGuckin states, "decided that the next freight was going to take [them] to Pocatello."[32] Although no one of this group could consider himself part of Nietzsche's "blond beasts" that London so admired, the men discovered their collectivity had strength and that they could *decide* that the next train would take them exactly where they wanted to go. Unlike London, who had to remain invisible and escape from the extended hands of the law, this group of revolutionaries chose to take on the crew. When they hopped the next freight and the trainmen demanded a dollar from each, they overpowered the conductor and his men. Ten miles out of the city, they then disabled the train by cutting off the air, allowing them time to jump off the train and disappear before it entered the yard.

This account illustrates the limitations and benefits of hobo solidarity. Because of their visibility on the first train, they were consequently seen and attacked by the gun-wielding agent. Because of their solidarity, though, they were able, for a time, to overpower the next crew and temporarily stop the train, ensuring their safety, freedom, and movement. Because of their numbers and visibility, they were able to not only upend the power dynamics of the train and command the crew, but also seize power over the machine itself, sabotaging it and escaping before they could be apprehended by reinforcements. In a TAZ-like moment, these men took advantage of their subcultural power, making themselves physically seen for a moment before, once again, disappearing into the night. These small uprisings gave them strength and confidence; through the sabotage of the train, their presence was felt even though they had physically disappeared.

The AWO "introduced an unprecedented level of structure and planning into I.W.W. harvest organizing," and as they began to be more successful in their membership drives, they colonized more spaces in the boxcars.[33] For many hobos this regulating of train space was beneficial because hoboing was dangerous. Hobos often were forced to pay a dollar or more to train crews, who saw them as easy marks. "Yeggs," or thieves, attacked hobos after a picking season was over, taking whole harvest salaries from them. Sadistic bulls were also often a problem, with the worst shooting unsuspecting hobos.[34] With the AWO gaining strength as their numbers grew, they were now in a position to actively protect hobos willing to be part of their organization. For example, some of the older, time-tested Wobblies joined together and decided that they would become the policing agents on the trains. McGuckin recounts, "Small units of not less than two or three were organized in such a way that each unit knew only itself. . . . Their purpose was to clean up the harvest fields of hold-up men, whether they were parts of train crews, railroad detectives, law officers, or just plain hold-up men. During the clean-up, freight trains might pull into their division points with a brakeman missing, never to be found. A railroad dick would be reported missing in the same way."[35]

According to McGuckin, Wobblies were willing to commit murder to keep these areas of the train "safe" for riders. This policing of boxcars was part of an IWW "800 mile picket line" strategy, controlling the railroads of the West by deciding who would be able to (illegally) ride the trains. The use of organized *persuasion* (physical as well as vocal) to enforce this picket line was, they felt, justified. It soon became apparent to many train riders that it would be advantageous to buy a "red card" to be safe from some of the more militant Wobbly members.[36]

Members of the IWW, by making themselves visible on the trains and in the jungles on the outskirts of town, created an imagined community in which hobos, by simply riding on trains, could see themselves as a part of a political organization engaged in a common purpose. The IWW stressed solidarity that in turn entailed responsibilities to the group. To disobey the laws could mean punishment, including expulsion from the train or possible physical injury. As Nels Anderson writes, "The I.W.W. has at times been able to exclude everyone who did not carry the red card of that organization."[37] The establishment of rules and fixing of borders forced regimentation on hobos that many rebelled against.

Scholars have linked the colonization of camps and trains by the IWW with strategies used by the federal government to locate and define the hobo. Ted Grossardt, a social geographer, writes, "Both the Federal government and the IWW attempted to project its presence into the same geographical space for different purposes."[38] In his view both the government and the IWW manipulated hobos in an attempt to delimit their movement. The hobo, who existed far from the public eye, was being fought over by the federal government and a revolutionary organization; both saw much to gain from controlling the transient worker population. Although their reasoning to do so was immensely divergent, the goal—to control the mobility and consequentially the political expressions of the itinerant worker—was important to both groups. Hobos found tangible relief through the efforts of the IWW; however, many also saw the limitations it placed on their movement. When the IWW was at its most influential, it could significantly control hobo jungles and gathering spaces and thus the movements of individual hobos.

## HOBO ORGANIZATIONS' DIFFERENT TRACKS

For Wobblies, hoboing was a way to get to a certain job or protest; it was not an essential defining quality. This mode of transportation was character building: the life of a bindlestiff made hobos tough and perfect for a revolutionary outfit. Hoboing, though, was a method of travel. For other organizations, being a hobo was not just a by-product of being a radical; it was in itself the reason for being a member. While most scholars of the hobo subculture examine the relationship between the hobo and the IWW, other successful organizations formed to cater to the hobo specifically, including the International Brotherhood Welfare Association (IBWA), the Migratory Workers Union, and the Ramblers.[39]

But why this intense scholarly focus on Wobblies and only a passing glance on these other organizations? One reason is obvious: the IWW produced real, tangible results affecting those who were *not* hobos, including farmers trying to get their crops in cheaply and on time as well as the police running agitators out of town. The Wobblies' actions were performed in the public domain. But for Lynne Marie Adrian, this "focus on the I.W.W. has kept scholars of the period from acknowledging the parallel development of an autonomous organizational movement in the hobo subculture. Consequently, the autonomy and distinctness of the hobo subculture has been severely underestimated." For Adrian, the focus on the IWW is primarily because they had nonhobo leadership who, while they might have *used* hobos for propaganda purposes, were "not an inherent part of the hobo subculture."[40]

The most significant of these other organizations was the one led by James Eads How, the "millionaire hobo" who was both the spokesperson and financial resource for the IBWA, a group organized exclusively for the betterment of the hobo. It advocated shorter workdays, the abolition of the "shark" employment agencies, free municipal facilities, unemployment insurance, and the implementation of other basic need-based facilities. How, who was influenced more by his religious beliefs than anarchist politics, clearly distinguished his group from other labor organizations;

his was exclusively an organization for the advancements of hobos. In a lead editorial for the *Hobo News* (which was the organ of the IBWA and financed by How), the paper declared adamantly, "The I.B.W.A. is not a Labor Union. It is a clearing house for Labor. It plows the field and plants the seeds so that Organized Labor can reap the benefit. It works toward one end and one end only and that is the complete emancipation of the Migratory Unskilled and often Unemployed workers."[41]

The IBWA was designed to help labor unions through educating workers in their rights or potential rights. It was not an organization determined to force a revolution; members felt that through education traveling men could become better politically aware hobos. The IBWA was primarily concerned with creating places for hobos to go during the winter months when they were trying to live on their stakes and waiting for the harvest cycle or industrial work to begin. Unlike the Salvation Army, who wanted to save the hobos' souls, the IBWA was a communal space where the doors were always swinging: come in for a bite to eat before heading out to look for a job; come in for a class on hostile rail junctures before heading out to catch a freight; come in to hear a professor talk about economics before heading out to the slave market.[42]

The focus of the IBWA, therefore, was on practical education. How and other well-known hobos such as Ben Reitman began to set up "Hobo colleges," designed to be "an intellectual and spiritual haven, a place where they could seek an education in a variety of subjects from law to economics, where they could make their own voices heard, and where in times of trouble, they could find sympathy and concern.[43] The education that the hobos received depended on a rotating list of "professors." Some, as Frank Beck's memoir *Hobohemia* attests, held degrees from academic institutions, and others were "specialists" in their own particular field. Jim Tully, for example, was on the staff and gave talks.[44] Depending on the night, the hobo would have the opportunity to grab a chair and listen to stories ranging from a published author's hobo travels to an accounting of the psychology of the migrant worker. These classes, however, were not lectures: if hobos disagreed with the speaker, they could add their own voices in the mix—their personal knowledge and willingness to speak were the only prerequisite to enter into the conversation. Hobo colleges were "part community center, part debating forum, part ego trip, part educational institution." This style of organization was popular among many hobos;

more than twenty local offices were founded in 1920, the most successful year.[45] Hobo colleges coincided nicely with the hobo lifestyle. If the hobo was in the area of a college, then he could join, have a discussion or debate, and then leave on the next train out of town.

The IBWA was therefore more of a fraternal organization instead of a militant political organization.[46] Members of the IWW, however, saw How as an eccentric millionaire who had no authentic connection to the working class. William Foster, a committed Wobbly, wrote that "the Industrial Workers of the World from 1905 on was the true organization of the floating workers, the hoboes of the West. Such bodies as [James] Eads How's and Jeff Davis' [International] Brotherhood Welfare Association were mere pretenders."[47] For Foster and other militant hobos, these "inauthentic" organizations were not politically structured to effect concrete changes for the transient worker. Thus, when the IWW had a strong influence on the hobo, the militant members saw any organization or individual unwilling to become radicalized as harmful to the movement and subject to censure and retribution.

For the more militant in the organization—especially those within the AWO arm of the IWW—those hobos who were not with the organization were against it. As Higbie summarizes, because the IWW "was open to all workers regardless of race, craft, or creed, so the logic went, anyone who refused to join was a scab. The result of this logic was that the line between convincing and coercing laborers to join the union sometimes was thin or nonexistent."[48] If a Wobbly found a hobo riding a train, then he needed to buy the red card and be part of the movement; if he did not, then he could be considered a scab and dangerous to all members of the working class.

In contrast to the IWW and the IBWA, other hobo organizations were distinctly antipolitical—their efforts were mainly to memorialize a subculture that they felt was disappearing. For example, Jeff Davis, a self-proclaimed "King of the Hoboes," formed the Hoboes of America. The organization, as Adrian explains, was "more like a fellowship organization in which men tell each other stories of the old exploits on the road, much like veterans' organizations can serve as forums for telling old war stories."[49] Davis himself was vehemently against the IWW and other types of organizations that could harm the image of the hobo in the public's eye. In a 1915 article in the *Independent*, Davis, who was opening a hotel for hobos, proclaimed, "This ain't goin' to be any hangout for cranks, either.

No 'bugology' or socialists, or anarchists. You treat the public right, and the public'll stand by you, 's our motto." To make this point clear, Davis hung a sign in the hotel lobby, stating, "RULES: Only real hoboes admitted here; no cranks nor preachers talkin' reform."[50]

All three groups wanted to organize the hobo for their own intended purposes, consequentially stratifying the political space in the boxcar. For members of the IWW, a hobo meant a migrant worker who could be used effectively on the frontlines of the class war. James Eads How and members of the IBWA thought that to be a hobo meant to be a transient worker who could be an educated hobo making individual, politically sound decisions. For members of Jeff Davis's Hoboes of America, to be a hobo meant to be a nonpolitical wanderer who was disappearing and quickly becoming a figure to be memorialized. The radical boxcar, therefore, was not a monolithic space but one of flux, and hobos who rode in this type of boxcar experienced this space in varying ways.

## THE POLITICIZED HOBO AS THE NEW HOPE OF THE ANTICAPITALIST MOVEMENT

If we return to *U.S.A.*, we can see how Dos Passos's hobo figures travel within this complex ideological terrain. Dos Passos certainly admired both the hobo and the IWW. Very perceptively, he chronicled the union's loss of vitality in 1918 by linking Mac's rejection of the IWW with the "death" of the American hobo.[51] As conscription led many men overseas to fight in Word War I and governmental forces attacked radical organizations, autonomy became a wistful idea. Both the radical and the hobo were seemingly no longer viable.

After working for the IWW for a time and listening to a speech by Big Bill Haywood, Mac decides to quit his job as an activist linotype operator to head back to his fiancée, Maisie, who has written to him that she is pregnant.[52] While the decision is difficult, he confesses to his fellow worker Ben Evans that although he believes fully in the fight, he is not a committed party man. When he leaves the Wobblies, Dos Passos has him immediately regain his hobo ways: in contrast to his passenger journey to Goldfield, he hops trains on his return trip. As he travels, he meets an old hobo. But unlike a previous "cheerful" old hobo who gave sage advice to him and Ike earlier in the narrative, in this parallel scene, the old man is deathly ill. The next morning Mac finds the weathered, sick man, who had been on the road for at least "seventeen years," dead.[53] Time has passed him by.

It seems, therefore, as if *U.S.A.* is ringing the death knell for the hobo along with that of the radical. The romanticism of Mac's earlier travels is gone; the sun-kissed boxcar of his first ride is replaced by the night's cold wind that leaves Mac "shivering in a fold of tarpaulin" with his "teeth chattering."[54] When Mac rejects the IWW to return to Maisie, Dos Passos shows us the consumptive face of a dead hobo. Mac's physical movement away from Big Bill Haywood (who himself will soon be exiled) and his fellow workers can certainly be read as his abandonment of the Wobbly cause, and, consequently, we could read this as the demise of the political radical. As Christine Photinos suggests, "Mac's narrative is . . . infused with nostalgia for a kind of male autonomy and freedom that Dos Passos associates with turn of the century hoboing."[55] Like Jeff Davis's view of the hobo as a proper subject for memorialization, the hobo is a relic, a character from an earlier era in America.

This reading is certainly prevalent among many scholars of *U.S.A.* The political hobo never had a chance, explains Frederick Feied in his reading of the hobo figure in the *U.S.A.* trilogy. While Dos Passos was obviously sympathetic to the Wobbly cause, Feied finds the hobos lacking any real insight into the nuances of class-based politics. "They are working stiffs, not intellectuals," Feied asserts, and Mac and his ilk could not fathom the strength of the oppositional power facing them. It was inevitable that their defeat, which was a defeat of the "America of Walt Whitman" and the "decline of political freedom in the United States," would result in the "gradual dissolution of hobo strength and the transformation of the onetime militant wobbly of its inception to the homeless and dispossessed vag of its conclusion."[56]

Does the vag character, as Denning writes, "mark the return of Mac," a return that would make the energetic Mac into a numb figure, cautiously begging for a ride on the side of the road? Is the *U.S.A.* trilogy indeed a narration of "the decline of the tramp from American hobo to beaten-down Vag," as Photinos states in her examination of the text? Did Mac, in other words, "sell out to the sons of bitches?"[57]

In my reading of this text, the answer is no, he does not. Mac's narrative does not conclude with this scene of the hobo's death; he is not the old hobo who is laid, uncovered, in a ditch beside the ballast, subject to vultures. And unlike the vag character, Mac is never pictured as scared or unconfident, waiting for someone to give him a ride. Mac refuses to "catch a westbound" train, nor does he live an unfulfilled bourgeois life with Maisie. Instead, after a short stay in his loveless marriage, Mac just goes.[58] But unlike the vag character, or the consumptive dying hobo he meets on his travels, this lack of keen direction is not accompanied by despair and death but by celebration. In a moment of epiphany, Mac suddenly realizes, "I'm free to see the country now, to work for the movement, to go on the bum again."[59] Mac's desire to remain politically active by his connection to *the movement* is embodied in his *physical movement.*

Although Mac worked hard while in Goldfield, when he leaves Maisie, he does not decide to rejoin "the boys" or even to find another IWW fight in the West. Instead, he travels to the U.S.-Mexico border. Mac is returning to a moment when he was with Ike, traveling in boxcars across national boundaries and discussing politics. It is certainly a retreat from the political activism that he was doing in Goldfield, but he is still talking about revolutionary politics while hoboing his way around the continent. At this historical moment when the IWW is being decimated and its leaders jailed or exiled, Dos Passos returns Mac to his hobo origins.

For critics who want to see Mac become a revolutionary martyr, or for those who see the trilogy as the squashing of the anticapitalist impulse, Mac, lifting his glass and toasting "to the workers, to the trade-unions, to the partido laborista, to the social revolution and the agraristas" while enjoying the economic benefits of owning his small bookstore, is an empty, pathetic figure.[60] Nonetheless, although he does not fight to his last breath for the revolution, it is clear that he never turns his back on revolutionary politics, either. Drinking and talking politics, Mac is doing what many hobos did, living off his "stake" before he continues his travels. There is no evidence in the text that while in Mexico Mac is just "faking" his belief and mouthing revolutionary credos for his own advantage. In fact, he has not changed from the young hobo in the beginning of *The 42nd Parallel* who finds great pleasure sitting in a grassy field talking politics to his friend Ike. Although he is not lying in a field under the warming sun waiting for a train to come to a stop, and is now in his own courtyard, surrounded by cats and friends, his speech is about radical politics. He is also still moving—heading from Juárez to Mexico City, from Mexico City to Vera Cruz, and from Vera Cruz perhaps back to Mexico City again. It is certainly not hard to imagine Mac grabbing hold of the bars of a boxcar and catching out soon after Dos Passos ends his narrative. As Big Bill Haywood flees imprisonment by narrowly eluding capture and escaping from the United States, and the Wobbly organization is systematically decimated by the full force of the U.S. government, Mac is still moving and talking, and his speech is one of revolution.

## THE REBIRTH OF THE HOBO

But to what end? Where does all this talking lead? As a hobo, Mac will not effect the same changes he did as a rank-and-file member of the IWW. For Barbara Foley, this leaves Mac a "marginalized expatriot" who has "wasted" his life. While it is true that Mac will not have the same influence outside the IWW as he did inside, to dismiss him altogether discounts the political dimensions of the hobo lifestyle. Mac has not been silenced, or stopped, when he leaves the IWW; the hobo in *U.S.A.* is certainly not dead. Lisa Nanney may be right that "the emergence of monopoly capitalism . . . threatens to overpower not just the labor movement or radical politics but also the possibility for any authentic belief or expression of belief in the original promises of America," but *U.S.A.* refuses to completely succumb to this nihilism and abdicate a belief in authentic political expression. The hobo exemplifies this American promise. The organized Left is in disarray, and *U.S.A.* plainly speaks to this predicament. But although Cowley states *U.S.A.* has no characters that show "the will to struggle ahead, the comradeship in struggle," Dos Passos uses the hobo to carry the radical through a time of abjection.[61] Although the organized Left was no match for capitalism and an oppressive state, Dos Passos, even at his most pessimistic, still believes in the interaction—the talking—that takes place among hobos in a boxcar as a political act. This conjoined act of speaking and moving is a rudimentary act to be sure, but one able to survive because of the hobos' invisible itinerancy. While Mac as a party man was not successful, Dos Passos never dismisses the political productivity of hobos traveling and speaking together.

This reading becomes clearer if we move to the hobo figures in Dos Passos's more experimental sections of *U.S.A.* The trilogy employs four distinctly different narrative forms: fictional narratives (such as Mac's); newspaper headlines and song collages titled Newsreels; short, poetic biographies; and experimental autobiographical stream-of-consciousness fragments titled the Camera Eye. Moglen, in *Mourning Modernity,* states that the author's experimental Camera Eye sections "recognize what is best in the United States, what is now imperiled and betrayed by the most powerful."[62] If we explore the Camera Eye sections, we see that Dos Passos, in the teeth of defeat, has relied on the hobo to continue the anticapitalist fight, and we can consequently read this text as one that, while never denying the extent to which the Left has been battered, also never allows itself to slip into abject defeatism. It is this role that articulates Dos Passos's boxcar politics found in *U.S.A.*

The hobo plays an important role in two of the Camera Eye sections. What we encounter here are fragmentary, stream-of-consciousness representations of important semiautobiographical moments in Dos Passos's own radicalization as a young man.[63] In Camera Eye (9), he recounts a time when he was working in a factory: "Up on the freight siding I got talking to a young guy couldn't have been much older 'n me was asleep in one of the boxcars asleep right there in the sun and the smell of cornstalks and the reek of rotting menhaden from the fertilizer factories he had curly hair and wisps of hay in it and through his open shirt you could see his body burned brown to the waist I guess he wasn't much account but he bummed all the way from Minnesota he was going south."[64] Staring at this sun-browned hobo who was his own age, Dos Passos first is surprised by his confidence, then rejects him ("I guess he wasn't much") before once again admiring the young man's freedom of movement. While the young Dos Passos was concerned with the awful smell of the factories, his "cabin full of mosquitoes," and the company's profit margin while working in the factory, the young hobo is confident in his ability to travel and take on temporary work to sustain himself.

Camera Eye (9) is positioned between Mac's narrative section, enthusiastically heading for the IWW fight in Goldfield, Nevada, and the Big Bill Haywood biography in which, at the end, the exiled "broken body" of the Wobbly leader has been buried outside of the United States. In Mac's narrative we see the idealistic impulse to join an organization to fight American capitalism and, to a degree, the result of this fight in the figure of a beaten and broken Haywood. In between these sections, we have a young hobo who is a confident traveler, moving easily throughout the country. This hobo, who had an influence on the author in his emergence as a radical, points to an alternative to the organized politics of the Wobblies that Mac will soon reject and the demise of Wobbly leadership Haywood's biography denotes.[65]

But while this young hobo travels for no overt political reason, in the penultimate Camera Eye (50), we see how this movement can be harnessed for political expression. Perhaps the most famous of all sections of *U.S.A.*, this Camera Eye recounts the heavy loss felt by those on the Left with the execution of the anarchists Sacco and Vanzetti. The most anthologized section of *U.S.A.*, Camera Eye (50) represents America split into two nations, with a seemingly clear winner and loser. But while this is a mournful recounting of a loss and therefore a heartfelt dirge filled with anger and resentment, it can also be read as one of hope in the possibilities of the future.

While "we stand defeated" is the line most often cited from this Camera Eye and the text itself, Dos Passos insists at the same time that the radical language of Americans has not been silenced because "the men in the deathhouse [Sacco and Vanzetti] made the old words new before they died." The "speech of the people," then, is not stifled. But who, exactly, is speaking this "language of the beaten nation," the language that has a radical political lineage but is also clearly the lingua franca of the moment? "But do they know that the old words of the immigrants are being renewed in the blood and agony tonight do they know that the old American speech of the haters of oppression is new tonight in the mouth of an old woman from Pittsburg of a husky boilermaker from Frisco who hopped freights clear from the Coast to come here in the mouth of a Back bay socialworker in the mouth of an Italian printer of a hobo from Arkansas the language of the beaten nation is not forgotten in our ears tonight." Dos Passos is clearly agonized over the death of the two anarchists, and this act of capital punishment crystallizes capitalism's power in *U.S.A.*, initiating the defeat of large radical political organizations like the IWW. The purging of radicals will be bloody and widespread, and Camera Eye (50), along with the bulk of *U.S.A.*, details the way the Left has been silenced. The men in the death house can no longer speak. The funeral procession consists of the defeated nation, "silent pale looking with scared eyes," staring at the coffins. The crowd, standing elbow to elbow, which formed to see the anarchists for the last time, is voiceless as well. But in one of the most hopeful of moments in the trilogy, in defiance of the "strangers who have bought laws . . . [and] hire the executioner to throw the switch," *U.S.A.* insists that despite the overwhelming suppression, there will be those who continue to speak the language of the radical movement.[66]

Out of the five whom Dos Passos mentions in this section who are speaking the people's language and making the "words new," two are hobos. They will be the ones who will continue the work of the executed anarchists. The hobo from Arkansas will "use the old words," but, reformed in his mouth from the agony of the executions, he will speak it with a new idiom.[67] In the face of extreme political repression, Dos Passos is inscribing within him the responsibility of continuing the work of the dead radicals by building the political community through his speech. Through this discourse, the long radical tradition within the United States will not die but will continue to spread as he moves throughout the country. The hobo, who is confined to neither one particular geographic area nor one political organization, affirms the duel power of movement and language. This affirmation does not deny the huge loss inflicted by the execution, nor does it discount the widespread suppression of radical organizations. But the focus on "the speech of the people" does concentrate our attention on the latent power of the oppressed. Unable to stop the execution (or American capitalism), these hobos can still speak about alternatives and thus, through this political act, create hopeful possibilities in the future. The radical movement is not fully defeated as long as there are people moving and speaking this language.

As discussed previously, London was also very interested in the language of hobos. Fascinated by the "vernacular" of the road kids, he, too, learned the words that were being spoken in the boxcar. But for him, this language was exclusionary and belonged only to those within his small subculture. Dos Passos, though, is doing something radically different in this section. The language of the boxcar is not exclusive; rather, Dos Passos is connecting the language of hobos with the "speech of the people" that he introduced at the beginning of this trilogy. For Dos Passos, language is inclusive, uniting people together in *U.S.A.*

This unauthorized use of language is a type of defiant resistance. After visiting Sacco and Vanzetti in prison, Dos Passos penned an article, "The Pit and the Pendulum," in which he wrote of the world that the two anarchists inhabited as they sat in jail waiting for their execution: "This is a world of phrases, prosecution, defiance, evidence, motion, irrelevant, incompetent and immaterial. For six years this man has lived within the law, tied tighter and tighter in the sticky filaments of law-words like a fly in the spiderweb. And the wrong set of words means the Chair. All the moves in the game are made for him, all he can do is sit helpless and wait, fastening his hopes on one set of phrases after another."[68]

Reading this section as it relates to Camera Eye (50), Thomas Strychacz situates the nonnative English–speaking Sacco and Vanzetti as victims of a legal language in which those who have the authority of legal words wield power over physical bodies. Sitting in jail, the men have to silently listen to their death sentence pronounced by a judge; abused physically through incarceration, these words were the conduit for state-sanctioned electrocution. Contrary to this incarceration and reliance on legal words, the hobos in Camera Eye (50) who survive by avoiding the law are able to "become mediums for a speech that transcends both individuality and the limited historical moment."[69] This active speech ruptures the legal power over words controlled by those in authority. By being "invisible" and creating these apertures, hobos offer utterances that the state cannot hear and therefore cannot silence. The anticapitalist movement is thus continually renewed and sustained.

Dos Passos's own words, as many critics have noted, could not make the words new again, and a distinct melancholic view of the radical movement is evident as his political ideas evolved from his involvement with the Communist Party as a young man to his support of the Vietnam War and adulation of William Buckley at the end of his life. His inability to continue speaking these radical words might be one reason why he ends the trilogy with the impotent "Vag." Dos Passos's hobos, however, are not like the vag figure, a diminished version of the hobo too scared to ride trains and who can no longer master the train. Despite this melancholic bookend to the trilogy, the hobo, as seen in Mac and in the Camera Eye sections, is still moving and speaking in the boxcars and jungles, renewing the radical political tradition. It is a basic step in any revolutionary process, but after the crushing blows felt by the Left, it is a crucial, preliminary rebuilding step. The belief in the original promise of America is present in the hobo from Arkansas or the train-hopping boilermaker from San Francisco as they keep riding and speaking their particular American radical idiom.

Dos Passos clearly respected the IWW, but when writing *U.S.A.*, he knew the devastating result of standing toe to toe with capitalism and handed the hobo the responsibility in keeping the radical tradition alive. While he wrote that it was the author's job, after the death of Sacco and Vanzetti, to write "so fiery and accurate," in a move that uses a particularly American train-hopping tradition, he has the poor, marginalized hobo speaking this language. Although it is not the formal language of the Wobblies or other radical organizations, it is an authentic American radical speech. As Strychacz succinctly writes of the hobos in Camera Eye (50), "Their speech is truly original insofar as it puts them in touch with a true starting point at which an infinitely renewable political entity and defining discourse was created."[70] This "speech of the people" is not the legalese of the state whose words connotes death sentences for the anarchists but a speech that survives along the rail lines throughout the United States. Although many languages (and lives) have been silenced, if one listens carefully enough, the "speech of the people" can be heard in the boxcar.

Chapter Five

# THE INTERRACIAL BOXCAR

## Scottsboro, the Great Depression, and *Wild Boys of the Road*

The various manifestations of boxcar politics found in the works of London, Tully, and Dos Passos, reveal its individualistic, communal, and radical attributes. Regardless of the differing political expressions of the hobo, though, a connecting tissue that has weaved through all three case studies is the way racial and gendered ideologies often hierarchized hobo space and infused it with danger and inconsistencies. Despite the boxcar having the potential for radical communality among marginalized individuals, hobo space often mirrored the racist and sexist practices found outside the boxcar. Solidarity among hobos was often challenged along these demarcations.

The infamous Scottsboro case, in which nine African American youths were falsely accused of raping two white women on a train, is a perfect example; it reveals that racial and gender components of hobo space are inherently part of all interactions among, and readings of, hobos. Much has been written about this case as an abhorrent miscarriage of justice, but buried within this narrative framing is the fact that all of the individuals caught up in this horrific melodrama were hobos. Focusing on this aspect of the case allows us to explore ways that worker solidarity within the boxcar can be eviscerated along racial and gendered lines—an argument initially used by activist and radical organizations who passionately reasoned during the trails that the nine African Americans, the white male accusers, and the two white females were all *workers* victimized by a capitalist system that used racial instigations to keep the working class in a perpetual fractured state.

## THE SCOTTSBORO CASE

On March 25, 1931, at 10:20 a.m., conductor Robert Turner watched a group of hobos hop on his freight train, which was bound from Chattanooga to Memphis along a southern route that took it through parts of Alabama. Thirty minutes after it left a stop in Stevenson, Alabama, a "startled station master looked up from his desk to see a ragged crew of hoboes, one holding his bleeding head."[1] The white hobos declared they were attacked by a group of black hobos, and they wanted to press charges. By then the train had already left the next station, Scottsboro—the seat of Alabama's Jackson County—so a call was placed down the line to Paint Rock, where, after the town sheriff had deputized all of the local white men, the train was stopped and thoroughly searched. Nine African American males and, to everyone's surprise, two white women, were found hiding inside. It did not take long before rape allegations were reported and Alabama's "peculiar" problem would be tried in courts and in newspapers for the rest of the decade.

This peculiar problem fixated attention on Alabama, placing both town and state under an unwanted microscope, revealing racist policies and practices intertwined with the daily and civic life of the South. Divested of its local moorings, the trials and subsequent retrials became part of a sad melodrama performed on the world's stage throughout the 1930s. For some, this case was one of the first shoots of the civil rights movement that blossomed in the 1960s; others saw this case as a horrific disgrace to southern white womanhood. Either way, Scottsboro evoked passionate opinions. Films and songs, plays and poetry, from such writers as Paul Peters and Langston Hughes were performed from street corners to theaters throughout the United States. Thousands filled squares, parks, and streets in huge rallies throughout the North, including ones that evolved into riots in Harlem. Outside the United States, unionized German workers broke windows of the American Embassy in Dresden, demanding that "their fellow workers" not be murdered by a racist court.[2] This peculiar problem that was in the news for the duration of the Great Depression was not (officially) concluded until July 13, 1950, when the last of the Scottsboro Nine went "free." Over half a century later, though, this case still resonates with many Americans, as evident in the numerous times the case has been linked to contemporary African American mistrials of justice. In 2010 the case that captivated the nation in the 1930s was being performed on Broadway.[3]

This peculiar problem and infamous case, when boiled down to its bare essentials, however, was fairly straightforward: hobos fighting on a train. Although certainly a common occurrence in boxcars since the time the golden spike was pounded into the ground at Promontory Summit, Utah, this was the only fight that garnered international headlines. Although in hindsight it is obvious why the Scottsboro case has become one of the most infamous trials in the twentieth century, reframing the discussion by examining it through the lens of the hobo subculture will reveal nuances of the case that have been mostly overlooked.

As discussed in my initial chapter on the subcultural politics of hopping a train, hobos did not have the same rights as citizens outside the boxcar; inside, hidden in the crevices of the train as they passed through towns in the middle of the night, they were invisible and outside the law. A few bloody hobos holding their heads in towns or even a few dead bodies on the side of the track did not cause alarm; like most on the margins of society, these transient homeless were problems only when a significant number lost their invisibility and forced themselves to be seen. This was exactly what these white hobos did when they lost the fight and were ejected from the train: they left the "invisible" world of the hobo subculture and entered the visible world of 1931 Alabama. How these poor men were visualized, though, was determined by who was gazing at them. Once emerging from the shadows of the boxcar, and their story interpreted, their status as hobos became irrelevant. They were read as white men beaten up by black men, and the mob that met the train in Paint Rock wanted "justice" for the upheaval of white supremacy. When it was found out that two white women hobos—Victoria Price and Ruby Bates—were also on the train, they too became the subject of this racist gaze. Although discovered in dirty overalls and caps, Bates and Price were (white) washed of their hobo pasts, becoming stand-ins for a mythical southern white womanhood. The families who came to picnic outside the courthouse in Scottsboro demanding their own lynch-style justice on the "boys" saw this case clearly in black and white. For them, this was not an issue of economics but an attack against white patriarchy.

Scottsboro is a story of racial injustice wherein white supremacist ideology was exposed as northern liberal Jewish lawyers argued in front of southern benches all the while young African American men languished in prison. But as much as the case ripped open the veneer of the tranquility that supposedly existed between the races in Alabama, revealing instead the bloody racial conflicts of quotidian life, what is apparent is that while traveling within the boxcar, the accusers, accused, and witnesses were similar: they were all hobos.

### *The Scottsboro Hobos*

A quick sketch of the nine African Americans reveals young men hoboing their way through the South, attempting to find work during the Great Depression. Clarence Norris had to drop out of school when he was young, consequently never learning how to read or write, and by thirteen had run away with other hobos. By the time he was pulled off the train in Paint Rock, he had spent close to five years working his way from town to town throughout the Southeast. Haywood Patterson was one of ten children who grew up poor in Chattanooga, trying to survive on his father's paycheck of twenty-eight dollars a week. When he was thirteen, he left school and began hopping trains. When Willie Roberson's grandmother died in 1930, he was placed with an aunt who could not care for him. She told him to hobo and find his own way; by the age of fifteen, he was on the road. Olen Montgomery, who had no sight in his left eye and only 10 percent in his right eye, was legally blind. He was hopping trains, trying to find work while making his way to Memphis to buy a pair of glasses. Charlie Weems was an orphan who dropped out of school in the fifth grade and began hopping trains, looking for jobs. Ozzie Powell, Eugene Williams, and brothers Andy and Roy Wright had similar stories, reflecting the larger reality of Depression-era America.[4]

These nine African American males found themselves from a very early age traveling the South in boxcars, jumping off in towns and cities, working a variety of jobs before jumping back onto freights and making their way to new towns. This perpetual quest for employment is the story of many men, women, boys, and girls in the 1920s and 1930s, with *Business Week* calling this particular type of transiency "one of the greatest interstate migrations since the gold rush." The story of these "pioneers without a frontier," however, has always been white-centric.[5] Paul Garon and Gene Tomko, who published a history of black hobos and their songs, state that the story of the Great Depression, its vast unemployment, and forced migrations have not been identified with the black population. "Perhaps this is the legacy of John Steinbeck, as well as Dorothea Lange and other Farm Security Administration photographers, but just as likely, it is the pervasive anti-black prejudice of America during the years of such troubling scarcity."[6] As Garon and Tomko emphatically reveal, the boxcar was a multiracial space. Although ignored, black hobos were on the road.

The first line in Woody Guthrie's memoir, *Bound for Glory*, begins with the observation, "I could see men of all colors bouncing along in the boxcar."[7] The historian Mark Wyman's well-researched revisionist history *Hoboes* details the wide variety of nationalities and ethnicities working their way around the country. Hyman's astute panoramic view shows the very apparent tensions and racial demarcations found on the road.[8] Numbers of nonwhite hobos (or any hobos for that matter), though, are almost impossible to be verified; for the most part, black hobos avoided any official trying to "count" them. As the case against the Scottsboro youths proves, it was especially beneficial for nonwhite train hoppers to remain in the crevices of the train and away from anyone trying to connect them to a particular place. Much like those traveling along the safe routes of the Underground Railroad a half century earlier, it behooved black hobos to become invisible when illegally traveling throughout the South. To find work, though, these hobos still needed to hop trains. One of the few studies during the Great Depression that examined African American transients was conducted outside the South by Herman Schubert in Buffalo in 1935; out of 2,308 interviews, 662 were with African Americans, with 50 percent of those unsuccessfully seeking work for at least two years.[9]

Besides exposing that nonwhite hobos were traveling throughout the South, with the discovery of Ruby Bates and Victoria Price on the train, the Scottsboro case also highlighted the fact that the hobo subculture was not exclusively male.[10] Much like the hobos she accused of rape, Victoria Price had to quit school at age ten, working to support a widowed mother. When the Depression hit in 1929, she could no longer find jobs in her town in Huntsville, Alabama (about forty miles from Scottsboro), and was forced to hop trains to find work, frequently staying in jungles with other hobos.[11] Price's riding companion, Ruby Bates, was also hoboing because she had been laid off from her mill job and was seeking employment.

Commenting on the Bates family, who was the only white family living on a block of dilapidated houses, one social worker stated, "Mill workers are as bad as Niggers . . . just lots of these women are nothing but prostitutes. They just have to be, I reckon, for nobody could live on the wages they make, and that's the only other way of making money open to them."[12] Parsing through the racist rhetoric, the social worker is making the link between sex workers, mill workers, and African Americans clear: all were marginalized in the town and shared the same economic base and social capital. The cotton mills where Price and Bates tried to find work were the same type of mills in which the nine accused "boys" searched for jobs. Price, who had been intermittently employed in the mills since the age of thirteen, at the time of her accusations, was unsuccessful at finding work at the Margaret Mill—a plant that was paying wages of only $1.25 per day for three days, every other week. "You know nobody can't live on wages like that," Price stated to a reporter.[13]

### *Hobos in the Depression-Era South*

Victoria Price was right. People were having great difficulty living on poverty wages, and many—white and black—had to take to the rails to find work. Like the interracial group of hobos in Alfred Maund's radical novel *The Big Boxcar* who all traveled together in fear of being caught by authorities, hobos, regardless of their race or gender, were forced to share their marginality as poor transient workers.[14] This marginality was hierarchal. Racist practices were clearly in play in the boxcar; Jim Crow laws were being unfairly enforced on the backs of black bodies whenever there were any disturbances of white supremacy. On the whole African Americans were subjected to much harsher penalties than their white counterparts. When caught, African Americans often served longer terms on chain gangs than their fellow white train riders; as vagrancy laws fed the convict lease system, many blacks returned to the same fields that had forcibly held their family members during slavery.[15] But despite African American hobos facing these additional physical and psychological injustices, all riders, regardless of race or gender, were subject to danger—of death, injury, or imprisonment.

Hopping trains was a perilous existence in prosperous times, but as more inexperienced riders headed to the rails to find work during the Great Depression, the numbers of deaths and dismemberments dramatically increased. The Interstate Commerce Commission annual reports show that during the years 1929 to 1939, a total of 24,647 trespassers were killed and 27,171 injured on railroad property. For a snapshot of the carnage, consider that in 1932, alone, of the 5,962 trespassers recorded as killed or injured in the first ten months of that year, 1,508 of them were under twenty-one.[16] While many lost their lives and limbs under the steel wheels of the train, those who survived often found themselves attempting to survive horrendous conditions.

When the white and black hobos hopped the slow-moving train emerging from Chattanooga's Southern Railroad yard situated on the border of the Tennessee-Alabama state line, not only were they faced with possible death and injury; they were also passing through two of the South's most vicious prison systems in the country. Ravaged by the Depression, able-bodied prisoners made money for monetarily strapped states, cities, and counties. In the same year that the Scottsboro youths were stopped in Paint Rock, the Associated General Contractors of America stated that seventy-five thousand convicts were employed in federal prisons, producing goods with a market value of $100 million. These estimates were for state and federal prisons only; there were 10,860 city and village prisons with approximately five hundred prisoners in each, as well as an additional 3,000 county prisons, many of whom also employed convict labor. In the South in particular, city and country prisoners were exploited by being forced to work on farms or building roads, resulting in millions of dollars of additional revenue for industries. The work was brutal and so were the conditions; in Tennessee the warden of a prison stated in 1931 that he frequently had inmates suffer through "30 to 40 blows with a heavy strap." This abuse was relegated not only to black prisoners but to all prisoners.[17] And while those individuals in federal, state, and county jails and reformatories ran the gamut from murderers to pedophiles, many in these prisons were convicted of being poor.

Among the hobos looking for work, oftentimes finding themselves in prisons for short, hard stretches of time, were teenagers. According to Daniel O'Connell, chief special agent of the Southern Pacific Company, a year after the Scottsboro Nine were arrested, 638,457 hobos were ejected from the company's trains and property (the Southern Pacific was only one of more than 130 major Class One railroad companies existing in the United States), and he estimated that 75 percent of those riders ranged in ages from sixteen to twenty-five years old. After the stock market crash of 1929, the Depression hit the economically marginalized the hardest. Six million children were living on relief, one in seven children under the age of eighteen. There were few opportunities at home for these young boys and girls, and even if their parents could afford to board them, often their schools were shuttered. In the South the situation was desperate: in Arkansas and Mississippi, for example, fewer than 5 percent of high school–aged African American youths were in school.[18] With few possibilities for jobs and education within their hometowns, these young, poor boys and girls turned to the road.

Although there were a number of transient youths who found that this path led them to jail, there were hundreds of thousands more who were undocumented travelers floating around the country looking for work. Consequently, there was a great fear of "youth in revolt," with numerous studies arguing for programs to delimit the mobility of the young. In the 1935 report *Youth in the Depression*, Kingsley Davis, the Hoover Institute senior researcher, wrote that if the American youth were not helped, the young "may take matters in their own hands and . . . revolution is not improbable."[19] While distinguishing American youths from young men and women in other nations, the premise of the polemic is clear: if the United States did not want the rise of a Nazi-like party to happen on American soil, substantial policy changes would need to be enacted immediately.

From this international perspective, Davis and other commentators, such as Lowell Norris, linked the teenagers on the move in the Great Depression with the hundreds of thousands of orphan children in the Soviet Union after World War I.[20] Over a million *Bezprizorni*, a term that could be translated as "wild children," were orphaned, and by 1922 many had formed large roving gangs of semi-organized thieves. To combat this national epidemic, the Soviet government instituted work camps. While successful, by the spring of 1928 there were still 250,000 lawless bands of children roaming the countryside, also the number of American teenagers estimated to be wandering the United States during the Great Depression.[21] *Road to Life* (1931), a Soviet propaganda film directed by Nikolia Ekk, centered on these wild children who, through the benefit of the state, were given a chance to escape the streets and reenter society—something that Roosevelt's Civilian Conservation Corps (CCC) would attempt to do later on in the decade in the United States.[22]

At the time of the initial Scottsboro trial, though, the CCC camps were not in place and the country was settling deep into the bone of the Great Depression. When that infamous boxcar traveled through Scottsboro, all the male hobos were in danger of ending on a chain gang and, depending on the bull who caught them, all the hobos—male and female, black and white—could have faced much worse fates. The accuser, accused, and witnesses on the train were all hobos and were part of the minority subculture of disenfranchised workers. This overarching view of the forced relationships among these hobos can be found in Kay Boyle's 1937 poem "A Communication to Nancy Cunard" that offers a pessimistic view of the Scottsboro trial. Although the overarching tone of the poem is of weariness at the racial injustice, a section alludes to the mutual marginality that all the hobos shared:

> Not the old or the young on it, nor people with any difference in their
> color or shape,
> Not girls or men, Negroes or white, but people with this in common:
> People that no one had use for, had nothing to give to, no place to offer
> But the cars of a freight train careening through Paint Rock, through
> Memphis,
> Through town after town without halting.[23]

In this poem the white male hobos who lost the fight, the white women hobos who cried rape, and the black hobos who were sentenced to die are in the same economic situation. They held no use value for those outside the car, and their only place in society was within boxcars, perpetually on the move. As the Boyle poem fantastically attests to, by remaining hidden in the train car that unendingly moves along the iron rails, the inhabitants embody a continuous liminal space. But while discounted as hobos, when the train was halted, their value became apparent. The hobos' bodies were geographically placed and racially categorized, and the white supremacist tropes of racial and gender separation supported in 1931 Alabama were firmly upheld. While separately, the white and black, male and female hobos faced similar punishments and dangers when hopping trains; when the train was stopped in Paint Rock, the analogous economic conditions of the hobos were dismissed in favor of their racial and gender differences. The hobos who lost the fight, therefore, felt confident when expelled from the train to go to the police and take advantage of their white privilege, a privilege that did not help them at other times when they were hoboing throughout the country.

## READING THE SCOTTSBORO TRIALS THROUGH A HOBO LENS

The train itself was an important material object during the trials. Lawyers argued over detailed diagrams and models, pinpointing the exact spots where all the hobos were (supposedly) discovered on the train. By the end of the trials, though, the impetus of why they were all there riding on the same train was minimized. The Communist Party USA (CPUSA) and other activists, however, made class disenfranchisement the primary issue when examining the Scottsboro case, focusing on the economic reasons that brought the participants to that particular train on that fateful day. While prosecutors and reporters framed the nine youths as "black brutes," "savages," and "animals," the initial defensive strategy was a clear, class-based Marxist position, defending the Scottsboro hobos not as "boys" but as "workers," thereby linking their position as transient laborers to workers of every race. While the defense's rhetoric was multivariate, Josephine Herbst in the July 1931 issue of the *New Masses* captures its core: "Some say this is not a labor case, but [the nine] were on the move because their families were poor and they had no work."[24]

A few weeks after the rape allegations were presented, the CPUSA's official papers, the *Liberator* and the *Labor Defender*, were calling into question the "legal lynching" taking place in the courtroom and organizing massive protests. B. D. Amis, the editor of the *Liberator*, wrote, "It would be impossible to imagine a case where there is so much reason to fight," and, through the party's legal arm, the International Labor Defense (ILD), they quickly mobilized.[25] Consistently outmaneuvering the NAACP, who was hesitant in its belief of the nine's innocence, the ILD grabbed control of the case. The CPUSA, which already had a toe hold in the region after launching a local antilynching campaign in response to multiple race-related murders in Emelle, offered, according to Robin Kelley, a "framework for understanding the roots of poverty and racism, linked local struggles to world politics . . . [and] created an atmosphere in which ordinary people could analyze, discuss and criticize the society in which they lived."[26] As an official for the ILD stated, "The issue of the oppression of Negroes is obviously an economic question," and in a two-pronged approach—fight in the courts and through mass action—the case would further expose and challenge American capitalism.[27] The Scottsboro case made, as William Maxwell states, "communism a household word in African American clubs, beauty shops, and churches and added color to the party's rank and file throughout the United States."[28]

The CPUSA's rhetoric, however, would change during the retrials, and as the battle for control of the defense with the NAACP grew tense, the ILD's strategy turned more paternalistic, focusing on the age of the "boys," primarily connecting them to their families and not to their status as disenfranchised workers. As they did so, they figuratively removed the youths from the trains and placed them in the dilapidated homes of their families. While this tactic changed the focus of the defense to one outside the purview of my argument, here I examine three early moments in the Scottsboro case where the nine's identities as hobos were placed in focus. Specifically, I want to highlight the way three individuals—William Patterson, Hollace Ransdall, and Eugene Gordon—argued the case in economic terms, placing on trial American capitalism's assault on the working class (with whom they counted the hobos a part), with its tiered racial hierarchy.

Barely a month after the train was stopped, William Patterson, a militant civil rights leader, connected the Scottsboro Nine to members of the working class in his *Labor Defender* article, "Judge Lynch Goes to Court." After stating that the rape charges were a systematic tool used by white capitalist society to terrorize blacks, Patterson used a Marxist interpretation to frame this railroading of justice. Tellingly, the word "boys" was never once used throughout the whole article. Instead, the nine were repeatedly described as "workers," whose crime was not rape but that they were "guilty of seeking work" as hobos. Patterson specifically analyzed the boxcar, commenting that the halting of the train was a way to separate workers from their jobs. And like the Boyle poem, he linked the black hobos with the white (male) hobos, illustrating how the train became another site infiltrated by capitalism's tentacles. The white hobos were also "victims" of the capitalist system that tricked them in believing in "white supremacy." The resulting "frenzy" of racial hatred that spewed forth from the presses was then explained as an inherent part of capitalism that kept "Negro workers" and, consequently, white workers who believed in "the great hoax of the ruling class," in their place. Patterson underlined the ways that capitalism exploited workers by fostering racial separation.[29]

While Patterson connected the black hobos with their white male counterparts, Hollace Ransdall, who spent ten days in Scottsboro for the American Civil Liberties Union interviewing local residents immediately after the arrest of the nine, linked Victoria Price and Ruby Bates as covictims to the capitalist system in her "Report on the Scottsboro, Ala. Case." Describing the nine as "illiterate jobless young itinerants," due to a lack of employment and educational opportunities, Ransdall detailed the socioeconomic realities of Ruby Bates and Victoria Price, writing that "economic scarcity has forced [them] across the great color barrier" and that all the participants were unemployed laborers searching for jobs. According to James Miller, Ransdall's report had "an electrifying impact upon the office of the American Civil Liberties Union, and its effect rippled outward, helping to shape Northern liberal and mainstream opinion."[30] While much more measured in its call to action than the articles and pleas coming from the CPUSA presses, Ransdall's report effectively extended Patterson's argument (which focused only on the white and black male hobos), pointing to both accusers and accused as exploited victims of white patriarchal capitalism, emplacing their shared position as transient workers squarely in the forefront of the report.

While Ransdall's report was muted, on the eve of the planned executions of the Scottsboro youths, Eugene Gordon, a noted labor journalist, loudly penned "A Call to Millions" in the *Labor Defender*, an angry diatribe against the attorney general of Alabama. I quote at length to exhibit the flavor of the column:

> He [the attorney general] gloats and slobbers in his glee at seeing workers burned to death like waste, like rubbish, like so many sacrificial beasts.

> He gloats and slobbers because these boys are workers, and he defies the working class because the boys are black workers. . . . He would make an example of these working class boys for black workers of the world to heed. Fellow workers of America, shall we let this thing be done? Is there a white worker within the United States who feels himself secure so long as any worker, white or black, is murdered as an example to teach YOU your place?[31]

Gordon—angrily and with a wide brush—was connecting this accusation of rape with the history of slavery in the United States, accusing the attorney general of denying the nine the ability to be free workers, using them as "sacrificial beasts," and metaphorically returning them to slavery. But the plea to white workers in this section highlights how slavery was both a racial and economic disenfranchisement. According to Gordon, execution of the nine was a systematic repressive response to not just black workers but all workers of every race.

Patterson, Ransdall, and Gordon contextualized the rape accusations as a class-based struggle, emphasizing the nine as members of the proletariat. In fact, the ILD's first observer of the trial was Douglas McKenzie, an organizer for the League of Struggle for Negro Rights, a radical group attempting to organize African American itinerant workers.[32] From the beginning then, for the CPUSA and other leftist organizations, this was primarily a case that involved workers who were violated, not "boys" falsely accused of raping white women. The CPUSA and other activist organizations articulated a hidden fear present in most discussions of hobos during the first part of the twentieth century: they were itinerant workers whose mobility offered possible disruptions to white capitalist society. What these writers did—along with many others—was to link black and white working-class bodies together, and, echoing the IWW mantra, suggest that they could become the vanguard of the coming revolution.

While race is obviously the linchpin in all these articles, these writers were also attempting to convince readers that the itinerant worker was a victim of capitalism and a disenfranchised member of the working class. An injury to those on the train, therefore, was an injury to all working peoples. This argument echoes the statements made by the Labor presses in the 1880s, as described in chapter 1. For example, in the radical *John Swinton's Paper*, an editorial by Swinton (a correspondent of Marx) discusses the plight of itinerant workers subjected to draconian tramp laws, stating, "But suppose the error of the tramp's ways is his inability to find work, on account of the state of things brought about by capitalism? In that case, it seems to us, the guilty parties who ought to be sent to the penitentiary are those who . . . are responsible for this social racket."[33] In both the 1880s and the 1930s, radical presses were showing that the plight of transient workers was a malicious corollary of capitalism and that the disenfranchisement of this subsection of the working class would lead to the alienation of the larger population. What is different about the propaganda found in the Labor presses of the nineteenth century and those found in the radical presses fifty years later is that the Scottsboro defenses revealed how racial violence is a particular capitalist tool of oppression used against the working class.

William Patterson, Hollace Ransdall, and Eugene Gordon certainly do not downplay the racial aspects of the Scottsboro case, but they contextualize racial injustice within a larger economic narrative. The "rape" that supposedly happened, hidden from view, was on a train moving across state lines. In essence, not only were black bodies "running away," they were committing an assault on white womanhood as they did so. Justice that had been meted out in previous circumstances—the local black bodies of the accused swinging from the town's trees where the "rape" took place—was instead tried in a southern courtroom by northern lawyers and angrily protested by people half a world away. The "justice" was no longer local, but part of an international dialogue.

The bodies moving throughout southern towns (and across state lines) undetected disturbed the hegemonic, ideological narrative of white, patriarchal capitalism. It also underlined southern legislatures' pre–Civil War discomfort with having a national networked rail system that allowed for the ease of bodies and goods to be transported across state lines. The nineteenth-century triumph of the rail, with its ability to annihilate space and time, posed a systematic vulnerability and social threat in 1931 Alabama. After the white, male hobos were ejected from the train by the Scottsboro Nine and the white, female hobos pulled from the car by the police mob, there was an attempt to restore this original narrative as all the players were roughly fit into racialized, social roles. As Caren Kaplan explains, those who travel "cannot escape the historical legacies of capitalist development and accumulation, of imperialist expansion and of inequalities of every kind." Within the machinations of capitalism, Kaplan contends that "the uneven operations . . . produce possibilities for some and delimit or obstruct opportunities for others."[34]

Although Kaplan is writing of leisurely travel—here Jim Crow laws would be a pertinent example of this type of obstruction—within the world of illegal travel during the Depression years where itinerant workers used the train as a way to procure jobs, these "uneven operations" for the white and black hobos showed that mobility was always a contested ideological space under capitalism. While the arrest of the young black males attempted to smooth this space, it was only partially successful, and after numerous trials and many years, the remaining of the Scottsboro Nine, bruised and battered, were released from prison. Although neither side could claim victory, the case has been referred to as an initial spark of the civil rights movement that struck down the Jim Crow laws, allowing, among many other things, white and black (paying) rail passengers to ride together.

What the Scottsboro case highlights, though, is that the subcultural world of the boxcar mirrors U.S. society's racial segregation in the 1930s. The initial fight happened because white and black hobos could not share the same space on a train. Activists and the CPUSA attempted to articulate the reasons for this contested space by highlighting the ways that capitalism used these ideological markers to rupture working-class solidarity. In the end, though, the defense, as well as the newspapers, moved away from examining what led these men and women to the boxcar during the Great Depression and instead focused almost exclusively on the racial and gender dynamics of the case.

The Scottsboro trials uncovered for the world the reality of racial strife and economic poverty in the South. But white and black hobos fighting in boxcars were not the only outcome of this shared space, and some texts focused on latent solidarity that could exist within an interracial boxcar. In this last third of the chapter, I would like to examine one popular text that imagined cross-racial solidarity.

## POPULAR REPRESENTATIONS OF THE HOBO

The hobo figure in 1930s film is a recognizable staple, where a montage of faux newspaper headlines, railroad tracks, and superimposed feet on a map was a common indication of the homeless transient. While films such as *Heroes for Sale* (1933) and *My Man Godfrey* (1936) have leads who are hobos, many other films have marginal hobo characters. Moviegoers, though, could see hobos even if they were not part of the film they paid money to see; these figures were featured in preshow newsreels in which reporters offered "man-on-the-street" interviews with hobos. As seen in period clips from the documentary *Riding the Rails: Teenagers on the Move in the Great Depression*, interviews with hobos in jungles or rail depots were a pertinent way to discuss the personal impact of the Great Depression on Americans.[35]

Moviegoers could also watch newsreels on the Scottsboro case throughout the decade, detailing the trial's numerous convictions and appeals. Radical film collectives, present from the beginning, also covered the case, documenting Scottsboro to rally the masses in support of the nine. The New York League, for example, directed and produced the films *Scottsboro Trial* (1932), *Scottsboro Demonstration* (1932), and *Washington Scottsboro Demonstration* (1932), examining the case as economic and racial injustice.[36] While these films were overtly political and reached a selective, small audience, there were also popular films that could be read as reimagining the Scottsboro incident. These films had a wider audience than the radical texts being produced, and although they ultimately could be conservative and reductive, some offered a counternarrative to the racial divisions both inside and outside the boxcar.

This counternarrative can be found in *Wild Boys of the Road*, William A. Wellman's 1933 Warner Brothers film that offers a glimpse of an interracial boxcar. While the film itself is certainly not radical and, in fact, its pro-NRA ending blatantly conservative, moments in the film articulate a potentiality for boxcar politics by reimagining a reaction to the Scottsboro "rape" as an interracial mode of resistive politics. While the actual rape on the train traveling through Scottsboro was a manufactured racialized fantasy that spoke to the reality of Alabama society in 1931, the fictional rape and consequential intervention of hobo characters in *Wild Boys of the Road* speaks of another possibility for working-class solidarity.[37]

### *The Interracial Boxcar in William Wellman's Hobo Films*

William "Wild Bill" Wellman directed more than eighty Hollywood films in a career that lasted almost four decades. Described as having an American personality that was a "quintessential combination of pagan and poet," over the course of his lengthy career, Wellman was "proudly a studio director."[38] After becoming disillusioned with Paramount Studios, Wellman was under contract with Warner Brothers in 1930, directing twenty-one films for the company in three years. The smallest of major studios, Warner Brothers made its name in the 1930s on "realistic," "ripped from the headlines" subject matter. The studio that produced many of the most iconoclastic gangster films, Warner Brothers also produced a variety of socially conscious films that specifically reflected on the fallout from the Great Depression, including *Wild Boys of the Road.*[39]

This film, however, was not Wellman's first depiction of the hobo lifestyle. His 1924 silent film *The Vagabond Trail* is a somewhat standard rags-to-riches trope of hobo films: in the hopes of finding a wayward brother, the main character, Donnegan (Buck Jones), must square off against an evil conductor who throws him off the train. Eventually, though, Donnegan survives his trials and learns life lessons from his time on the road; by the end of the film he is married and domesticated. While this film enacts simplistic gendered clichés of the hobo lifestyle, Wellman's next film would begin to push these stereotypes, exploring interracial solidarity among the subculture.[40]

Four years after *The Vagabond Trail,* Wellman directed *Beggars of Life,* based on the hobo author Jim Tully (who also cowrote the screenplay). The film, a loose adaptation of the book (see chapter 3) follows a young woman, Nancy (Louise Brooks), who kills her abusive foster father when he attempts to sexually assault her. With the help of Jim (Richard Arlen), a kind-hearted hobo who falls in love with her, Nancy hops freights and enters into the dangerous community of hobos. Discovered as a woman (she is wearing men's clothes to protect her identity) by Oklahoma Red (Wallace Beery), a hard-drinking, gun-wielding, violent leader of the hobos, Nancy finds herself in danger as the rest of the hobos drunkenly leer at her. When Jim attempts to protect her, Red holds a kangaroo court in the moving boxcar that, although played for laughs, may result in a gang rape of Nancy. Jim is "convicted" by the court and about to be killed when Nancy, playing on the sexual ambitions of the "Arkansaw Snake" (Robert Perry), causes a fight in the boxcar, and the two are able to escape. In this film, the hobos are thoughtless and dangerous drunken louts who are slaves to their desires. The train car is a place of division where there is no solidarity—leadership is determined by who has a gun (and alcohol). All potential rapists, these hobos are manipulated and easily fooled.[41]

In the midst of this unflattering description of the hobo subculture, Wellman embeds a surprising scene where, after escaping from the train and hiding in a railway shack, Nancy and Jim meet an African American hobo and his white, disabled companion who have been hopping trains together. As the white man is dying, he calls out for his companion and the title card reads, "Where's your hand black man, I'm afraid." As the black hobo forages for food to restore his partner, the white hobo dies. This relationship, although certainly not the focus of the film, is shot as a melodramatic interracial relationship based on transient mutualism.[42] The scene particularly stands out when compared to the drunken, selfish hobos in the railroad car. Although this is a small moment in the film, this type of solidarity is on full display in *Wild Boys of the Road.*

The hobos who take center stage in *Wild Boys of the Road* are very different from the hobos found in Wellman's *Beggars of Life.* While both films employ hobos, kangaroo courts, murders, and rape, the hobos in *Wild Boys of the Road* are clearly different. The film is narratively straightforward. Eddie (Frankie Darro) and Tommy (Edwin Phillips) are two average American kids who like to go to dances and drive around with their girlfriends in Eddie's beat-up car. As the Depression grabs hold of their families and the patriarchal households are turned upside down, the two boys decide that they will not be familial burdens and strike out on their own. Ironically whistling, "we're in the money," Eddie sells his car, and the two hop trains to look for jobs. After a restless night on a train, they meet Sally (Dorothy Coonan Wellman), who is hoboing to meet up with a long-lost Aunt Carrie (Minna Gombell) in Chicago. Soon they are part of a loose gang of teenage hobos traveling around the country looking for work. Their gang, which crosses ethnic, gender, and racial boundaries, works together looking for work and food, while also begging and stealing. They are an American form of the *Bezprizorni.*[43]

Unlike some of Wellman's other films in which the group members are mindless drones—as are the hobos in *Beggars of Life*, the American voting populace in *The President Vanishes* (1934), and the bloodthirsty mob in *The Ox-Bow Incident* (1943)—the hobos are favorably shot throughout *Wild Boys of the Road.* In one particularly poignant scene, the shot is a medium close-up of the group huddled together on a flatcar in the middle of a rainstorm (rain is a common motif in Wellman's films). The group, shoulder to shoulder and knee to knee, sways back and forth in one movement as the train hurdles down the tracks. In this scene, the solidarity is functional; they are in this position for warmth. They are powerless to the conditions (the rainstorm), and the mood is one of resignation as they endure their time on the rails together, heading into an unknown future. In this scene, there is no dialogue, just the shuttling, grinding sounds of the train and the downpour of the rain.

But this powerlessness and group dynamism change very quickly as the group communally finds its voice. The train is stopped by the railroad police, who order the young hobos to get off the train. They meekly comply and, dejected, meet an older hobo who informs them that they are far from any town. Staring at the group, he then questions why they left the train in the first place, bluntly stating, "You have an army don't you?" The term *army*, derogatorily used by politicians and journalists to imply an organized violent band of criminals, is being appropriated by the old hobo to show the latent power that the young itinerants embody. Suddenly, they realize their strength. Even though they are marginalized and seemingly powerless, they immediately begin to work together. They head back to the train and, with newfound conviction, declare to the police that they are commandeering the train. A comic fight takes place as a refrigerator car is opened and eggs, vegetables, and fruit are thrown at the baton-wielding police; the wild boys and girls are working together effectively—including a scene in which African American hobos are fighting alongside Swedish, Jewish, and Italian hobos. The cops are defeated, and the wild boys and girls are able to travel.

This scene, along with comparable scenes throughout the film, shows these interracial and interethnic relationships in complicated and contradictory ways. The film employs racial stereotypes; for example, during the fight African American hobos toss a watermelon down onto the head of a white cop while laughingly shouting, "A gift from Dixie." Clearly using the watermelon as a racist prop for laughs, Wellman then complicates the stereotype by having the young black hobos unafraid to use this symbol against the police while fighting alongside their fellow white hobos for a space on the train. Unlike the Jim Crow laws that separate the white and black travelers or the Scottsboro train where white and black hobos refused to ride peacefully together, these itinerants will share the same boxcar without any overt racial divides. The examples of this interracial solidarity are many: early in the film as the gang waits for a train, the first shot of the group is of an African American boy who joins the other hobos in good-naturedly teasing their white counterparts. Toward the end of the film when the hobos have built a "sewer city," the black hobos are entrepreneurs, opening a DIY laundromat, similar to the white youths who set up their own businesses. In the film there is no indication of a strict divide between black hobos and white hobos; when Tommy, who has lost a leg, receives the stolen prosthetic that the group has procured for him, the African American hobos are there among the group, cheering on the disabled young man. In a film that both employs and then undercuts racial stereotypes, Wellman portrays a boxcar in which transient youths are working together, crossing normative racial and gender boundaries.

### *Reimagining the Scottsboro Rape*

In *Wild Boys of the Road*, after the young hobos win the battle and a space to ride, the train pulls away from the impotent police waiting on the side of the tracks, and the hobos are seen laughing in the boxcar, giddy with their newfound power. Like the previously discussed scene in the rain where the hobos were huddled, swaying as one body to the rhythm of the train car, in this scene, they are again close together, rubbing elbows. This time, though, they are in control of their environment, standing up and laughing. That is, until they see one of their traveling companions on the floor, crying and hurt. She tells the group that during the fight she was trapped by a brakeman (Ward Bond) and assaulted. Left alone in the train car and without the protection of the hobo subculture, she was vulnerable and could not defend herself. Wanting justice, some of the hobos think about reporting the assault to the police, but the idea is quickly discounted because they realize they are outside the law.

Their solidarity in the fight against the police has changed them, and they understand their power: they can take care of the situation themselves. Wellman underlines the group dynamics of the scene as these wild youths on the train become a single body taking on the conductor. After the young hobos discovered their sexually assaulted friend, the trainman, who is on the roof, looks down at the gang and says, "Who broke into the car?" Eddie takes ownership, and as the brakeman swings down into the boxcar, he squares up with the larger man. The brakeman punches Eddie, who falls to the side with a bloody nose. It is the group that then takes on the brakeman, with arms coming in from all angles to land a punch, eventually throwing him out of the speeding car and killing him.

The trainman is able to defeat the single, individual hobo (Eddie) just as he was able to assault the single, vulnerable female hobo; the collective body is needed to exact their revenge. Unlike the mob scenes in most of Wellman's films that show the group easily manipulated, these young hobos are able to work together.

Earl Baldwin's screenplay, which was heavily edited by Warner Brothers because they feared that the graphic bleak nature would lead to "premature births" from the shocked audience, differed greatly from the finished film.[44] In his version, when the young hobos board the liberated train, the traumatized girl has committed suicide by hanging herself. Capturing the conductor, the hobos hold a kangaroo court. But unlike the pseudo-humorous court held in *Beggars of Life* that portrays the hobo subculture as a collection of sexually deviant, violent drunkards, the hobos in *Wild Boys of the Road* are organized and conduct a trial in which they try the conductor for rape and murder. They convict and kill him. In this version they act as a unified body replicating a court system and administering their harsh sentence. In both the screenplay and the film, the hobos have a solidarity that transcends race and gender. While Wellman's racial and gender politics are certainly complicated, and he was far from a civil rights activist or a feminist, the way he uses the hobos shows possibilities of solidarity within the boxcar.

To highlight the uniqueness of this scene, let us briefly turn to other texts in which black and white hobos intermingle in the same boxcar. *Sister of the Road*, marketed as "the frank, uncensored story of a wandering woman of the underworld," was purported to be the autobiography of Bertha Thompson. In fact, Ben Reitman wrote and submitted the manuscript to Lippincott in 1934 (although it was not published until 1937). Joanne Hall's archival research of Reitman's papers has traced the history of the writing of this book, exploring the way Reitman used Thompson to promote an "aura of sexual promiscuity with which the female hobo is surrounded." In addition to analyzing the published version of the book, Hall also uncovers an expunged scene that harkens directly to the Scottsboro train car. In the scene unnamed African American males violate Thompson, her friend Maggie, and other riding companions. Described in animalistic stereotypes, the young men board the train and rape the women.

Just as the "attack" in the train stopped in Paint Rock became a national rape fantasy played out on the front pages of southern newspapers, in *Sister of the Road* Reitman's scene also became a rape fantasy. Instead of a lynch mob demanding justice for an attack on white womanhood, Reitman has the two women enjoy the assault: one woman, describing the attack to her father, says that they were "beautifully and satisfactorily raped." Thompson refers to the incident as "exciting," refusing to identify her attackers.[45] In the Scottsboro courtroom, attempts were made to remove the hobo identities of Victoria Price and Ruby Bates to construct them as victims of African American sexual aggression; in Reitman's book the hobo identities of the women are securely fashioned, and their "deviancy" allows them to "enjoy" the attack. The scene is shocking on a number of levels; this book, although sensational, has numerous progressive sentiments. Reitman, after all, defended the hobo subculture in numerous books and articles and yet, in describing the relationship between black and white rail riders, the racial space of the boxcar becomes a stratified space of a sexual assault.

A different reversal of the Scottsboro incident can be read in Nelson Algren's first novel, *Somebody in Boots*, a Depression-era book published in 1935. Cass McKay, the central character, is brought up in a dysfunctional and destitute family, and after his father is arrested for murder, he is forced to take to the road as a hobo, searching for work. In one scene early in the novel, he is in a boxcar traveling through east Texas with a group of hobos, including a strong-willed Wobbly and an African American female, when the railroad police confront them. The Wobbly calls for solidarity among the workers, telling them that their numbers will protect them against the police force. Singing "Casey Jones" quietly, the hobos try to be brave, but at the first sign of trouble, they hide in the corners of the boxcar as the old Wobbly, left alone, is quickly removed from the train. The rest are locked in the boxcar so they can be more easily arrested further down the line. As the train moves slowly along the tracks, the hobos manage to burn their way out of the moving boxcar, and Cass finds himself with a few hobos, including the woman, walking toward the town.[46]

It does not take long for the men to become animalistic, surrounding the girl "bark[ing] laughter." Calling her "nigger gal" and "nervy black heifer," the main antagonist tries to pin her to the ground. She resists and is about to escape when another hobo grabs her legs and forces her down, whereby all members of the group, including Cass, proceed to gang-rape the woman. This scene, in a novel filled with pessimistic views of the interactions of hobos, racially reverses the rape of the Scottsboro incident. Instead of black men raping white women, white men gang-rape a black female who was hoboing her way to New Orleans to find work after the death of her husband. In a style as stark as the subject matter, Algren simply states of the attackers, with an ironic nod to Hemingway, "They were all of them men; they were men without women."[47]

In Algren's novel the hobos are impotent in their resistance to power; the old Wobbly rallying the men to stand up to the police is parroted by the hobos, but there are no genuine political ties or class solidarity that bind them. These hobos, who would not stand together with the Wobbly to defend themselves, join together to enact violence on the body of a fellow train rider. The cultural historian Richard Pells writes of the worldview of the novel, "Algren suspected that 'the people' were not incipient socialists but potential brown shirts who might come together solely for an orgy of looting and arson. Otherwise they would remain fragmentary individuals, drifting helplessly down the road to nowhere."[48] Unlike Reitman or Algren, who reference the Scottsboro incident to divide the boxcar among gender and racial lines in their texts, Wellman, on the screen, uses the sexual assault to show racial and gender solidarity among a group of marginalized individuals joining together to communally take revenge.

### *Wild Boys of the Road* and Scottsboro

In the Scottsboro case Alabama prosecutors knew that the white, southern juries would see the black hobos' fight with the white hobos as both a reason for the rape as well as evidence that the rape occurred.[49] In other words, once they fought the white hobos on the train and disturbed the order of white supremacy, it would only be logical that they would then partake in the rape of white women. According to Files Crenshaw and Kenneth Miller, authors of *Scottsboro: The Firebrand of Communism*, a racist "evaluation" of the trials published in 1936, the nine were not workers and "nowhere in the record is there anything to indicate that any of them were even remotely connected with Southern Industry." The nine, by being hobos, are figuratively seen as runaway slaves whose mobility on the train allowed for a manifestation of base lusts for white women and desired violence against white men. The black hobos needed to be placed within the Alabama courtroom and sentenced to death to delimit their movements before their travels would "inspire" other blacks, leading to a "stake in the very heart of the solid South."[50] According to this racist and classist logic, the nine's original crime was their invisible mobility; the need to see their black bodies and regulate them was not only justified, but imperative.

*Wild Boys of the Road*, though, transforms key aspects found in the Scottsboro case, as black and white, male and female hobos respond to a rape allegation and offer an alternative outcome. The film, which opened the same year as *King Kong*, with its racist images of wild savages and a lustful beast, points to the possibilities of an interracial boxcar transformed as a space for collective subcultural resistance. Instead of white hobos attacking black hobos or black male hobos raping white, female hobos, in this film we have black and white, male and female transients all standing together in the subcultural world of the boxcar, taking on railroad authorities and administering their own justice. The interracial group dynamic in this mainstream Hollywood film reveals the possibilities of a manifestation of an interracial boxcar politics. The wild boys and girls are guilty only of being poor, but in their poverty they find a positive communal mobility.

The train, though, both in the film and in reality, must stop eventually, and after the hobos have killed the brakeman rapist, the train enters the Chicago yard and the police who are waiting for them will be no match for the group. Once the train stops moving, the subcultural power of the hobos is diminished. Tommy loses his leg as a result of leaping off the train, the "sewer city" where the wild boys and girls created their own town (reminiscent of the Bonus Army Hoovervilles erected in the shadow of the White House in 1932) was violently hosed down by the police, and Eddie gets caught up with gangsters and mistakenly attempts to rob a theater.

With the three facing an extended sentence, the kindhearted judge surprisingly gives leniency to the group because, as the judge states, with a poster of the NRA in the background, "Things are simply going to get better." Reviewers from the *New York Times* to Wellman himself have read the ending as inconsistent with the narrative of the rest of the film.[51] The original script included Eddie being shot and thrown into juvenile jail, while Tommy and Sally were given long sentences in juvenile detention.

But Warner Brothers rejected this ending as being too bleak. While the revised ending might be more hopeful for the audiences anxious for FDR's policies to "make things better," germane to this argument, the reshot ending undercuts the solidarity of the hobos in the boxcar. While traveling, the interracial group worked together and fought for one another. In the courtroom scene, it is only the three of them and the kindly judge who whimsically gives them a free pass. Capitalism is not challenged or exposed, but with this ending, it is shown as a benign, paternalistic, white-centric entity.

This ending blunted the progressive moments of the film and contained the wild boys within a narrative reminiscent of the tramp stories of the late nineteenth century made popular by Horatio Alger. In these popular serials, there is usually an intervention of a rich benefactor able to look past the grimy cheeks of a young transient, see his moral uprightness, and save the virtuous (white) boy from poverty. These stories, as Christine Photinos explains, "promise a kind of middle-class correction," and the ending of *Wild Boys of the Road* certainly fulfills this promise: the judge is able to see the virtue in Eddie and return him back to his father, who (according to the judge) will find a job and regain his patriarchal role in the family.[52] Erased from the film are the multiple boys and girls who shared the boxcar with Eddie. What about the African American youths, or the young girl who was sexually assaulted? Would they find their way into a sympathetic courtroom? Although this arbitrary doling out of "justice" was seen by contemporary reviewers as selling out a story that had broad social implications and making it a "rather pointless yarn," for the Scottsboro youths and countless other hobos riding the rails, the idea that justice was not fair but gendered and white-centric reflected the reality of their day-to-day lives.[53]

## MARGINALIZED SUBCULTURAL SPACE WITHIN THE INTERRACIAL BOXCAR

The hobo, a part of a pool of cheap migrant labor in the late nineteenth and twentieth centuries, was marginalized within the working class. Twice marginalized for their economic situation and race, black hobos had only a finger grip on the lowest rung in the working-class hierarchy. Clarence Lee, who was riding freights at the time of the Scottsboro case, states this feeling clearly, "When I was riding the freight trains, I didn't feel like an American Citizen. I felt like an outcast."[54] When the Scottsboro case first started making the news, black hobos on trains in the South often found that their riding days were over. Lee, Bumblee Bee Slim, and Blind Arvella Grey all narrowly escaped lynch mobs who were arbitrarily searching for black hobo "rapists." These and other black hobos would feel like an "outcast among outcasts."[55]

Garon and Tomko recount in their history of the black hobo that there was a sense of racial egalitarianism among some hobos traveling together, which Wellman captures in his film.[56] But like a rocky boxcar ride, the racial dynamics could change quickly and without warning. This was the case for Harry Haywood, the Communist Party's "foremost theorist on the black self-determination thesis" and vocal defender of the Scottsboro Nine. Haywood personally knew the travails of the black hobo, and the Scottsboro trials represented for him "but a single expression of the whole system of national oppression of the Negro People"; in numerous articles he clearly points out the way that these hobos were used as pawns by the white capitalist system.[57] His personal experiences allowed him to understand the many obstacles that these transient workers were facing. In his autobiography, *Black Bolshevik*, Haywood describes his first trip from Chicago to Beloit, Wisconsin, where, afraid of being injured, he was tutored by a white hobo who helped him hop the train before generously instructing him on the ways to survive while riding boxcars. Along with twelve other hobos, they rode peacefully together. The train, though, was stopped, and when a black man was discovered in the group, Haywood was ordered to spend the rest of the trip shoveling coal for the fireman. This illustrates the contours of the racial components of boxcar politics. Traveling together, the hobos were helpful to one another as they made their way along the iron rails. Once they were discovered and stopped, however, racist practices were reinstated, and the black hobo was required to bear the brunt of the labor and hostility.[58]

Chapter Six

# THE SPIRITUAL BOXCAR

## Lostness in *On the Road* and the End of the Political Hobo

The Scottsboro Nine were hoboing for reasons of economic survival, attempting to become invisible and avoid racist legal and extralegal practices. When they were caught and brought into the harsh light of the American justice system, the color of their skins made their hobo identities mostly irrelevant. In their defense, radical presses and the Communist Party USA attempted to make clearly legible the nine's woring-class allegiances: these were young African American laborers who had been denied their right to work.

The legal travails for these men lasted for years. But as the last of the Scottsboro Nine still languished in prison awaiting release, Jack Kerouac toed the asphalt at the edge of a highway and threw his thumb out, looking for a ride that would take him from New York's Bear Mountain region to his friend on the West Coast. During his travels, and his numerous subsequent published and unpublished texts about these wanderings, Kerouac created a significantly different hobo figure that did not resemble the Scottsboro Nine or any of the other hobos previously analyzed in this book. Kerouac's hobos are neither looking for jobs nor linked to any semblance of a working-class culture. They do not partake in radical union culture (like Dos Passos's hobos), nor are they members of a marginalized community helping one another survive (like Tully's hobos). They are not even arch-individualists trying to rise in the stratified hobo world (like London's profresh hobos). In Kerouac's hands, there is no subculture to begin with: they are individualists portrayed as ghosts, spiritual guides circulating around the country ready to lead those who can recognize them. These hobos are not of the world, and they offer no commentary on the state of the floating proletariat. Instead, in the immediate post–World War II American landscape, Kerouac's boxcar space is a romanticized ideal of nostalgic masculinity that depoliticizes hobos, transforming them into spirit wanderers. Kerouac's hobos do not partake in a boxcar politics; rather, contextualized within a historic moment in which the railroad is in decline, the car culture reigns supreme, and fewer flesh-and-blood hobos are found in train yards, the type of hobo Kerouac imagined exemplifies the end of boxcar politics.

Consequently, Kerouac's hobos do not point to a new type of hobo figure, waiting to be birthed in the turbulent times ahead; his hobos will not take part in the "rucksack revolution" that Japhy Ryder dreams about in *The Dharma Bums*, foreshadowing the 1960s counterculture.[1] The social, political, and technological upheavals that will transform the United States in the second half of the twentieth century will also transform the railroad industry and consequently the hobo subculture; neither the train nor the train hopper will emerge the same. While a new type of rail rider will be found in a boxcar in the second half of the twentieth century through to our present day, Kerouac's hobos bookend a hobo epoch: at a time when the railroad was in steep decline and the car was becoming a symbol of American freedom, Kerouac glances in a car's rearview mirror and sees the "poor forlorn" hobo, presenting him in his novels and essays as a ghost that haunts midcentury America.[2]

This haunting leads to revelation: the ghostly hobos embody the elusive "it" that Dean Moriarty and Sal Paradise long for in their numerous trips throughout *On the Road*. This metaphysical state is not to be found in any particular geographic destination: Kerouac tells us that we will not find "it" on any map because, as Dean explains, "it" can happen only when time stops and the world fades away. As Kerouac's biographer Gerald Nicosia states, "One could only find it by coasting from moment to moment with the flux of mind. It represented the dissolution of time and the immediate experience of immortality."[3] As Kerouac's texts show, to reach this elusive, ecstatic state, one must disengage with both geography and time. He uses the hobo to exemplify an ontological lostness, an ecstatic state that allows for dissociation from the world. In Kerouac's hands, this alienation works to depoliticize the hobo figure, making him a disoriented "little bum" who, as a spiritual guide, holds the key (perhaps) to the greater mysteries of life but who is perpetually alone and impotent in his political voice. In a similar vein as Dos Passos does in *U.S.A.*, Kerouac writes nostalgically about the hobo; but, unlike Dos Passos, Kerouac embodies the hobo without any historical or political lineage or any future possibilities. He is a ghost of a mythical American beatific past.

Early on in the novel, Dean is asked by Carlo Marx, "Whither goest thou, America, in thy shiny car in the night?"—linking the (unknown) future of the United States with the automobile.[4] When this question is asked, the train culture has been displaced by the automobile culture, and Kerouac's hobos do not readily fit within midcentury America. By the time *On the Road* is published, the hobo subculture is "dead," and Kerouac has transformed the transient worker, who was part of a vibrant subcultural community throughout the late nineteenth and early twentieth centuries, into a spiritual guide with no class allegiance or recognition. Kerouac creates a "hobo confabulation," transforming the hobo figure into a sympathetic ghost—but one that does not have any political relevancy in Cold War America.

## HOBOS AND AN ALTERNATE VISION OF AMERICA

Whether hopping a ride in the back of a pickup speeding throughout the Midwest, swaying to a tenor man speaking into his instrument, or riding as a passenger in a beat-up car, Sal Paradise, the narrator of *On the Road*, is searching for the elusive "it" that both Dean and Sal are struggling to embody. Although they begin to enter this state during their travels, neither is completely successful. They are searchers, wanderers in the "Great American Night," but only those whom they revere as gods are able to hold onto "it" for an extended period. There are brief elusive moments, though, in which Sal touches on this ecstatic state. Traveling across the country, Kerouac details one of these moments: "I had reached the point of ecstasy that I always wanted to reach, which was a complete step across chronological time into timeless shadows, and wonderment in the bleakness of the mortal realm, and the sensation of death kicking at my heels to move on, with a phantom dogging its own heels, and myself hurrying to a plank where all the angels dove off and flew into the holy void of uncreated emptiness, the potent and inconceivable radiances shining in bright Mind Essence, innumerable lotus-lands falling open in the magic mothswarm of heaven."[5] Ecstasy is a timeless state of being, and this is Sal's ecstatic moment in which time stands still, and he is a part of the "holy void of uncreated emptiness." But while Kerouac wrote that his life's goal was "eternal ecstasy, now and forever," Sal cannot hold onto "it" and is forced to return back to "chronological time" to find his friends and discuss these visions. That is why, throughout the book, Sal is traveling after the "mad ones" who he believes might cross into "timeless shadows."[6]

While Slim Gaillard, the famous jazz musician whom Kerouac immortalizes, could hold onto "it" precisely because he could play a note for so long and so true, losing himself in the music that he created, in *On the Road*, hobos are also some of the few characters able to embody this state. In fact, Kerouac's overall vision for *On the Road*, according to Nicosia, was that "the whole book was to be like a hobo song."[7] These wanderers, although somewhat marginal characters, hold key roles in the text. What ostensibly drives Sal and Dean to the road is the romanticized search for Old Dean Moriarty, who taught Dean his hobo ways before abandoning him as a child. It is this same old, alcoholic, ghostlike hobo whom Sal is distinctly thinking about in the final paragraph of the novel. Between these two bookends, hobos continually appear at other important moments. After meeting Terry, a love interest, and excitedly beginning his (short-lived) career as a cotton picker, Sal looks out from his hotel window and sees an "SP freight going by with hundreds of hobos reclining on the flatcars and rolling merrily along." He is galvanized: "'Damn!' I yelled. 'Hooee!' It *is* the promised land."[8] The idyllic vision of working with a member of the fellahin leads Sal to imagine a large number of hobos traveling in a relaxed state across the "promised land": Kerouac links this idyllic view of American agriculture with the "merry" hobos. Although he would quickly become exhausted with the work that placed him among the racialized working class, his romantic view of hobos traveling in boxcars (his hobos are never seen actually working) never tires.

On his very first journey in *On the Road*, Sal meets a cowboy who tells him, "I used to hop freights at least once a month. In those days you'd see hundreds of men riding a flatcar or in a boxcar . . . going from one place to another and some of them just wandering. It was like that all over the West."[9] These boxcar wanderers belonged to a different era (and geographic area for the northeastern-born-and-raised Kerouac)—a recent past that he holds up as a nostalgic ideal. For Kerouac, hobos were not part of the working class but separate from society, playing by their own set of rules. They suffered, but in their suffering, an alternate vision of America was formed. It was an aesthetic vision that Kerouac first glimpsed in the books of Thomas Wolfe: America was a poem, not a place to work for a paycheck. After reading Melville at age sixteen, and inspired by Depression era–riding hobos, the would-be writer wrote in his journal that, in Bartleby-like fashion, he "preferred not to" work.[10] Kerouac was not interested in the ways hobos procured employment (his own father suffered greatly in his many unsuccessful attempts to secure jobs), but it was their ability to remove themselves from a working life that fascinated the young artist.

Kerouac details his distinct view of the hobo more specifically in his ominously titled article, "The Vanishing American Hobo," in which he writes, "The hobo is born of Pride having nothing to do with a community but with himself and other hobos and maybe a dog. . . . Proud was the way the hobo walked through a town by the back doors where pies were cooling on window sills."[11] For Kerouac, these are self-important individualists, and he creates an otherworldly aura around them. Whether it is old Dean Moriarty, the "father [they] never found," or the unnamed "hundreds" of hobos traveling past his motel window, these men are always in perpetual motion, mostly unreachable, except in passing glimpses.[12] Due to their amorphousness, they lose their corpus and instead become symbols, grails that get Sal and Dean on the road or keep them there. Hobos appear briefly before disappearing from view. Sal can only attempt to follow.

Kerouac, for all his traveling, distances himself from this group, writing, "I myself was a hobo but only of sorts. . . . I was not a real hobo with no hope ever except that secret eternal hope you get sleeping in empty boxcars."[13] This unwillingness to grab the hobo title is significant because, although Kerouac hopped trains throughout his life, especially when he was living on the West Coast, he knows he is not like these men.[14] While there is a deep respect for these hope-filled wanderers, Kerouac understands that these hobos—like the gods whom he admires—are not part of his world but of "the eternal." They are ghosts, and Kerouac, with his corporal desires, is not one of them.

But hobos—and trains—continue to have a strong influence. In *On the Road,* when told by Roland Major that he needs to give up hopping trains, Sal replies, "I know that. It's just that I love boxcars and I love to read the names on them like Missouri Pacific, Great Northern, Rock Island Line. By Gad, Major, if I could tell you everything that happened to me hitching here."[15] For Sal, hopping trains leads to stories, and boxcars create an entry point for these stories to be formed; watching trains pass him by is thus conceived as a literary event. This word-centric motive to hop trains is one of the reasons that Kerouac cites he was not a "real" hobo, because, as he states, "I knew some day my literary efforts would be rewarded by social protection."[16] While Dos Passos's hobos speak the "speech of the people," combining language and movement that would help spread the anticapitalist movement throughout the United States, Kerouac's hobos point inward toward a spiritual understanding of self. His hobos, like all the mad ones who people the storyline of *On the Road,* reinforce that, for Kerouac, travel directly relates to a lostness, a temporal geographic disconnection. Kerouac's hobos lose themselves and exist in the "timeless shadows" of the ecstatic state, offering a spiritual roadmap for Kerouac to follow. This role of the hobo is most clearly understood in the figure of a wandering hobo searching for a magical bridge.

## THE GHOST OF THE SUSQUEHANNA

Special among the other hobos in *On the Road* is the Ghost of the Susquehanna, a recurring figure in the texts of Kerouac.[17] Unlike most of the other hobos we glimpse in this book, the ghost allows Sal to walk next to him. It is not a positive interaction. Frustrated and trying to get home, Sal meets the "shriveled old man" of about sixty years old along the side of a road. On closer inspection of the old man, Sal sees a "semi-respectable walking hobo of some kind" who promises there will be a bridge that they can cross. Sal walks for some time, trying to follow the ghost, but a physical bridge never materializes. Frustrated at the circular conversation of the hobo, he leaves the "little madman" and quickly gets a ride from a passing motorist that will lead him back toward his home in Queens. Cushioned in the front seat of the car, he soon rides past the "poor forlorn man, poor lost sometimeboy, now broken ghost of the penniless wilds." The hobo is "lost," Sal is heading home, and the whole meeting is described as a "sad endeavor."[18]

Seen, at first, as a confused homeless man, on reflection the old hobo takes on mythical proportions. In his conversation with the ghost, Sal is offered a chance "to cross a bridge," but, weary from travel and desiring to get home, he misses the ecstatic moment being offered to him until it is too late. Although this old hobo was seemingly confused, Kerouac writes of him as a prophet, a man forever tramping across the land laden with his visions and "madness." Early in the text, Sal, talking with friends, anticipates this meeting, writing, "All we could do was yell . . . eastward over the Plains, where somewhere an old man with white hair was probably walking toward us with the Word, and would arrive any moment and make us silent."[19] When Sal discovers the old man in the East, however, he is not silent before the Word. Instead, he keeps interrupting the hobo with questions about accurate directions and specific roads. Sal is frustrated because, even though the old hobo says he is trying to head to "Canady" and they keep walking, Sal realizes that the old man is heading the wrong way—at least in a strict geographic sense. Following him along the side of the road, Sal is lost and confused, trying to look ahead into the "inky night" to see the physical bridge that the old man says is ahead of them. Frustrated by being lost and homesick, Sal leaves the hobo, leaves the Word that would silence him, and finds a driver who knows the right direction to take him to the place (home) within which he so desperately wants to find solace.

For someone who will always be identified with flux, Kerouac was, in fact, concerned with permanence. Home, for him, referred to a place in Queens (or his numerous other abodes he shared with family), where his mother made his lunches and a crucifix hung over his bed. John Clellon Holmes, his friend and fellow Beat writer, wrote that Kerouac was "the seeker after continuity who, no matter how rootless his life may seem, has always known that our anguish is uprootedness."[20] This tension between stability (home) and lostness weaves itself throughout the novel; Kerouac even composed a hobo theme song for *On the Road* that speaks to this fractured state: "Home in Missoula, home in Truckee, home in Wounded Knee, home in Ogallala, home I'll never be, home I'll never be."[21] Kerouac's desire for home is in direct tension with his desire for ecstasy—the narrator's name itself contains the pun: for Sal, paradise is lost. When the old hobo meets Sal and speaks of a bridge, he is helping Sal become ontologically lost. The ghost is offering Kerouac a way to get back home—a spiritual "home" that relates to his Franco-Canadian roots.[22] The bridge that the old man mumbles about does not have any geographic physicality, nor does it exist in chronological time; rather, it is a bridge that one will find only when one has embraced lostness.

After returning to his home in Ozone Park, Kerouac wrote in his journal about his experience meeting the ghost. His description of the ghost is similar to his depiction in *On the Road*, with one added detail. More so than in the novel, Kerouac recounts in detail the mighty Susquehanna River, a lonely and haunted river continuously flowing along its path. His intertwining descriptions of the ghost with the Susquehanna River at times make it hard to tell when he is writing about the hobo and when he is discussing the river. They both have an eternal quality: their motion constant, their parallel journeys solitary. The descriptions of both are underwritten with elements of violence; to follow either one is to risk (bodily) death. But walking alongside both the hobo and the river invites visions for Kerouac, and as he listens to the old man discussing the trains that he had hopped in his life (and the mythical bridge in this journal version leads to a train yard that can take them anywhere), he is able to have a shamanistic vision of the man as prophet.[23]

Norma Walrath Goldstein writes in her article about the Ghost of the Susquehanna that "the bridge image is not necessarily linked to a place but to an essence, an idea or spiritual state. The directionlessness of the old man supports this theme and the old wanderer teaches Sal that the wilderness of America cannot be defined by place like east or west, reinforcing the notion that their quest is a spiritual one befitting a ghost."[24] To embrace being lost is to accept a rupture from geography and time. When one is lost in this way, one loses one's identity. This, for Kerouac, is ecstasy.

Analyzing this relationship between subjectivity and physicality, Elspeth Probyn explicates the need to understand ourselves in terms of our location, writing, "Profoundly, we experience our subjectivities, the ways in which we are positioned in regard to ourselves as subjects, in terms of both space and time. How can it be otherwise, given that our bodies and our sense of ourselves are in constant interaction with how and where we are placed?"[25] In other words, as spatial geographers will tell us, where we are is who we are. If identities are connected to places, then Kerouac (at times) wants to undefine himself to free himself. It is a way to reach the ecstatic moment where his wanderings are leading him.

This feeling of lostness happens to Sal in the often-quoted opening pages of *On the Road.* In his initial journey, when Sal arrives in the West and sees the Mississippi River for the first time, the sight is an important moment for him and his life as a writer. Exhausted, when he is turned away from the YMCA, he finds a cheap motel near railroad tracks.[26] Waking up, he has a moment where he is not quite sure where he is. I quote here at length:

> I woke up as the sun was reddening; and that was the one distinct time in my life, the strangest moment of all, when I didn't know who I was—I was far away from home, haunted and tired with travel, in a cheap hotel room I'd never seen, hearing the hiss of steam outside, and the creak of the old wood of the hotel, and footsteps upstairs, and all the sad sounds, and I looked at the cracked high ceilings and really didn't know who I was for about fifteen strange seconds. I wasn't scared; I was just somebody else, some stranger, and my whole life was a haunted life, the life of a ghost. I was halfway across America, at the dividing line between the East of my youth and the West of my future, and maybe that's why it happened right there and then, that strange red afternoon.[27]

It is in this moment when he is in between geographic areas, when he can locate himself neither in time nor in a particular place, that he becomes, like the old man wandering on the side of the road, a ghost. He is lost, and, because of his lostness, he loses his identity and becomes a stranger to the life he has been leading. As Nicosia writes of this pivotal moment in the author's life, "He was no longer Jack Kerouac the mill town athlete but some new Kerouac, a seeker of America . . . but with two World Wars and a sexual revolution complicating his identity." For Kerouac this was not a frightening experience but a momentary freeing from geographic placeness. As Jeffrey Andrew Weinstock writes about this state, "Geographic lostness contributes to a sense of temporal lostness, and the two together participate in the development of a profound sense of ontological lostness—the sense not just of being lost in the world, but the loss of the world altogether."[28] Kerouac, at certain moments, is able to achieve this state of ontological lostness, and while he is not able to stay lost, and instead sadly slinks back to a recognized place—his home—at the end of all his cross-country journeys, the old ghostly hobo fully exists in this ecstatic realm. Though Sal does not realize it while he is with the old man—the thoughts of home are too strong—he has regrets almost as soon as he sees the hobo in the rearview mirror.

Nicosia reads the Ghost of the Susquehanna as a warning figure for Kerouac, writing, "After several months of wandering, Jack must have found the old man an ominous reminder of what he could easily become, were it not for the clean bed, good meals and ordered life his mother held in wait."[29] I also read the ghost as a warning figure, but contrary to Nicosia, I see the ghost as a warning *not* to head home. Kerouac describes leaving the old man as his "day of the Laodiceans."[30] Biblical references abound in all of Kerouac's works, but this reference is particularly enlightening. The Laodiceans, who are found in the Book of Revelations, are described as spiritually blind, mistakenly viewing themselves as favored in the sight of God. But, in God's eyes they are wretched and miserable creatures, poor in spirit and soul. In other words, the Laodiceans do not see the truth in front of them until it is too late. Traveling away from the old man, heading in the "right" direction that he could chart with a map, and soon to be dropped off at one of the most famous of geographic markers—Times Square—Sal suddenly realizes he has been blind and did not "see" the hobo. Tired, hungry, and cold, he heads home defeated. At this low point in Sal's life, he was looking for directions on a map instead of embracing the ontological lostness that the hobo represents.

Gilles Deleuze reads *On the Road* as a novel of deterritorialization. Kerouac's writing is not a mere representation of an America that the author sees as he wanders across the American landscape. It is neither a simple portrayal of a land nor a description of the contours of a geographic area. It is not even a re-creation of a trip through fantastical stories. Rather, it is a creation, Deleuze suggests, of a whole new world. Through their journeys, Sal and Dean, the philosopher contends, "create a new Earth," and they do so through deterritorialization, a breaking away from the more hierarchal ways of traveling involving maps that contain vertical and horizontal lines on a grid. Instead, *On the Road* is "a flight towards the West, the discovery that the true East is in the West, the sense of the frontiers as something to cross, to push back, to go beyond. *The becoming is geographical.*"[31] When Sal becomes lost, there is a displacement of established mappable borders that place the land into observable and countable areas and thus the creation of a new earth. As Sal wakes up in a motel room and is caught for fifteen seconds in a space where he is a ghost, he is experiencing a type of ontological lostness and becoming something different, something new. As his biographer notes, Kerouac "didn't write to know the world but to know his visions of the world," and at this moment Sal's lostness allows him to become a ghost at the "dividing line" of his life.[32]

Lostness causes much anxiety, however, and when Sal meets the ghost who offers him a chance to become lost, he is unable to break away from geography and his identity. When he does experience this ecstatic state, Sal cannot handle it. As every trip that he takes in *On the Road* begins with excitement and enthusiasm filled with innumerable possibilities (a type of rebirth), all his trips end with an intense sadness and a slinking back to a place he recognizes and knows—his home (a type of death). Sal states of one of his journeys, "I had my home to go to, my place to lay my head down and figure out the losses and figure out the gains that I knew was in there somewhere too."[33] He needs to reestablish his identity by subtracting the losses from the gains and placing himself, once again, in a specific recognized geographic place; a place where he grew up and whose umbilical cord stretched into the West of his travels. Even though Sal desires the lostness that the old hobo experiences and that he himself had experienced during the fifteen seconds in the motel room, in *On the Road* he is unable to embrace the Ghost of the Susquehanna and the ontological lostness the hobo represents.

For Kerouac, the hobo is a nostalgically tinged, mystic symbol not bound by class. The old hobo is, after all, a "ghost," a remnant—or reminder—of something from the past haunting the present. Although in reality there were still men and women riding trains and searching for work and a place to sleep for the night, when Sal was in the passenger side of whatever car Dean was able to get his hands on, the hobo was already relegated to America's past. The once-revered hobo is "made to slink," and the "death" of the hobo subculture leads Kerouac to conclude despairingly,

> As far as I am concerned the only thing to do is sit in a room and get drunk and give up your hoboing and your camping ambitions because there aint a sheriff or fire warden in any of the new fifty states who will let you cook a little meal over some burning sticks in the tule brake or the hidden valley or anyplace any more because he has nothing to do but

> pick on what he sees out there on the landscape moving independently of the gasoline power army police station—I have no ax to grind: I'm simply going to another world.

Having the police identify and round up anyone who is "lost" leads Kerouac to sit in his room and drink heavily, dreaming of another world. As he writes, "The hobo is Virgil, he leadeth," and the Ghost of the Susquehanna leads to a mystical state.[34] But in this essay that prophesizes his own death, he pessimistically realizes that the old madman hobo searching for bridges will never bring the Word specifically to him.

While as a young boy growing up in Lowell, Massachusetts, Kerouac admired the local hobos who had become famous for traveling cross-country, stating to a friend that "there was no better life" for him. As a young writer, finding himself employed by the railroads, he felt an affinity toward hobos, sleeping among them instead of staying in hotels. Nine years before his death, though, Kerouac realized that "the woods are full of wardens" and that the hobo could no longer move freely in America.[35] In *On the Road* Sal could not reach the ecstatic state that the Ghost of the Susquehanna offered him; a few years later, in 1960, when Kerouac published "The Vanishing American Hobo" in *Holiday,* he pessimistically views the hobo as gone forever. At the heart of the essay, written with the (uncredited) help of Allen Ginsberg, Peter Orlovsky, and Gregory Corso, is the rapid decay of America.[36] The great "raw body of America" that Kerouac celebrates in *On the Road* has been under surveillance, and those who step outside the norm are prodded by a police state until they give up their perceived outlaw ways. The hobo, in its ghostlike form, exemplifies an America that has disappeared. Kerouac is relegated to a nostalgic mythologizing of the hobo figure that has already disappeared from the American landscape. It is this depoliticized view of the hobo that still reverberates. A more complicated examination of Kerouac's view of the hobo—a view distinctly intertwined with nostalgic ideas of a mythical American manhood—allows us to understand a general way that hobo in the present day is understood.

## KEROUAC'S NOSTALGIC VIEW OF THE HOBO

With Dean and Sal always willing to push themselves and their cars to the breaking point, it seems inevitable that *On the Road* would be seen as celebrating car culture. But while the automobile is often a conduit for their restless wanderings across the United States and Mexico, there was, in fact, much ambivalence on Kerouac's part toward the car and a more wistful nostalgic longing for the train. This ambivalence that Kerouac felt toward the automobile is undergirded by the fact that Sal hates to drive, and he is very rarely behind the steering wheels of the cars he finds himself in. This is Dean's responsibility, and Sal relegates this authority, "driving" the story only later when he is in front of his typewriter. If the car represented the future, Kerouac is yearning for a mythical American past.

The automobiles in *On the Road* get Sal and Dean to places, but they do so with America flying by in a blur as Dean "balls" the motor, exhausting (and usually damaging) one car before quickly abandoning it for an interchangeable one. Much like the women in the novel, the cars are afterthoughts, used for their own selfish pleasures before being discarded. Subjected to their male gaze, there is no authentic connection to the actual automobiles. This can be seen in a passage from *Visions of Cody*, a book that parallels the narrative of *On the Road* but is told in a more graphic, personal way. Here Kerouac, in one of the few moments we see him sitting behind a steering wheel, responds to the standardization of geographic areas across the United States as a result of the growth of the highway-motor complex—the standardization that Dean in *On the Road* embraces. Kerouac writes of driving into a town:

> Mainly, though, this is, a sad *white* outside-of-town intersection open-spaced, stuccoed like buildings on Arapahoe Street in Cody's Denver, this is the openspace whiteness which is always situated *exactly halfway* between the country and downtown, so that when you come in to a new city you always have to cross snowy suburban intersections like this—I've seen a building, originally redbrick one-story warehouse, located exactly at this halfway spot between the highways of the land and the dense buildings downtown and it was painted white but had failed and the red-brick showed through—to make a startling sight in all the pure hotdog roadstand and motel whiteness and in fact the gravel is almost white in these nameless districts of USA.[37]

In this "halfway spot" (reminiscent of the "dividing line" between the East of his youth and the West of his future), it is the whiteness that Kerouac laments here, both with its ideological racialized implications and its literal reality: the actual painting over the vibrancy of a red brick building with a standard white sameness. Kerouac reveals his affinity for the old, the supposedly replaceable, the purposely forgotten and carelessly relegated, and in a beautiful metaphor shows how that which is replaced never fully disappears. The ghost of the brick remains, bleeding back through the paint.

The hobo holds the same resonant quality for Kerouac as this redness from the brick wall: both enter within the text as a reminder of the past onto which he wants to hold. For an author who wrote the novels of the Duluoz Legend to capture his personal, cultural, and imagined history, Kerouac uses the hobo to offer a way back into his own and America's past. And just as he does with the Duluoz Legend, Kerouac takes a history (the hobo subculture) and elevates it to epic proportions.[38] Locating Dean's hobo father, therefore, becomes an overarching quest for their travels. The hobos on the South Pacific train that he sees out of his motel room window become nothing less than an idyllic vision of paradise. And the Ghost of the Susquehanna is not just a poor, disoriented homeless man but a visionary, a seeker of the truth. The hobo—and the constant mentions of railroading throughout *On the Road*—is part of the legend that Kerouac creates. It is a vision that contains no mention of work, no desire for community. The hobos are all ghostlike in the ways that they are part of the present but in a translucent, amorphous way.

It is no surprise that in *On the Road*, the "greatest ride" of Sal's life is found not in one of Dean's stolen cars but rather in the back of a truck that has more in common with a boxcar than an automobile. It is Sal's first foray into the West, and he gets a ride on an empty flatbed truck in Nebraska, making it all the way to Cheyenne, Wyoming. Although Sal is riding in a truck, Kerouac describes it as "riding a railroad train, just as steady and just as straight." Here, he also meets a "thirty-year-old hobo," Mississippi Gene, whose clothes are black from the soot of the railroads. The hobo is a fatherly figure and has a "charge," a young boy who is also riding the rails because he is trying to escape trouble. As opposed to the other "boys" in the flatbed, Mississippi Gene is a dynamic figure, one who has "buddhistic" qualities. The hobo embodies the "wise and tired old Negro" and is described as a mystical guiding figure for Sal in this scene; never really known (he is quiet and serene), but Gene assists Sal as "the verdant farmfields of the Platte began to disappear," helping him understand land that he has never encountered. Having prophetic qualities, Gene also gives mysterious advice about places that Sal should see, where "most of the boys pass thru and always meet there." When he sings a simple hobo song, Sal's love for the man grows. This boxcar journey—albeit in the back of a flatbed truck—is an important moment for Sal. And because the journey has just begun, as opposed to his experience with the Ghost of the Susquehanna when he was at the end of a trip, he is open to the hobo's words.[39]

Mississippi Gene is based on a man whom Kerouac never met but was told stories about when he was a resident in a psychiatric ward. While being evaluated in a naval hospital, Kerouac met William Holmes Hubbard, nicknamed Big Slim, a gregarious part-time oil worker who had hoboed for most of his life.[40] Slim mischievously told Kerouac that they should use the hospital's butter knives to "break the locks and hop freights to Butte, Montana, to meet another hobo buddy, Mississippi Gene."[41] While they never did, as Kerouac spins the tale in *On the Road*, he conjures up the old, wise hobo as a spiritual guide, blessing his journey as he is introduced to the West. The beauty of the ride in this scene is sharply contrasted with the ugliness of the next scene, when Sal leaves Mississippi Gene and heads to the bars in Cheyenne. It is Wild West week, and when Sal hops down from his ride, he finds himself in a simulation of the West, with fat, sweaty tourists in absurd outfits pushing past him and firing blank pistols in the air. The bourgeois are impotent, the West is inauthentic, and, unlike Mississippi Gene, the bars hold no enlightenment. The West that Kerouac conjures cannot be found in the simulated West of Cheyenne; while both are invented simulacrums, they do not mesh, and after such promise at the beginning of his journey, Sal eventually heads back east to his mother's house.

In the former scene, though, Mississippi Gene is an anachronistic figure quite different from the other boys on the flatbed. Kerouac elevates Mississippi Gene to a type of otherworldly character, where his hobo qualities are intertwined with his buddhistic essence. The truck becomes a train, and the homeless man becomes a mystic. Although Mississippi Gene has a link to the marginalized transient America that Sal romantically idolizes, Kerouac elevates the hobo from a historical rendering and instead creates a new figure. Mississippi Gene emerges from an identifiable hobo caricature but is transformed into something familiar but otherworldly: a ghost.

## HARRY PARTCH, NOSTALGIA, AND HOBO CONFABULATIONS

Kerouac's hobos are mystic figures with no political corpus. The Ghost of the Susquehanna, Mississippi Gene, and Kerouac's other hobos have helped transform representations of the hobo from political actors on the margins of society into ghostly, apolitical caricatures. Seemingly not part of any class and emptied of historical realities, in Kerouac's hands they are mystics, individually roaming the United States. The closest comparison of this type of hobo figure can be found not within the pages of a novel but in the words and music of Harry Partch, an experimental composer who, like Kerouac, created ghostlike hobo characters that led to a state of lostness. Particularly, Partch's *U.S. Highball*, the "first underground masterpiece in American music," is aligned with the hobo motif of *On the Road*. The twenty-six-minute composition is a "hobo confabulation" in which Partch relies heavily on his own hobo experiences traveling from 1935 to 1941 throughout the United States, lyrically rendering his diary reminisces to shape his hobo figure.

Much like Kerouac's hobos, Partch's figures, rooted in authentic experiences, are symbolically changed. First written in 1943 and rewritten in 1955, *U.S. Highball* is an aural montage in which dissonant sounds disrupt the chronological progression of the protagonist, Slim, who is leaving California and hoboing his way to Chicago. Slim's narrative interactions with other hobos and his bawdy and sometimes playful observations, though, are distorted by the particular compositional method. *U.S. Highball* is composed of short sections ("songs") made up of "verses" that are initially played before being repeated, although with different tonal groupings.[42] The tone of the repeated sections change, often becoming tenser, as the music places the words in unfamiliar context. This is similar to Kerouac's own prose style, in which he repeatedly writes of, for example, his experiences with the Ghost of the Susquehanna over the course of multiple books, but with each rendering, slightly changing the figure to fit a particular mood. Another example is in his beautiful stream-of-consciousness short story, "October in the Railroad Earth," wherein the rhythm of the long, ungrammatical sentences that often roll on for pages at a time are driven by the industrial staccato beat of freight trains. The sentences' formal structure and the story's ideas are cyclical, and, through the repetition, meaning continually builds.[43]

In Partch's hands, the familiar names of cities and towns often take on an ominous feel; for others, the alliteration and the multiplicity of the composition makes unknown cities seemingly familiar. The hobo is moving from one geographic area to another, but Slim, and the listener, becomes lost as the world disappears and the places passing by become otherworldly. Partch, who had previously written about the hobo at greater length in "Bitter Music," a journal he kept during the mid-1930s, acknowledges the temporal and geographic discordance of *U.S. Highball*, stating that "the strictly literal time and place of its concept form merely the flight deck for what follows."[44] The verses of the songs are snatches of conversation that Partch wrote down verbatim while he was on the road, but the composition loses the quality of a transcript of authentic hobo life. Instead, an imaginary hobo appears like a ghost through the musical intonations. Geographic locations start shimmering; the places are somewhat familiar but just slightly off: instead of California or Chicago, the singers (mis)pronounce the words—Californiel, Chi (pause) cago—before singing them again in a slightly varied way. There is mistiness to the words sung throughout the composition, and, as a listener, it is impossible to separate the snippets of the hobo conversation that Partch copied down in his notebooks from his artistic manipulations of them. Kerouac often used this methodology as well. Late in his life, he composed a song titled "The Midnight Ghost," which he recorded on his home tape recorder. The song is a reminiscence of a freight train ride he took from San Francisco to Los Angeles. Kerouac makes poetry of the names of the towns that he passed, eventually inventing new names and new towns, relying on sounds to create meaning.[45]

Like Kerouac's hobos, Partch's confabulation creates the false memory of a realized recent past with the (anti)epic quality that the hobos embody. The narrative shape disappears throughout the composition, and the aural montage of nonlinear conversations and haphazard geographic markers leaves an impression of lostness: Slim does not exist in any place but, like a ghost, appears and disappears throughout the United States. Slim is divided into "imaginary selves" that do not speak to the cultural and political heritage of the hobo but rather to the musicality that the language intones. As Partch explains, "A peculiar introspective intensity, a peculiar humor, a peculiar drama, and a peculiar urgency . . . integrates and intensifies the fragments of word thoughts, remarks, and signs into an account."[46]

For Partch, this account lends itself to a particular strand of American music. Slim, like the Ghost of the Susquehanna, like Old Dean Moriarty, like the hundreds of hobos riding on a South Pacific freight passing Sal's window, does not have a particular corporal history but is a ghost that haunts the present.

While *U.S. Highball* might be "unique in twentieth-century music," and *On the Road* was heralded as birthing a unique "bop prose," part of their artistic experimentation removed the hobo from a cultural history that had a distinct working-class, train-centered materiality, offering instead ontologically lost, individualized figures.[47] Like Dos Passos, there is a focus on hobos, movement, and language, but while Dos Passos's *U.S.A.* trilogy insists that the hobo's words would move others to resist the state, in Kerouac's hands, the hobo lives in a stateless existence. Kerouac's and Partch's manipulations of their respective travel memories have created hobo confabulations that are symbolically rich but lack political agency. Kerouac's hobos' individualism, their mystic qualities, and their lack of recognizable working-class history point to the hobo not as a resisting figure but as a spectral one.

## GHOSTS, INDIVIDUALISM, AND MALE POWER

Far from being radical, these spectral figures are lost father figures that conjure a mythical American manhood. Kerouac's anticonsumerist stance can and should be read as politically motivated in a postwar moment that closed itself off in tightly guarded suburbs. But just as important, this stance should be understood as individually motivated: Kerouac is concerned with singular utterances, not collective refusals.

Scholars, and the Beats themselves, however, attempt to collectivize Kerouac's individualism within a generational movement. Jason Spangler interrelates Kerouac's *On the Road* with John Steinbeck's *The Grapes of Wrath*, attempting to show that the former has deep roots in the latter and that both works collectivize the resistance of the characters into a type of humanist politics. For Spangler, Dean and Sal's traversing the United States taps into the "shared cultural trauma" of the Great Depression, and throughout the novel they "encounter people who serve as the walking scars of America's struggle through the 1930s." As the economic boom enveloped the United States after World War II, creating a type of national cultural amnesia, *On the Road* reminds readers that "the remnants of the 1930s still exist." Constructing a link between Steinbeck's Oakies and Kerouac's hobos, Spangler suggests that both Steinbeck's and Kerouac's novels are political in the sense that both advocate for a shared "universal soul" that can heal the fractured nation—be it in the Great Depression or the Cold War.[48]

Putting aside what I feel is a significant misreading of Steinbeck's novel, Spangler is correct that the haunted specter of the Great Depression certainly does weave itself through the novel. But unlike the overt working-class solidarity performed in Tom Joad's famous "I'll be there" speech to his mother that destabilizes the individual in favor of a collective response to the Great Depression, Kerouac's characters favor the individual as *separated* from the collective. Contrary to Spangler's view, Dean did not "embrace collectivity"; rather, through his magnetic personality and manipulative ways, Dean, like Sal, used people for his own personal satisfaction.[49] This is true for Kerouac's writing style, as well—while he was orbiting within a milieu of writers and artists, the term *Beat Generation* is a misnomer; Kerouac was not part of a collective but an individual following after the "mad ones," writing down what he saw and heard, reconfiguring the details to create his own personal Duluoz myth.

Instead of categorizing Kerouac's politics within an ambiguous spiritual "universal soul," Mary Paniccia Carden reads *On the Road* more specifically in terms of a gendered politics "that evades the restrictions of a bourgeois-driven patriarchal culture without abandoning traditional patriarchal prerogatives of male power." In this way, Dean and Sal are still read as rejecting the materialism that is one of the tenets of capitalism and the American Dream. But this materialistic rejection is framed within a paradigm of traditional, white male narratives of self-determination and conquest that ultimately do not reject the society they are traveling through but selfishly manipulate it among gendered and racial lines. By devaluing normalized capitalist success stories in *On the Road*, Kerouac advocates for a consumption-based ethos (cars, women, racialized others) that manifests itself as an attempted authentic expression of American manhood. The voracious consumption is celebrated and seemingly without cost. Dean is not rejecting a free market system; he is employing it, selling his good looks and compelling personality for sex, cars, and drugs. As Carden explains, "Cassady glories in his unlimited and unsanctioned consumption of the ultimate icons of capitalist economy based on male dominance—cars and women."[50] As a poor, white, uneducated male from a dysfunctional family, Dean takes an alternative route to achieve his "success" in a capitalist economy. Rejecting bourgeois marriage and financial responsibility, Dean renews an American manhood that, according to Sal, "offers a new call and . . . a new horizon."[51] For these wanderers, it is a manhood that needed to be repaired.

While Dean's hobo father is missing and the search for him is tangentially what keeps them on the road, Kerouac's loss of a father figure also greatly impacts his road life. The opening line of the *On the Road: The Original Scroll* conjures a lost father: "I first met Neal not long after my father died. . . . I had just gotten over a serious illness that I won't get into except that it really had something to do with my father's death and my awful feeling that everything was dead."[52] But while Kerouac sees this replacing of missing or dead fathers as a renewal that employs a homoerotic brotherhood of sexually liberated males joining together to alleviate the strain of "wives and woes," the new American manhood celebrates a selfish, individualized consumption that, far from being a desire for a "universal soul," is not even collectivized along lines of masculine solidarity.[53] Toward the end of the novel, as Dean steals a few dollars from an infirm Sal and leaves him alone in Mexico while heading back to the United States to unite with a bride-to-be, the individualized, hyperkinetic, consumerist indulging continues unabated.

If we return to the Ghost of the Susquehanna and the other hobo characters who haunt *On the Road*, we see a different form of American masculinity that, unlike Dean's "new horizon" of the American male, bridges Sal to a mythical, lost American manhood. The missing or dead white male father figures becomes a ghost that haunts the characters, and Kerouac slides this paternal loss of an idealized fictional manhood into the ragged figure of the hobo. Kerouac transforms this father figure into a spectral guide who offers a path to a timeless, ecstatic state of being. It is, though, a path that Sal ultimately cannot accept. Kerouac's own father was a Franco-American printer grounded in an ethnic working-class community and, as much as he displaces the working-class lineage in the hobo figures he conjures, Kerouac cannot follow them to an ecstatic state. As Justin Trudeau writes, "This is a point that Kerouac returns to throughout the novel, as the lesson of the ghost won't go away because neither Jack nor Neal is able to successfully cross the bridge out of their bodily inheritance."[54] Kerouac was neither able to embrace the ghost and cross the bridge to "eternal ecstasy" nor able to break the embrace of the spectral haunting of white, patriarchal capitalism. While he rejects its materialism, his travels are paved by patriarchal entitlements of white, male power.

In the preface to *Big Sur*, Kerouac writes, "In my old age I intend to collect all my work and re-insert my pantheon of uniform names, leave the long shelf of books there, and die happy."[55] The corpus of these autobiographical texts, which he labeled the "Duluoz Legend" (perhaps itself a ghost haunting a bookstore in St. Petersburg, Florida), offers insight into a literary life within a postwar America that had transformed itself from the poverty of the Great Depression to a robust national economy, from a country in love with trains to one in love with cars.[56] Kerouac uses the hobo figure to epitomize the spectral aspects of these earlier times in the present moment, but the figure ultimately is about the individual and not about a collectivized generation. Far from being seen as a member of an army of tramps who were to be eradicated one arsenic-laced pie at a time, Kerouac's hobos are apolitical individuals. Perfect as spiritual guides, they are disconnected from the working class. In Kerouac's America, the boxcars are still shuttling around the country, but they are filled with ghosts.

# AFTERWORD

## The End of Boxcar Politics

The cultural historian Mark Wyman appropriates the scientific term *symbiosis* to describe the special relationship between the hobo and the railroads in which "two dissimilar organisms [form] an intimate association that is necessary for the survival of each." The railroads were essential to the agricultural health of the United States, and hobos allowed for this health to blossom. Without railroads crops would not get to the supermarkets in distant cities and towns of the United States, but without hobos those crops would never have made it onto the railroads in the first place. But the health of both declined as the trucking conglomeration siphoned off much of the hauling business from the railroads and the "gasoline tramps" began replacing hobos in the fields.[1]

As Jack Kerouac was developing his Ghost of the Susquehanna figure in the middle of the twentieth century, the hobo in popular culture was already becoming a nostalgic entity. Hobos were still being employed in literature—even in radical texts—but, just like in *On the Road*, they were mostly disconnected from a distinct working-class lineage. For example, Alfred Maund's *The Big Boxcar*, published the same year that Viking accepted *On the Road*, utilizes the hobo motif and contains plenty of boxcars and train hopping within its pages. Maund, a southern Marxist writer active in labor and civil rights movements, does not tie, however, his hobos (male and female, white and black) to a working-class tradition; instead, he uses the train as a metaphor for a country rumbling toward a troubling future in Cold War America. Maund's hobos are not looking for jobs; they are looking to escape.

By the time Kerouac and Maund were writing, the symbiosis between the hobo and the train was in a fractured state, and the relationship between the hobo and the floating proletariat subculture was mostly severed. The car was the primary mover of the nation, the railroad was a shell of its former self, and the hobo was considered by many to have disappeared. This death of the hobo was prophesied early on; in the 1920s Fred Cummings, a representative of Colorado beet farmers, articulating a desperate need for relaxed immigration laws, stated to a senatorial committee that the hobo was simply "gone."[2] While Cummings was pleading for laws that would allow for the influx of cheap labor (at the expense of union labor), by the 1950s, when Kerouac was frantically traveling throughout the United States in one rundown car after another, the hobo, like the train, belonged to a different era.

## THE RISE OF THE CAR

After suffering from constant police and neighborhood surveillance, Kerouac realized he had to give up his hobo ways "around 1956."[3] Two events might have helped him come to this conclusion. First, in that year Viking finally accepted *On the Road* (although it was not published until 1957), bringing the Beat Generation officially into the national spotlight.[4] While this outward interest had serious negative consequences for Kerouac's own writing capability, it also birthed numerous admirers eager to mimic Sal and his friends' cross-country trips by hopping into their own cars and traveling on the open road. These roads would be easier to find because the second event, the signing of the Federal Aid Highway Act of 1956 by Dwight Eisenhower, would create a forty-one-thousand-mile interstate highway system, the largest public works project up to that time in the United States. Paul Boyer, a cultural historian, states that this defining act "reshaped American life and brought Americans' love affair with the automobile to its pinnacle of besotted infatuation."[5] The automobile, a symbol of potential freedom for the nation gripped in the

Cold War era of automated realties, "served to lessen the rather harsh realities of a competitive capitalist system with its class structure, repetition, dehumanization, and repressive impulses."[6] In essence, then, while *On the Road* has been seen as a countercultural novel that spawned beatniks, it also celebrated a car culture that was very much in line with normalized American values. Car culture allowed us to become, to use Cotton Seiler's terminology, a "republic of drivers," but it was a republic that celebrated individual movements rather than shared rides.[7]

In the 1950s stock imagery of the car on an unending road was like the train in John Gast's iconoclastic painting, *American Progress;* both were popular objects that symbolized the nation's evolution. A Ford advertisement from 1951 exemplifies this belief: "Today the American Road has no end; the road that went nowhere now goes everywhere. . . . The wheels move on endlessly, always moving, always forward—and always lengthening the American Road."[8] As the ad covertly shows, there is a symbiotic relationship between the car and the state. The car that represents freedom is able to stay in motion only because of government-funded roads; more "freedom" (more miles on a car's odometer) experienced by more drivers will consequently result in more roads being built. As Phil Patton writes, "The automobile and its highway froze the values of the frontier by making movement a permanent state of mind, turning migration into circulation."[9] Dean and Sal's circuitous rides, looked at from this perspective, were part of a 1950s-style manifest destiny to pave the frontier in concrete and asphalt, settling the wild roads and stabilizing them for the family sedans that soon would be following their paths.

If the highway, as Jeff Brouws, Bernd Polster, and Phil Patton describe it, is the "nervous system of the body politic, the body economic, the body cultural," than the Federal Aid Highway Act of 1956 speaks to a type of standardized care in place to regulate the American body.[10] Fast food restaurants homogenized their architecture to reassure drivers that the places where they were eating on the sides of the highways were the same ones they knew in their own towns. Shopping malls with similar layouts sprouted outside of city centers, shifting commerce from central business districts to outlying areas. Suburbs, with their quickly built, uniform floor plans, sprang up, and, as Jane Holtz Kay states, the "asphalt exodus" brought capital and mobility from city centers to racially homogeneous neighboring communities. Photography and films, although occasionally revealing the dangers of travel, mostly used standard shots celebrating American freedom and mobility. Tellingly, in *On the Road* Dean, the supposed symbol of anticonformity, embraces this standardization, stating, "We know America, we're at home; I can go anywhere and get what I want because it's the same in every corner."[11] While his actions might befit a "Holy Goof," he knows that his goofing will be performed in similar places throughout the United States.

This connection between the automobile, government, and business is best expressed by George Humphrey, Eisenhower's secretary of treasury, who explicitly articulates the central importance of the automobile in American life, stating, "America lives on wheels, and we have . . . to keep America living on wheels and keep the kind and form of life we want."[12] What Humphrey's statement, Eisenhower's national commitment to highway building, and Kerouac's culturally significant car-themed freedom cemented in the 1950s was a national embrace of the automobile and, consequently, a rejection of the railroad. Humphrey's statement was not just political bombast: the particular "wheels" that would produce a specific "form of life" were found on the automobile, and that significantly changed the daily lives of many U.S. citizens.[13] Clearly reminiscent of the rhetoric of railroad promoters in the late nineteenth century, by the time Kerouac leaves the Ghost of the Susquehanna on the side of the road, it is the car that is heralded as the fundamental technological advancement that will (again) change the United States.

By the last year of the nineteenth century, there were 2,500 cars being produced by thirty U.S. companies; ten years later there were almost a half million.[14] In 1914, with few roads paved well enough for an automobile to travel on, over a million Americans owned motor cars—even though fewer than half a million Americans earned enough money to pay federal income taxes. The car was a symbol that was a "more impressive piece of machinery than a radio, more personal in its impact than a skyscraper or dynamo, and certainly more tangible than electricity."[15] Building on this interest, the 1920s saw a huge demand by the car-buying public and record profits for the automobile industrial complex that consolidated the steel, glass, and petroleum industries, a major factor of the booming decade.[16] And although the years of the Great Depression might be viscerally remembered through the prism of broken-down jalopies packed with families' possessions in John Steinbeck's *The Grapes of Wrath*, these automobiles offered a way off their repossessed farms: revenues from state fuel taxes increased exponentially from 1929 to 1932, while other state tax revenues were dramatically reduced.[17]

By the time Sal was traveling with Dean in the 1940s, the country's first superhighway, the Pennsylvania Turnpike, had opened, ushering in the new decade. People wanted cars, and senators found themselves demanding numerous "road bills" to pass through Congress. Although production was severely halted during the war, when World War II ended and the Beat Generation was discussing their "movement" in newspaper articles, prime-time talk shows, and literary magazines, the demand for cars reached a fever pitch.[18] Detroit's automobile giants were making record profits, and the car was king.

## THE DECLINE OF THE RAILROAD

While the car grew in popularity over many decades, with a metamorphic ascension in the wake of World War II, the railroad was declining in an equally long and sharp trajectory. In 1932 Senator James Couzens stated, "Our railroads . . . fulfilled a great purpose, but if we had no railroads today, we never would think it necessary to build them."[19] In love with automobiles, the country was turning its back on the train, as the railroad, which was the pinnacle of technological invention in the late nineteenth century, was seen as archaic by the time Kerouac was traveling throughout the United States. The railroads were America's first big business and were the main player in altering the United States from an agrarian nation to an international commercial power; yet by the time President Wilson commandeered the railroads in 1917 for the war effort, the industry was a shell of itself. Although World War II was financially lucrative for the industry, and railroads were responsible for moving most of the passengers and freight for the wartime effort, when GIs returned from the war, many were excited to buy their own automobiles to travel around, rather than wait at a station for a train.[20]

Railroads, perhaps the greatest symbol of capitalist expansion in the United States, were also the poster child for corporate greed; the owners of the companies were, after all, labeled "robber barons" for a reason. As the new megabusinesses of the highway-motor complex grew, the railroads became a prime target of the popular press. The main point of contention centered on a populist-driven idea of "freedom" that the car (supposedly) offered, and this was in direct opposition to the "oppressive" nature of the railroad.

This selling of freedom is at the heart of a Chevrolet ad from 1924 that equates the driver of an automobile with the head of a railroad company: "Every owner is, in effect, a railroad president, operating individually on an elective schedule. . . . The once poor laborer . . . is now a capitalist."[21] Invoking the American Dream and building on the populist sentiment of the time, advertisers wanted American consumers to believe that buying an automobile was a tangible way to strike back at the railroads, thereby, as Edith Wharton stated, "freeing us from the compulsions and contacts of the railway, the bondage to fixed hours and beaten track."[22] Thomas MacDonald, the president of the Federal Bureau of Public Roads, also used this populist rhetoric when trying to gain support for a roads bill, stating that public roads were an inalienable human right, while private rails were a privilege based on fare. The car, although securely enmeshed in the highway-motor complex, was seen as an individualized antidote to the greedy capitalists of the railroads. Case in point: while the railroads aided the North in defeating the South, thus preserving the Union, according to MacDonald, "The intersectional misunderstanding which gave rise to [the Civil War] could not have reached the critical stage of war had it been possible as it is now for the Southern planter to spend his summer in Maine and the New England businessman to journey southward in his own car for . . . a winter vacation in Florida."[23] According to this class- and race-based logic, the North won because of the railroad, but the war would never have been fought if the car had been invented sooner.

Just as the railroads were believed to bring forth progressive changes to the United States in the nineteenth century, in the twentieth century faith in the automobile was seemingly limitless. Railroads were linear, and one had to be beholden to the machine, with its schedule and iron roads taking the passenger to particular places. In contrast, the car offered innumerable possibilities limited only by the drivers' imaginations.

## THE HOBO DISAPPEARS

The rise of the automobile and the decline of the railroad marked a seismic shift in the way the country—both its people and its freight—moved throughout the United States. The effects of this change would be felt in myriad sectors throughout the country, including the hobo population. In the late nineteenth century, when the railroad consolidated the agribusiness of the United States, the marginalized hobo was both a consequence of, and a resistance to, the rise of finance capitalism. But the decline of the railroad, and the factors that contributed to this decline, also marked the waning of the subculture.

After World War II there was a major shift in the labor markets, as farm wages fell much lower than industrial wages—hobos who often would winter in cities on stakes they made through the rest of the year found themselves settling down in those cities and finding continuous employment. Other hobos who traveled around the country discovered by the mid 1920s that a "new class" of rubber tramps were taking their jobs because foremen wanted local people who could drive to and from work.[24] Fredrick Mills stated that it was "impossible to hobo in peace" in the second decade of the twentieth century because of the number of cars being used by itinerants to get to their next job.[25] At this juncture there was also a seismic ethnic and racial switch in laborers, as Mexicans became the fastest-growing group of migrant workers; from 1910 to 1930, a total of 750,000 Mexicans entered the American labor market.[26] Having their own cultural practices, many of these foreign-born laborers did not ride trains to get to their jobs. By the time American soldiers returned home from the war, it was nonnative, migrant workers who traveled by car and not by train who were seen as essential to the agricultural health of the nation. Time and technology was passing the hobo by.

Although the "poor laborer" of the aforementioned Chevrolet ad might not ever become a railroad president as the glossy advertisement proclaimed, an inexpensive car might help him receive a fruit-picking job ahead of the hobo hopping off a train. But even if the hobo had been able to get to a farm before his rival "rubber tramp," as agribusiness became more mechanized, there were fewer jobs to be had, and, consequently, many hobos left the road and stayed in cities, picking up factory jobs. By the 1940s the farm-laboring population was in deep decline.[27]

The shift in labor also solidified the out-of-placeness of the hobo; while the hobo was always a marginalized figure in labor politics, working-class issues "became associated with this particular historical and geographic juncture: urban, heavy industry, male bread winners." After the suppression of the Industrial Workers of the World devastated its rank and file along with its leadership, the hobo lost its main political champion. Hobos, whose identities were connected to being both laborers and rail riders, did not fit into labor negotiations. And while it may be true that, as Frank Tobias Higbie writes, "the fate of capitalism was challenged more by the intellectual hobo than by the working-class tough or the degraded floating laborer," the hobo by the middle of the twentieth century had mostly disappeared.[28] Wyman states that "fifty years earlier the appearance of the steam locomotive had marked the close of the pioneer epoch and launched the second period of western history, now the internal combustion engine, with its automobile and tractor offspring, signaled that another new era was aborning."[29] Like Kerouac's Ghost of the Susquehanna, the hobo was left in the exhaust of the passing automobile.

## THE END OF THE HOBO EPOCH . . . BUT THE TRAIN HOPPER LIVES ON

With the introduction of the transcontinental railroad in the 1860s, the train was heralded as a premier symbol of technological advancement, but by the middle of the twentieth century, accentuated by Eisenhower's Federal Aid Highway Act of 1956, the symbol was tarnished. By the 1970s the rail infrastructure in the United States was in disrepair and the train an anachronistic afterthought. As high-speed rails and aerodynamic trains make the front pages of newspapers in the present day, the nineteenth-century image of the train—huge, powerful, lumbering—is relegated to a previous era whose transportation, and implementation of capitalism, has been dismissed for a sleeker model.

This does not mean, however, that there are not people in the present day sneaking on trains in the middle of the night, making their way across the country. But these train hoppers are enacting a different form of politics than the hobos discussed within the pages of this study. When the hobo is mentioned in the present day, most often nostalgic imagery is invoked, complete with a handkerchief bindle and long, white beard—and not the image of the working-class transient worker.

The impending death of the "authentic" hobo has been a constant in most rail-riding memoirs, with each generation of riders proclaiming the subculture to be in the throes of taking its last breath. For example, in the

1940s Ben Benson, who had been traveling since 1898 and who wrote a book about a hobo trip in which he traveled from coast to coast with less than a dollar in his pockets, wrote in the *Hobo News* a message to young men (and only men) thinking about living their life on the road: "If this was the beginning of the century I was talking to you boys: I would advise you all to hit the road. But, I regret to say, 'Them days are gone forever!'" For Benson, who believed that traveling the rails for a few years made boys become well-rounded men, this particular rite of passage, in his opinion, was lost forever in the United States.[30]

With each new decade, however, the hobo is raised from the grave only to be proclaimed, once again, moribund. This is especially true if we examine the texts written in the past thirty years. In 1993 Dale Maharidge's book, titled *The Last Great American Hobo*, pronounced that Montana Blackie was the last of the dying breed. Three years later Jacqueline Schmidt, after spending time with older hobos, proclaimed in the title of her memoir that the subculture was "done and been." Ted Conover, a journalist who in the early 1980s hopped trains with hobos around the United States, wrote in the preface to the 2001 edition to *Rolling Nowhere* that in the twenty years since the recording of his book, "the world of hoboes with road names who cooked in jungles with 'gunboats' (coffee cans) is a thing of the past." The life histories of older hobos recorded in 2003 in Cliff Williams's *One More Train to Ride* are primarily remembrances of a vibrant subculture. This feeling of loss is a recurring sentiment in *Riding toward Everywhere*, William T. Vollman's 2008 memoir of his failed search at finding the hobo archetype in the train yards and boxcars of a post-9/11 America.[31]

All these books have at their core older white males described as the last holdovers from a previous era. Even Eddy Joe Cotton's 2002 memoir, *Hobo*, although subtitled "A Young Man's Thoughts on Trains and Tramping in America," has an older hobo, Alabama, featured prominently in the book. A surrogate for Cotton's own absent father (the book is reminiscent of *On the Road* on many levels), the older man speaks of the hobo lifestyle as belonging to a bygone era in which he is one of the few remaining of a subculture in decline. Cotton, hopping trains for the first time at the turn of the twenty-first century, listens attentively to the stories of the older hobo. In one particular scene, Alabama is frustrated when he arrives at a jungle that he has been using sporadically over many years and finds that other rail riders have not properly maintained it. Shaking his head sadly, he states, "It ain't what it used to be."[32] In *Hobo*, a misogynistic road diary in which the author finds his place in America by participating in alcohol-induced sexual adventures, Cotton justifies his own road trips by linking his present movements to a defined past that has been already memorialized within the United States. Alabama's long hobo résumé and his acceptance of the young author allow Cotton to place himself in a mythical, historical lineage. He can use the paternalistic advice of the older man to underwrite his own personal travel narrative.

In these texts detailing the impending death of the hobo, Maharidge, Schmidt, Williams, Vollman, and Cotton lament the loss of a white, male, outsider subculture.[33] By proclaiming the death of the hobo, these writers are molding the individuals whom they highlight to fit recognizable vagabondage narratives that coalesce into culturally acceptable norms of white American masculinity. Anyone who does not fit in these recognizable caricatures, whether because of race or gender, is sidelined in the narrative.[34] Although the poverty that the particular riders endure is certainly noted and, like many observations of homeless people, fetishized, the lives of these men who can tolerate life on the margins of society are folded into American exceptionalist travel narratives that reveal more about a cultural desire to memorialize the past than to speak to the present. With this memorializing there is a shaving of the complex past of the hobo subculture and a smoothing of the thorny exterior of the hobo into an identifiable, likeable character: they are older, white, unemployed, apolitical males who are the "last" of a dying breed.

The death of the "last" hobo is, however, not the end of the rail-riding subculture or the train. In 2010 trains transported more than 200 billion tons of freight across the United States (and Canada), and improvements have slowly been made to the rail infrastructure in the United States.[35] There are also current-day rail riders, sometimes labeled *gutterpunks* or *crusties*, presently making their way across the United States in the recesses of boxcars. Some of these riders are like Jessica Hahn, who found a welcoming, although ultimately destructive, community of fellow train riders when traveling the United States in the 1990s. Others, such as Sascha DuBrul, are self-labeled anarchists consciously using train hopping to foster TAZ-like movements throughout the country in the twenty-first century. Others are like Michael Brody, who in 2013 published a celebratory photography book on train hoppers titled *A Period of Juvenile Prosperity*, or like Daniel Skaggs, whose film *Freeload* is a contemplative reflection of his years hopping trains. Still others are like Christopher Artis and Medeana Hendershot, who died in Lakeland, Florida, in 2011, when they were crushed in the coal car in which they were traveling. They were rail riders because they liked the romanticized freedom associated with the train-hopping subculture.[36] The present-day train-hopping scene existing among riders, trains, and the large rail-riding subculture is a complex set of negotiated interactions performed during a cultural moment very different from the interactions that existed among hobos in the late nineteenth and early twentieth century outlined in *Boxcar Politics*. These new rail riders' relationship to work and to the working class has changed, just as notions of the working class itself have evolved in this period of late capitalism.[37] A sophisticated interpretative methodology is needed as contemporary scholars begin to analyze the current rail-riding subculture and the politics of train hopping in the twenty-first century. To understand the present-day moment, though, it behooves scholars to examine the politics of train hoppers in light of the past.

At the end of the nineteenth century, hobos were seen as members of a thieving army infiltrating cities and towns, and harsh "tramp" laws were consequently enacted so that the transients' movements could be curtailed. Examining hobo memoirs at the turn of the twenty-first century, this attempt to stop them has been successful as all but a few have disappeared. The older men who remain are lauded for their survivalist capabilities and placed into acceptable narratives of white masculinity. What this study of the political nature of hopping trains from the introduction of the transcontinental railroad to the Federal Aid Highway Act of 1956 shows is that the accepted narrative of the hobo leaves out a complex history of negotiated interactions among a vibrant, transient working-class subculture that does not fit neatly into these caricatures.

The simple fact that scholars are still debating whether or not the hobo belongs in the working class is a perfect illustration of the way the hobo—as opposed to, for example, the factory worker—has been depoliticized.[38] The hobos found throughout the United States over a century ago were a multifaceted community that created hobo spaces in boxcars, expressing counterhegemonic, resistive lifestyles to the alienating effects of capitalism as embodied by the railroad. By exploring lived and theoretical communal relationships formed within the boxcars by these transient workers, a far more diverse and complicated working-class figure emerges. Although marginalized in the social and political history of working-class literature, in the flesh, they were an integral part of the political economy of the United States, and their labor was instrumental as the country transitioned from an agricultural-based society to an industrial one. As a figure, read through the lens of subcultural theory, these mobile transient workers offer a particular strand of resistance to capitalism. Together, this complex intertwining of flesh and symbol can be narratively read as boxcar politics.

# NOTES

## INTRODUCTION

1. Laura Hapke, *Labor's Text: The Worker in American Fiction* (New Brunswick, N.J.: Rutgers University Press, 2001), 14.
2. Richard White, *Railroaded: The Transcontinentals and the Making of Modern America* (New York: Norton, 2011), xxiv.
3. Nels Anderson, *The Hobo: The Sociology of the Homeless Man* (Chicago: University of Chicago Press, 1923), 230; Frank Tobias Higbie, *Indispensable Outcasts: Hobo Workers and Community in the American Midwest, 1880–1930* (Urbana: University of Illinois Press, 2003); Tim Creswell, *The Tramp in America* (London: Reaktion Books, 2001); Todd DePastino, *Citizen Hobo: How a Century of Homelessness Shaped America* (Chicago: University of Chicago Press, 2003); Mark Wyman, *Hoboes: Bindlestiffs, Fruit Tramps, and the Harvesting of the West* (New York: Hill and Wang, 2011).
4. Mari Jo Buhle, Paul Buhle, and Dan Georgakas, eds., *Encyclopedia of the American Left* (New York: Oxford University Press, 1998).
5. What makes a text part of working-class literature is a complex and highly debated one. For an overview, see Paul Buhle, "American Exceptionalism," in Buhle, Buhle, and Georgakas, *Encyclopedia of the American Left*, 20–22; Paul Lauter, "American Proletarianism," in *The Columbia History of the American Novel*, ed. Emory Elliott, Cathy N. Davidson, Patrick O'Donnell, Valerie Smith, and Christopher P. Wilson

(New York: Columbia University Press, 1991), 331–56; Patricia Cayo Sexton, *The War on Labor and the Left: Understanding America's Unique Conservatism* (Boulder: Westview, 1991); Janet Zandy, *Calling Home: Working-Class Women's Writing* (New Brunswick, N.J.: Rutgers University Press, 1990), 1–19. Although these are important debates, this study is not concerned with finding the dividing line between proletariat and lumpen proletariat writings and locates the hobo securely within the working class. For a compact synopsis of the various etymologies of the term *hobo,* see William Sayers, "Contested Etymologies of Some English Words in the Popular Register," *Studia Neophilologica* 80, no. 1 (June 2008): 15–29.

6. Alberto Melucci, "The Symbolic Challenge of Contemporary Movements," *Social Research* (Winter 1985): 789–816.
7. Creswell, *Tramp in America,* 10–11.
8. Ken Gelder, *Subcultures: Cultural Histories and Social Practice* (New York: Routledge, 2007), 5, 83–107.
9. Thorstein Veblen defines finance capitalism in *The Theory of Business Enterprise* (New Brunswick, N.J.: Transaction Books, 1904). For a reading of Veblen's texts and an overview of finance capitalism, see James V. Cornehls, "Veblen's Theory of Finance Capitalism and Contemporary Corporate America," *Journal of Economic Issues* 38, no. 1 (2004): 29–58.
10. Sherry Lee Linkon and John Russo, "Border Crossings: Interdisciplinarity in New Working-Class Studies," *Labor History* 53, no. 3 (2012), 374; Michel de Certeau, *Heterologies: Discourse on the Other* (Minneapolis: University of Minnesota Press, 1986), 10–14.

## 1. VIEWS FROM THE BOXCAR

1. Ben Reitman quoted in Nels Anderson, *On Hobos and Homelessness,* ed. Raffaele Rauty (Chicago: University of Chicago Press, 1998), 3.
2. Nels Anderson, *The Hobo: The Sociology of the Homeless Man* (Chicago: University of Chicago Press, 1923), 41.
3. Michael Denning, *Mechanic Accents: Dime Novels and Working-Class Culture in America* (London: Verso, 1987), 149.
4. Christine Photinos, "The Figure of the Tramp in Gilded Age Success Narratives," *Journal of Popular Culture* 40, no. 6 (2007): 995.
5. Horatio Alger, *Tony the Tramp; or, Right Is Might* (New York: New York Book Company, 1909); Lee O. Harris, *The Man Who Tramps: A Story of Today* (Indianapolis: Douglas and Carlon, 1878), 267; Denning, *Mechanic Accents,* 151; Bret Harte, "My Friend the Tramp" (1877), in *The Writings of Bret Harte,* vol. 11 (Boston: Houghton Mifflin, 1907), 98–110; Laura Browder, *Slippery Characters: Ethnic Impersonators and American Identities* (Chapel Hill: University of North Carolina, 2000), 175.
6. Tim Creswell, *The Tramp in America* (London: Reaktion Books, 2001), 10–14.
7. Josiah Flynt, "The American Tramp," *Contemporary Review* 60 (August 1891): 251; Todd DePastino, *Citizen Hobo: How a Century of Homelessness Shaped America* (Chicago: University of Chicago Press, 2003), 64–65. Josiah Flynt had a major impact on readers' views of the tramp or hobo figure, writing most famously *Tramping with Tramps: Studies and Sketches of Vagabond Life* (1899; repr., n.p.: Ulan,

2011) and having numerous publications in popular magazines such as the *Century.* Flynt also was read by Jack London and Jim Tully, among others examined in this monograph.

8. Carlos A. Schwantes, "The Concept of the Wageworkers' Frontier: A Framework for Future Research," *Western Historical Quarterly* 18, no. 1 (1987), 39–55. See Mark Wyman, *Hoboes: Bindlestiffs, Fruit Tramps, and the Harvesting of the West* (New York: Hill and Wang, 2011) for a thorough examination of the ethnic and racial composition of agricultural laborers in the late nineteenth and early twentieth centuries. The hobo subculture was neither exclusively white nor male, nor even composed exclusively of adults.
9. Robert H. Wiebe writes that the migrant workers were the "indispensable outcasts of rural America." *The Search for Order, 1877–1920* (New York: Macmillan, 1967), 17. Frank Tobias Higbie's astute history of the midwestern hobo community takes its name from Wiebe's phrase. David Montgomery, *The Fall of the House of Labor: The Workplace, the State, and American Labor Activism, 1865–1925* (Cambridge: Cambridge University Press, 1987), 59–60.
10. Frank Tobias Higbie, *Indispensable Outcasts: Hobo Workers and Community in the American Midwest, 1880–1930* (Urbana: University of Illinois Press, 2003), 8.
11. John J. McCook, "A Tramp Census and Its Revelations," *Forum* 15 (1893): 753–66; Alice Solenberger, *One Thousand Homeless Men: A Study of Original Records* (New York: Charities Publication Committee, 1911); Gregory R. Woirol, *In the Floating Army: F. C. Mills on Itinerant Life in California, 1914* (Urbana: University of Illinois Press, 1992).
12. Clarence S. Thompson, "Tramping as a Pastime," *Charities and the Commons* 16 (September 22, 1906): 619.
13. Montgomery, *Fall of the House*, 78.
14. See John Lennon, "Too Dirty to Be a 'Bo? Gutterpunks, Hobos, and Subcultural Negotiations of Identity," in *Youth Subcultures: Exploring Underground America*, ed. Arielle Greenberg (New York: Longman, 2007), 212–23.
15. DePastino, *Citizen Hobo*, 8.
16. David Rothman, *The Discovery of the Asylum: Social Order and Disorder in the New Republic* (Piscataway, N.J.: Transaction, 1971), 162.
17. Anderson, *Hobo*, 82–83. For a detailed examination of the way the homeless are perceived by those outside of the community, see Kathleen R. Arnold's *Homelessness, Citizenship and Identity: The Uncanniness of Late Modernity* (Albany: State University of New York Press, 2004).
18. See Creswell, *Tramp in America*, 138–43.
19. "The Tramp," *New York Times*, August 8, 1875. Although the *Times* article did not specifically state methods for eliminating the wandering poor, many devised plans to do so. For examples, see Kenneth Allsop, *Hard Travellin': The Hobo and His History* (New York: New American Library, 1967), 59, 118.
20. Allsop, *Hard Travellin'*, 110, quoting "Ways of Dealing with the Hobo," *Chicago Tribune*, July 12, 1877.
21. Michael Davis, "Forced to Tramp: The Perspective of the Labor Press, 1870–1900," in *Walking to Work: Tramps in America 1790–1935*, ed. Eric H. Monkkonen (Lincoln: University of Nebraska Press, 1984), 160.

22. Davis, "Forced to Tramp," 144, quoting *National Labor Tribune,* August 17, 1875.
23. Davis, "Forced to Tramp," 144, quoting *Journal of United Labor,* December 1883, 604.
24. Gibbs Smith, *Joe Hill* (Layton: Utah: Smith, 1969), 35–36; untitled article, *Industrial Worker,* May 22, 1913. Although originally composed for Northern troops, its popularity was so great that both Union and Confederate soldiers sang it while heading into battle. For a discussion of Joe Hill and his songs, see William M. Adler, *The Man Who Never Died: The Life, Times and Legacy of Joe Hill, American Labor Icon* (New York: Bloomsbury, 2011), 91–201.
25. Davis, "Forced to Tramp," 144, quoting *Journal of the Knights of Labor,* November 2, 1893.
26. Jack London, *War of the Classes* (New York: Macmillan, 1905), 95.
27. Karl Marx, *Capital,* vol. 1, trans. Ben Fowkes (London: Penguin, 1976), 794–95.
28. London, *War of the Classes,* 95.
29. Eric Monkkonen, introduction to *Walking to Work,* 5, 14.
30. Richard Oestreicher, *Solidarity and Fragmentation: Working People and Class Consciousness in Detroit, 1875–1900* (Urbana: University of Illinois Press, 1990).
31. George McNeill, *The Labor Movement: The Problem of Today* (Boston: Bridgman, 1887), 459.
32. Davis, "Forced to Tramp," 149, quoting *John Swinton's Paper,* December 6, 1885, and May 24, 1885.
33. Davis, "Forced to Tramp," 157, quoting *National Labor Tribune,* December 1, 1877.
34. Creswell, *Tramp in America,* 49.
35. Paul Ringenbach, *Tramps and Reformers, 1873–1896: The Discovery of Unemployment in New York* (Westport, Conn.: Greenwood, 1973).
36. Creswell, *Tramp in America,* 48–57.
37. Davis, "Forced to Tramp," 161.
38. Joanne Hall, "The Wanderer Contained: Issues of 'Inside' and 'Outside' in Relation to Harold Gray's *Little Orphan Annie* and Marilynne Robinson's *Housekeeping,*" *Critical Survey* 18, no. 3 (2006): 39.
39. Frank C. Laubach, *Why There Are Vagrants: A Study Based upon an Examination of One Hundred Men* (New York: Columbia University Press, 1916), 71.
40. For a detailed contextual analysis of the female tramp figure, see Tim Cresswell's "Embodiment, Power and the Politics of Mobility: The Case of Female Tramps and Hobos," *Transactions of the Institute of British Geographers* 24, no. 2 (1999): 175–92.
41. Lynn Weiner, "Sisters of the Road: Women Transients and Tramps," in Monkkonen, *Walking to Work,* 178, quoting McCook, "Tramp Census," 753–56.
42. Anderson, *Hobo,* 137.
43. Cliff Maxwell, "Lady Vagabonds," *Scribner's Magazine,* March 1929, 292.
44. Hall, "Wanderer Contained," 37–50; Hall, "Sisters of the Road? The Construction of Female Hobo Identity in the Autobiographies of Ethel Lynn, Barbara Starke and 'Box-car' Bertha Thompson," *Women's Studies* 39, no. 3 (2010): 216.
45. Hall, "Sisters of the Road?," 225–33, 224. For an analysis of the novel, see 221–25.
46. Weiner, "Sisters of the Road," 176–77.
47. For an analysis of the way lesbian hobos have been portrayed, see J. R. Roberts [Barbara Rae Henry], "Lesbian Hoboes: Their Lives and Times," *Dyke* 5 (Fall 1977), 39–47.

48. Alexander Keyssar, *Out of Work: The First Century of Unemployment in Massachusetts* (Cambridge: Cambridge University Press, 1986), 118–19.
49. Stephan Thernstrom and Peter R. Knights, "Men in Motion: Some Data and Speculations about Urban Population Mobility in Nineteenth-Century America," *Journal of Interdisciplinary History* 1, no. 1 (1970): 7–35.
50. Higbie, *Indispensable Outcasts*, 176.
51. Montgomery, *Fall of the House*, 87.
52. Kenneth L. Kusmer, *Down and Out, on the Road: The Homeless in American History* (London: Oxford University Press, 2002), 64; Kusmer, *Down and Out*, 62, quoting Charles B. George, *Forty Years on the Rail* (Chicago: Belford, Clarke, 1888), 182. Certainly, this allowance to ride was not always a selfless act of kindness by trainmen, and there was often a price to be paid for riding illegally on trains, with trainmen grafting hobos on numerous occasions. Ranging in prices, these "fares" depended on the hobos' ethnicity, gender, and age, and also whether or not they were former railroad employees. For a detailed exploration of the relationship between trainmen and hobos, see Kusmer, *Down and Out*, 57–72; Shelton Stromquist, *A Generation of Boomers: The Pattern of Railroad Labor Conflict in Nineteenth-Century America* (Urbana: University of Illinois Press, 1993), 192.
53. Ernesto Laclau and Chantal Mouffe, *Hegemony and Socialist Strategy: Towards a Radical Democratic Politics* (London: Verso, 2001), 178.
54. Robert G. Athearn, *The Mythic West in Twentieth-Century America* (Lawrence: University Press of Kansas, 1986), 48.
55. Stephen E. Ambrose, *Nothing Like It in the World: The Men Who Built the Transcontinental Railroad, 1863–1869* (New York: Simon and Schuster, 2001), 369. Besides class, railroad cars, like most places in the nineteenth-century United States, also were segregated by race and sex. For a thorough discussion, see James W. Ely's *Railroads and American Law* (Lawrence: University Press of Kansas, 2001) and Barbara Young Welke's *Recasting American Liberty: Gender, Race, Law and the Railroad Revolution, 1865–1920* (Cambridge: Cambridge University Press, 2001).
56. For two texts that detail this transformation, see Carlos A. Schwantes and James P. Ronda, *The West the Railroads Made* (Seattle: University of Washington Press, 2008); and Richard White, *Railroaded: The Transcontinentals and the Making of Modern America* (New York: Norton, 2011).
57. Lynne Kirby, *Parallel Tracks: The Railroad and Silent Cinema* (Durham, N.C.: Duke University Press, 1997), 200, quoting "The Railroad System and the Railroad Journey," *American Railroad Journal and General Advertiser*, January 2, 1847, 9.
58. See Joseph L. Schott's *Rails across Panama: The Story of the Building of the Panama Railroad, 1849–1855* (Indianapolis: Bobbs-Merrill, 1967) for a detailed examination of one of these proposed lines.
59. Sarah H. Gordon, *Passage to Union: How the Railroads Transformed American Life, 1829–1929* (Chicago: Dee, 1996), 5. For a description of these short-line trains, see George Estes, "The Rawhide Railroad," in *Treasury of Railroad Folklore: The Stories, Tall Tales, Ballads and Songs of the American Railroad Traditions*, ed. Benjamin Albert Botkin and Alvin Harlow (New York: Bonanza Books, 1989), 270.
60. Gordon, *Passage to Union*, 135.
61. William G. Thomas, *The Iron Way: Railroads, the Civil War, and the Making of Modern America* (New Haven, Conn.: Yale University Press, 2011), 1–17.

62. William R. Everdell, *The First Moderns: Profiles in the Origins in Twentieth-Century Thought* (Chicago: University of Chicago Press, 1997), 4.
63. Kirby, *Parallel Tracks*, 199.
64. White, *Railroaded*, 490.
65. Ibid., xxii.
66. Charles Francis Adams Jr., Henry Adams, and Francis Amasa Walker, *Chapters of Erie and Other Essays* (Boston: Osgood, 1871), 98.
67. Henry Adams, *The Education of Henry Adams: An Autobiography* (New York: Houghton Mifflin, 1918), 240; Daniel R. Headrick, *The Tools of Empire: Technology and European Imperialism in the Nineteenth Century* (New York: Oxford University Press, 1981), 187.
68. Frank Norris, *The Octopus: A Story of California* (Garden City: Doubleday, 1901), 46.
69. Sigmund Freud, *Moses and Monotheism*, trans. Katherine Jones (New York: Vintage, 1939), 84. For a historical rendering and theoretical extrapolation of the shock and trauma, including an analysis of the "railway brain" and how this affected individuals riding railroads, see Kirby, *Parallel Tracks*, 19–75. For a detailed description of how another naturalist writer, Theodore Dreiser, used the narrative of the railroad and the laborer as a way to reconceptualize American masculine psyche and physical injuries in an age of industrial expansion, see Jennifer Travis, "Injury's Accountant: Theodore Dreiser and the Railroad," *Studies in American Naturalism* 3, no. 1 (2008): 42–59.
70. Norris, *Octopus*, 48.
71. See Michael O'Malley, *Keeping Watch: A History of American Time* (New York: Viking, 1990), 172; Eviatar Zerubavel, "The Standardization of Time: A Sociohistorical Perspective, *American Journal of Sociology* 88, no. 1 (July 1982): 1–23; and Kirby, *Parallel Tracks*, 48–57.
72. Frederick Jackson Turner, *The Frontier in American History* (1920; repr., Mineola, N.Y.: Courier Dover, 2012), 38.
73. Albert Fishlow, "Productivity and Technological Change in the Railroad Sector, 1840–1910," in *Output, Employment and Productivity in the United States after 1800*, ed. Dorothy S. Brady (Cambridge: National Bureau of Economic Research Books, 1966), 588.
74. Henry Nash Smith, *Virgin Land: The American West as Symbol and Myth* (Cambridge: Harvard University Press, 1950). For two examples of the way the railroads created new social and economic avenues for a subsection of African Americans and wealthy white women, see Larry Tye, *Rising from the Rails: Pullman Porters and the Making of the Black Middle Class* (New York: Holt, 2004); and Amy Richter, *Home on the Rails: Women, the Railroad, and the Rise of Public Domesticity* (Durham: University of North Carolina Press, 2005) for two examples of the way the railroads created new social and economic avenues for a subsection of African Americans and wealthy white women.
75. Richard Slotkin's trilogy, *Regeneration through Violence: The Mythology of the American Frontier, 1600–1860* (Norman: University of Oklahoma Press, 1973); *The Fatal Environment: The Myth of the Frontier in the Age of Industrialization, 1800–1890* (Norman: University of Oklahoma Press, 1985); and *Gunfighter Nation: The Myth of the Frontier in Twentieth-Century America* (New York: Atheneum, 1992),

consists of classic texts that explore the myths of the frontier and the borderland area between space and time.

76. See Wolfgang Schivelbusch, *The Railway Journey: The Industrialization and Perception of Time and Space* (Berkeley: University of California Press, 1987), 37, for an example of the anxiety railroads caused in Europe. Many questions were raised by transcontinental railroads, including how trains could alter the sovereignty of a bordered nation-state.
77. Slotkin, *Regeneration through Violence*, 215.
78. Stromquist, *Generation of Boomers*, 11.
79. Page Smith, *The Shaping of America: A People's History of the Young Republic*, vol. 3 (New York: McGraw-Hill, 1980), 89; Schivelbusch, *The Railway Journey*, 34, quoting "Reports of the Commissioners Appointed to Consider and Recommend a General System of Railways for Ireland," *Quarterly Review* 63 (January 1839): 9.
80. Christine Photinos, "Tracking Changes in Jack London's Representation of the Railroad Tramp," *Journal of American Culture* 30, no. 2 (2007): 175–86.
81. For a detailed examination of the myth around Roosevelt's personal transformation, see Slotkin, *Gunfighter Nation*, 29–62.
82. Aharon Appelfeld, *The Iron Tracks*, trans. Jeffrey M. Green (New York: Schocken, 1998).
83. Michel de Certeau, *The Practice of Everyday Life*, trans. Steven Rendall (1984; repr., Berkeley: University of California Press, 2011), 111.
84. Mark Simpson, *Trafficking Subjects: The Politics of Mobility in Nineteenth-Century America* (Minneapolis: University of Minnesota Press, 2005), 93; See Doreen Massey, *For Space* (Los Angeles: Sage, 2005), for a detailed examination of power as it relates to spatial constructs.
85. De Certeau, *Practice of Everyday Life*, 111.
86. Ibid., 37, 113; emphasis added.
87. For example, in a luxury car commercial that was widely shown in the first decade of the twenty-first century, a sleek, shiny car is placed in the middle of a loud, chaotic construction sight. In the first frame, the car's windows are down and the noise of the industrial world is grating and disturbing. With a flick of a switch, however, the windows rise and the noise is replaced with soft classical music. The noise belongs to the uncivilized and unsafe world under construction; the sound belongs to the world of the (high-priced) civilized and ordered car environment.
88. Dick Hebdidge, *Subculture: The Meaning of Style* (London: Routledge, 1979), 90.
89. Jim Tully, *Beggars of Life: A Hobo Autobiography* (1924), ed. Paul J. Bauer and Mark Dawidziak (Kent, Ohio: Kent State University Press, 2010), 230.
90. Thousand-mile paper is the rough brown paper that railroad companies line their cars with to protect both merchandise and the car from damage. Hobos tore this paper off the walls and used it for insulation in the cold weather. See Meynardie Blanchard, *Rails, Trails and Other Tales* (Bloomington: Xlibris, 2010), 131.
91. De Certeau, *Practice of Everyday Life*, 113. An example of the hobos' unofficial status is epitomized by the countless "tramp graves" found along the railroad tracks of the United States. Having no form of identification and no recognizable next of kin, many hobos were buried just a few feet from the tracks in unmarked graves by railroad workers or townspeople after they were found dead.

92. Michel Foucault, *Discipline and Punish: The Birth of the Prison*, trans. Alan Sheridan (1975; repr., New York: Vintage, 2005), 162.
93. Allsop, *Hard Travellin'*, 159. For an informative, albeit sensational, description of the horrors of riding this way, see George Millburn's *Hoboes and Harlots* (New York: Lion Books, 1954), 15–25. This type of violence is portrayed in the popular movie *Emperor of the North* (Christopher Knopf, directed by Robert Aldrich [Los Angeles, Calif.: Twentieth Century Fox, 1973], VHS), in which Ernest Borgnine plays the sadistic bull who tries to throw the adventurous hobo (Lee Marvin) off his train. Jack London, in his hobo memoir, *The Road*, also has many good descriptions of how hostile train crews would get unwanted riders off their trains (*Emperor of the North* was loosely based on some of the chapters of *The Road*).
94. De Certeau, *The Writing of History*, trans. Tom Conley (New York: Columbia University Press, 1988), 4.
95. Mark Simpson, "Travel's Disciplines," *Canadian Review of American Studies* 26, no. 2 (1996): 90; Anson Rabinbach, *The Human Motor: Energy, Fatigue, and the Origins of Modernity* (Berkeley: University of California Press, 1990), 167.
96. Mark Seltzer, *Bodies and Machines* (New York: Routledge, 1992), 17–18, 13.
97. Denning, *Mechanic Accents*, 163. For Eric Hobsbawm's original terminology and analysis, see his *Bandits* (New York: Delacorte, 1969).
98. Talmadge Wright, *Out of Place: Homeless Mobilizations, Subcities, and Contested Landscapes* (Albany: State University of New York Press, 1997), 1–2.
99. Ibid., 6.
100. For an analysis of the nineteenth-century tramp laws, see Creswell, *Tramp in America*, 110–30. It is, of course, not only the state that acts on the body of the homeless; teenagers with gasoline and matches in their hands also have a potential target.
101. James C. Scott, *Weapons of the Weak: Everyday Forms of Peasant Resistance* (New Haven, Conn.: Yale University Press, 1987); Scott, *Domination and the Arts of Resistance: Hidden Transcripts* (New Haven, Conn.: Yale University Press, 1992).
102. De Certeau, *Practice of Everyday Life*, 114.
103. Charles W. Chesnutt, *The Marrow of Tradition* (1901; New York: Penguin, 1993), 58–59.
104. Ibid., 55. The practice of racial segregation on southern lines varied greatly—there was an economic cost on the part of the companies for having to connect extra cars for African American passengers. See Ely, *Railroads and American Law*, 138–43.
105. Chesnutt, *Marrow of Tradition*, 62.
106. Laura Hapke, *Labor's Text: The Worker in American Fiction* (New Brunswick, N.J.: Rutgers University Press, 2001), 133. For a detailed examination of militant southern black dockworkers, see Eric Arnesen, *Waterfront Workers of New Orleans: Race, Class and Politics, 1863–1923* (Urbana: University of Illinois Press, 1994).
107. John Fiske, *Understanding Popular Culture*, rev. ed. (New York: Routledge, 2010), 19.
108. De Certeau, *Practice of Everyday Life*, 37.
109. Eric J. Sundquist, *To Wake Up the Nations: Race in the Making of American Literature* (Cambridge: Harvard University Press, 1993), 442.

110. Hapke, *Labor's Text*, 133.
111. Ken Gelder, ed., *The Subcultures Reader*, 2nd ed. (New York: Routledge, 2006), 1, 3.
112. Browder, *Slippery Characters*, 175.
113. David Muggleton and Rupert Weinzierl, "What Is 'Post-subcultural Studies' Anyway," in *The Post-Subcultures Reader*, ed. Muggleton and Weinzierl (Oxford: Berg, 2003), 3–26.
114. John Irwin, *Scenes* (New York: Sage, 1977), 18.
115. Michel Maffesoli, *The Time of Tribes: The Decline of Individualism in Mass Society* (New York: Sage, 1990), 98.
116. See Graham St. John, *Technomad: Global Raving Countercultures* (Sheffield, U.K.: Equinox, 2009); Oliver Marchart, *Post-Foundational Political Thought: Political Difference in Nancy, Lefort, Badiou and Laclau* (Edinburgh: Edinburgh University Press, 2007); Stephen Duncombe, *Notes from Underground: Zines and the Politics of Alternative Culture* (London: Verso, 1997); David Muggleton, *Inside Subculture: The Postmodern Meaning of Style* (Oxford: Berg, 2002). Duncombe's examination of the zine subculture is particularly insightful. Using the archaic form of print in an electronic world, Duncombe understands the zine community as a network of individuals linked not by the rigidity of their stances but by "alternative" styles and subject matter. In essence, it is their particular marginalities (be it racial, sexual, class) that connect them. These zine writers and readers form a "shadow America," creating a subcultural geography that can paradoxically link minority subcultures throughout the United States in both practical and ideological ways.
117. This is the argument made by many post-Marxist scholars about identity-based theorists. See Alain Touraine, *The Post-Industrial Society: Tomorrow's Social History; Classes, Conflicts, and Culture in the Programmed Society* (New York: Random House, 1971); Alberto Melucci, *Nomads of the Present: Social Movements and Individual Needs in Contemporary Society*, ed. John Keane and Paul Mier (Philadelphia: Temple University Press, 1989); and Laclau and Mouffe, *Hegemony and Socialist Strategy*.
118. Andy Bennett, "The Post-subcultural Turn: Some Reflections 10 Years On," *Journal of Youth Studies* 14, no. 5 (2011), 493–506.
119. See, for example, John Urry, *Mobilities* (Cambridge: Polity Press, 2007); James Clifford, *Routes: Travel and Translation in the Late Twentieth Century* (Cambridge: Harvard University Press, 1997); and Marc Augé, *Non-Places: An Introduction to Supermodernity*, trans. John Howe (London: Verso, 1995).
120. Annemarie Mol and John Law, "Regions, Networks and Fluids: Anaemia and Social Topology," *Social Studies of Science* 24, no. 4 (1994): 643.
121. John Urry, *Sociology beyond Societies: Mobilities for the Twenty-First Century* (London: Routledge, 2000), 357.
122. Hakim Bey, *T. A. Z.: Temporary Autonomous Zone, Ontological Anarchy and Poetic Terrorism* (Brooklyn: Autonomedia, 1985), 98–101.

## 2. THE CRAMPED BOXCAR

1. Huck Gutman, ed., *As Others Read Us: International Perspectives on American Literature* (Amherst: University of Massachusetts Press, 1991), 5–6; Jonathan Auerbach, *Male Call: Becoming Jack London* (Durham, N.C.: Duke University Press,

1996), 5; Michael Denning, *Mechanic Accents* (London: Verso, 1987). Denning traces the rise of the reading culture among the working class as adventure texts became readily available for a minimal sum.

2. Jeanne Campbell Reesman, "Prospects for the Study of Jack London," *Resources for American Literary Study* 25, no. 2 (1999): 147. There is no shortage of London biographies. Here is a small sample (in chronological order): Charmian Kittredge London, *The Book of Jack London*, 2 vols. (New York: Century, 1921); Joan London, *Jack London and His Times: An Unconventional Biography* (New York: Doubleday, 1939); Philip Foner, *Jack London: American Rebel* (Boston: Citadel, 1947); Richard O'Connor, *Jack London: A Biography* (New York: Little, Brown, 1964); Daniel Osborn Dryer, *Jack London: A Biography* (New York: Scholastic, 1997); Alex Kershaw, *Jack London: A Life* (New York: St. Martin's, 1997); and Clarice Stasz, *Jack London's Women* (Amherst: University of Massachusetts Press, 2001); Jeanne Campbell Reesman, *Jack London's Racial Lives: A Critical Biography* (Athens: University of Georgia Press, 2009); Campbell Reesman, *Jack London: Photographer* (Athens: University of Georgia Press, 2010).
3. See Richard W. Etulain, *Jack London on the Road: The Tramp Diary, and Other Hobo Writings* (Logan: Utah State University Press, 1979), 29–60, for a complete reprint of London's tramp diary, in which he recounts his experiences with Kelly's army. (I use the spelling "Kelly" throughout this book, although in published documents and criticism it appears as both "Kelly" and "Kelley.") For details of the publishing history of *The Road*, see Christine Photinos, "Tracking Changes in Jack London's Representation of the Railroad Tramp," *Journal of American Culture* 30, no. 2 (2007): 175–86.
4. Clarice Stasz, *American Dreamers: Charmian and Jack London* (New York: St. Martin's, 1988), 53; Frederick Feied, *No Pie in the Sky: The Hobo as American Cultural Hero in the Works of Jack London, John Dos Passos, and Jack Kerouac* (New York: Citadel, 1964), 28; Earle Labor, *Jack London* (Woodbridge: Twayne, 1995), 32.
5. Etulain, *Jack London on the Road*, 17–27.
6. Photinos, "Tracking Changes," 177; Eric H. Monkkonen, *Police in Urban America, 1860–1920* (Cambridge: Cambridge University Press, 1981), 142.
7. Jack London, *Revolution and Other Essays* (New York: Macmillan, 1910), 298. For a contextualization of London's position as an apprentice, see Todd DePastino, ed., *The Road*, by Jack London (New Brunswick, N.J.: Rutgers University Press, 2006), xi–xlix.
8. Jack London, "The Apostate," *Woman's Home Companion* 33 (September 1906): 5–7, 49.
9. Mark Simpson, "Travel's Disciplines," *Canadian Review of American Studies* 26, no. 2 (1996): 92; Photinos, "Tracking Changes," 177.
10. This discrepancy between our readings may be the result of the "ideological incoherence" of London that Simpson highlights in "Travel's Disciplines," 83–116. London's views change throughout his life, and while Simpson and Photinos read this short story in light of naturalistic fiction, I read it through London's view of the tramp figure he describes in *The Road* (New York: Macmillan, 1907).
11. DePastino, *Road*, xi.
12. Jack London, *Road*, 56.
13. DePastino, *Road*, xxiii.

14. American Social History Project, *Who Built America? Working People and the Nation's Economy, Politics, Culture, and Society,* vol. 2, *From the Gilded Age to the Present* (New York, Pantheon Books, 1989), 138; Carlos A. Schwantes, *Coxey's Army: An American Odyssey* (Lincoln: University of Nebraska Press, 1985), 13.
15. Schwantes, *Coxey's Army,* 32.
16. Western contingents were organized specifically as industrial armies and not as commonweals of Christ. For a detailed description of the western armies, see Todd DePastino, *Citizen Hobo: How a Century of Homelessness Shaped America* (Chicago: University of Chicago Press, 2003), 59–71.
17. Schwantes, *Coxey's Army,* 116, quoting *Omaha Bee,* April 15, 1894.
18. Schwantes, *Coxey's Army,* 195.
19. Nels Anderson, *The American Hobo* (Netherlands: Brill, 1975), ix.
20. Frank Tobias Higbie, *Indispensable Outcasts: Hobo Workers and Community in the American Midwest, 1880–1930* (Urbana: University of Illinois Press, 2003), 7, 19.
21. DePastino, *Citizen Hobo,* 15.
22. Kenneth L. Kusmer, *Down and Out, on the Road: The Homeless in American History* (London: Oxford University Press, 2002), 123–25.
23. Ibid., 132.
24. For details of Jack London's early life as an oyster pirate, see Joan London, *Jack London and His Times,* 39–53,
25. London, *Road,* 158, 159. In his early tramp short stories, which he wrote for his high school newspaper, the *Aegis,* London would attempt to capture this language. See "'Frisco Kid's' Story" and "And 'Frisco Kid Came Back" in Earle Labor, Robert C. Leitz III, and I. Milo Shepard, eds., *The Complete Short Stories of Jack London,* vol. 1 (Stanford, Calif.: Stanford University Press, 1993), 6–8, 27–29.
26. London, *Road,* 163.
27. In *The Road,* London describes the "gay-cat" as "short-horns, *chechaquos,* new chums, and tenderfeet" (173). The "prushun" was a young, inexperienced traveler, and a "punk" was in the "possession" of the profresh. London's discussion of the prushan makes no mention of the sexual relations that often existed between the prushan and the older hobo, who was also known as a "wolf." For a discussion of hobo sexuality, see Thomas Minehan, *Boy and Girl Tramps in America* (New York: Grosset and Dunlap, 1934); and Nels Anderson, *The Hobo: The Sociology of the Homeless Man* (Chicago: University of Chicago Press, 1923), 144–49.
28. Etulain, *Jack London on the Road,* 95. For an analysis of London's misreading of Nietzsche, see Katherine M. Littell, "The 'Nietzschean' and the Individualist in Jack London's Socialist Writings," *Jack London Newsletter* 15 (May–August 1982): 76–91; and Carolyn Johnston, *Jack London: An American Radical?* (Westport, Conn.: Greenwood, 1984), 10.
29. Begging, mentioned in most hobo autobiographies, is a substantial issue that novice hobos must face. For two such examples, see John Worby, *The Other Half: The Autobiography of a Tramp* (New York: Furman, 1937), 54; and Woody Guthrie, *Bound for Glory* (New York: Dutton, 1943), 201.
30. Jim Tully, *Beggars of Life: A Hobo Autobiography* (1924; Oakland, Calif.: Nabat / AK, 2004), 1.
31. William A. Bailey, *Bill Bailey Came Home* (Logan: Utah State University Press, 1973), 152, 156.

32. Charles P. Barth, *Hobo Trail to Nowhere* (Philadelphia: Whitmore, 1969), 10; Archie Lawson, *Freight Trains West* (Sacramento: Lucas, 1980), 20; Jack Black, *You Can't Win* (1923; Oakland, Calif.: Nabat / AK, 2000), 62.
33. Etulain, *Jack London on the Road,* 95.
34. Jack London, *The Call of the Wild* (1903; New York: Puffin Books, 1994), 13.
35. London, *Road,* 60–67.
36. Ted Grossardt, "Harvest(ing) Hoboes: The Production of Labor Organization through the Wheat Harvest," *Agricultural History* 70, no. 2 (1996): 285; Cresswell, *The Tramp in America* (London: Reaktion Books, 2001), 48–86.
37. London, *Road,* 24.
38. Ibid., 32.
39. Ibid.
40. Ibid., 34, 41, 50. DePastino, in his introduction to *The Road* (xi–xlix), makes the salient argument that London's disengagement with working-class society could be argued as an implicit commentary on capitalism. *The Road* barely mentions any jobs that London had when on the road. This downplaying of the work he needed to do to survive allows London to present a masculine ideal of hoboing; he would not work for anyone else (a type of submissiveness) but instead must survive by his own wits, nostalgically pointing to an earlier time of republican, Jeffersonian idealism.
41. For a discussion of de Certeau and railroad space, see chapter 1.
42. Schwantes, *Coxey's Army,* 100–101.
43. Donald Le Crone McMurry, *Coxey's Army: The Study of the Industrial Army Movement of 1894* (Boston: Little, 1929), 154.
44. Joan London, *Jack London and His Times,* 72; Richard White, *Railroaded: The Transcontinentals and the Making of Modern America* (New York: Norton, 2011), 215. The sympathy was complicated and multilayered. For an interesting view of Coxey's army in the popular press, see the dime novel *On to Washington; or, Old Cap. Collier with the Coxey Army,* Old Cap, Collier Library #545 (May 30, 1894), which both sympathizes with the men marching on Washington but also questions their validity and purpose. For an analysis of the story, see Denning, *Mechanic Accents,* 154–56.
45. McMurry, *Coxey's Army,* 154–55.
46. William Peterson, "Kelly and His Men," *Palimpsest* 52 (June 1971), 302, quoting *Iowa State Registry,* May 4, 1894; Thorstein Veblen, "Army of the Commonweal," *Journal of Political Economy* 2 (June 1894): 456–61; editorial, *New York Times,* May 1, 1894, 4; "The Whipping Post for Tramps," *Century* 49 (1895): 794.
47. For a detail of Kelly's ordered, daily regiment, see Peterson, "Kelly and His Men," 289–304. Regimental order under harsh conditions enhanced public sympathy for the army. For examples of sympathetic editorials of the march, see Schwantes, *Coxey's Army,* 104.
48. Johnston, *Jack London,* 11; Joan London, *Jack London and His Times,* 70–71.
49. Etulain, *Jack London on the Road,* 2.
50. McMurry, *Coxey's Army,* 157.
51. Ibid., 164; Carl Browne, *When Coxey's "Army" Marcht* [*sic*] *on Washington, 1894,* ed. William McDevitt (San Francisco: McDevitt, 1944), 11.
52. McMurry, *Coxey's Army,* 197–226. Train stealing was a common event among many of the western industrial armies, with more than *fifty* train thefts reported.

53. For a detail of the pledge, see Peterson, "Kelly and His Men," 300, quoting *Weekly Gate City,* May 24, 1894.
54. London, *Road,* 183; 185.
55. Ibid., 183.
56. Joan London, *Jack London and His Times,* 84.
57. William McDevitt, "Did Jack London Join the Industrial Army?," in Browne, *When Coxey's "Army" Marcht,* 29.
58. London, *Road,* 95.

## 3. THE POLYPHONIC BOXCAR

1. Paul J. Bauer and Mark Dawidziak, *Jim Tully: American Writer, Irish Rover, Hollywood Brawler* (Kent, Ohio: Kent State University Press, 2011), 110–14.
2. Ibid., 44, 80, 2.
3. Ibid., 186.
4. Ibid., 111–13.
5. Jim Tully, "Jack London: A Baffled Greatness," *Literary Digest International Book Review,* June 23, 1923, 226.
6. Todd DePastino, ed., *The Road,* by Jack London (New Brunswick, N.J.: Rutgers University Press, 2006), xl; Jack London, "To the Editorial Department, *Cosmopolitan,*" December 17, 1906, in *The Letters of Jack London,* vol. 2, ed. Earle Labor, Robert C. Leitz, and Milo Shephard (Stanford, Calif.: Stanford University Press, 1988), 654–55. For a detailed description of the origins of London's *The Road,* see Christine Photinos, "Tracking Changes in Jack London's Representation of the Railroad Tramp," *Journal of American Culture* 30, no. 2 (2007): 175–86.
7. DePastino, in his introduction to *The Road,* makes a compelling argument that London's profresh characters had an "undertone of self criticism" (xlii) and were a literary rebellion against Victorian manners and tastes. Tully, though, did not acknowledge these undertones; he saw only a braggart who romanticized the road.
8. Janet Zandy, *Hands: Physical Labor, Class, and Cultural Work* (New Brunswick, N.J.: Rutgers University Press, 2004), 90.
9. Jim Tully, *Beggars of Life: A Hobo Autobiography* (1924; repr., Oakland, Calif.: Nabat / AK, 204), 6.
10. Ibid., 12, 10.
11. Tully had made three shorter train-hopping trips, but this was his first sustained hobo experience. See Bauer and Dawidziak, *Jim Tully,* 11, for a description of these earlier "failed" attempts.
12. *Beggars of Life,* directed by William A. Wellman (Los Angeles: Paramount Pictures, 1928).
13. Even when Hemingway writes specifically about hobo characters, they are mostly stories of masculinity and not stories of the working-class subculture. His most famous hobos in "The Battler" are case in point. A former boxer who needs to be physically controlled, the hobo is mentally unstable and unfit to be around civilization any longer. Nick, hoboing his way to maturity, leaves behind the boxer and his caretaker. *In Our Time* (New York: Boni and Liveright, 1925).
14. Merritt Y. Hughes, "Jim Tully: Poet or Picaro?" *Sewanee Review* 37, no. 4 (1929): 393.
15. Contrary to the view that Tully was apolitical, throughout his life Tully was

involved in political causes, including being a sponsor for the Committee to Defend America by Keeping Out of the War, as well as writing beautifully and passionately about the horrors of the death penalty. For a discussion of Tully's complicated relationship to political causes, see Bauer and Dawidziak's *Jim Tully,* especially 157–65, 197–201, 219–27, and 272–82.

16. Bauer and Dawidziak, *Jim Tully,* 203, quoting J. M., *New Republic,* February 1926.
17. Tully, *Beggars of Life,* 85.
18. Ibid., 168, 170.
19. Ibid., 168.
20. William Brevda, *Harry Kemp: The Last Bohemian* (Cranbury, N.J.: Associated University Presses, 1986), 19.
21. Harry Kemp, *Tramping on Life: An Autobiographical Narrative* (New York: Boni and Liveright, 1922), 132.
22. Ibid., 133
23. Arthur Compton-Rickett, *The Vagabond in Literature* (London: Dent, 1906), 6.
24. Michael Johnson, "Review of Harry Kemp," *American Studies* 27, no. 2 (1986): 67.
25. Walt Whitman, *Democratic Vistas: The Original Edition in Facsimile,* ed. Ed Folsom (Iowa City: University of Iowa Press, 2010), 19. The original edition of *Democratic Vistas* appeared in 1870.
26. Nicolas Mills, *The Crowd in American Literature* (Baton Rouge: Louisiana State University Press, 1986), 12; Michael Hardt and Antonio Negri, *Multitude: War and Democracy in the Age of Empire* (New York: Penguin, 2004), 99; Richard Sennett, *The Fall of the Public Man* (New York: Knopf, 1977), 299; Daria Frezza, *The Leader and the Crowd: Democracy in American Public Discourse 1880–1941,* trans. Martha King (Athens: University of Georgia Press, 2007), 55, quoting Gustave Le Bon, *Psychologie Des Foules* (Paris: Revue, 1896), 50.
27. Frezza, *Leader and the Crowd,* 32.
28. Bauer and Dawidziak, *Jim Tully,* 75–79, 103.
29. Jim Tully, "A Declaration," *Smart Set,* December 1923, 105–6.
30. Hardt and Negri, *Multitude,* 99, 100, 162, 105.
31. Ibid., 137, 131, 103. For a discussion of the differences between the Centre for Contemporary Cultural Studies and post-subculture scholars, see chapter 1.
32. Hardt and Negri, *Multitude,* 212.
33. Tully, *Beggars of Life,* 22, 25.
34. Ibid., 64.
35. Ginette Verstraete, "Railroading America: Towards a Material Study of the Nation," *Theory Culture Society* 19, no. 5–6 (2002): 145.
36. For this monumental work and his definition of "interstitial group," see Frederic Milton Thrasher, *The Gang: A Study of 1,313 Gangs in Chicago* (Chicago: University of Chicago Press, 1927).
37. Nels Anderson, *The Hobo: The Sociology of the Homeless Man* (Chicago: University of Chicago Press, 1923).
38. Ibid., 19; Ken Gelder, *Subcultures: Cultural Histories and Social Practice* (New York: Routledge, 2007), 33. In *Beggars of Life,* 125–32, Tully recounts the murder of African American hobos at the hands of Oklahoma Red, which was ostensibly about stolen liquor but was mostly a racially motivated murder. He also recounts the lynching of another African American as he was trying to escape a posse.

39. Tully, *Beggars of Life*, 142.
40. Jules J. Wanderer, "Hobo Signs: Embodied Metaphors and Metonymies," *American Journal of Semiotics* 17, no. 4 (2001): 133.
41. For a discussion of freight train graffiti, see Jeff Ferrell's "Freight Train Graffiti: Subculture, Crime, Dislocation," *Justice Quarterly* 15, no. 4 (1998): 587–608; and Matthew Burns, "We Were Here: Marks, Monikers, and the Boxcar Art Tradition" (master's thesis, Lehigh University, 2005). For an excellent resource on hobo graffiti and boxcar art, see Bill Daniel, *Mostly True* (New York: Microcosm, 2008); and *Who is Bozo Texino? The Secret History of Graffiti*, directed by Bill Daniel (San Francisco: Wild Sages, 2005), DVD.
42. Verstraete, "Railroading America," 150.
43. Tully, *Beggars of Life*, 169.

## 4. THE RADICALIZED BOXCAR

1. John Dos Passos, "Sacco and Vanzetti," review of *The Life and Death of Sacco and Vanzetti*, by Eugene Lyons, *New Masses*, November 1927, 25.
2. Jean Paul Sartre, *Literary and Philosophical Essays*, trans. Annette Michelson (New York: Macmillan, 1955), 96; Malcolm Cowley, "John Dos Passos: The Poet and the World," *New Republic* 70 (April 27, 1932): 300; T. K. Whipple, "Dos Passos and the *U.S.A.*," *Nation*, February 19, 1938, 211; Lionel Trilling, "The America of John Dos Passos," *Partisan Review* 4 (April 1938): 29.
3. Alfred Kazin, *On Native Grounds: An Interpretation of Modern American Prose Literature* (New York: Harcourt Brace Jovanovich, 1942), 276; John William Ward, *Red, White, and Blue: Men, Books, and Ideas in American Culture* (New York: Oxford University Press, 1969), 39; Ian Colley, *Dos Passos and the Fiction of Despair* (New York: Rowman and Littlefield, 1978).
4. John Dos Passos, *The Big Money* (1936; repr., New York: Mariner Books, 2000), 372.
5. Lisa Nanney, *John Dos Passos Revisited* (New York: Twayne, 1998), 177.
6. John Dos Passos, *U.S.A.*, vol. 1, *The 42nd Parallel* (1930; Boston: Houghton Mifflin, 1960), 3.
7. John Dos Passos, *The 42nd Parallel* (1930; New York: Mariner Books, 2000), 4, 10, 8. All subsequent citations refer to this edition.
8. Ibid., 28.
9. Soon after taking the job, there is another train travel experience for young Mac. Although frightened, he is more comfortable and in control than on his first trip. After some trepidation, he has the courage to sell Doc Bingham's books to the passengers. Each time that Mac heads on a train, there is a growth process where Mac learns how to control his situation, culminating in his ability to hop trains as a hobo.
10. Dos Passos, *42nd Parallel*, 41, 46.
11. Ibid., 48.
12. William T. Vollman, *Riding toward Everywhere* (New York: HarperCollins), 2009.
13. Dos Passos, *42nd Parallel*, 11, 48.
14. Kingsley Widmer, *The Literary Rebel* (Carbondale: Southern Illinois University Press, 1965), 95.
15. Ralph Chaplin, *Wobbly: The Rough-and-Tumble Story of an American Radical*

(Chicago: University of Chicago Press, 1948), 88; Charles Ashleigh, "The Floater," *International Socialist Review* 15 (July 1914): 36.

16. Dos Passos, *42nd Parallel*, 60. For more information on hobos' cyclical poverty, see Nels Anderson's *The Hobo: The Sociology of the Homeless Man* (Chicago: University of Chicago Press, 1923), 40–60.
17. Dos Passos, *42nd Parallel*, 71.
18. Upton Sinclair, *Jimmie Higgins: A Story* (1919; repr., Middlesex: Echo Library, 2006), 138.
19. Dos Passos quoted in Granville Hicks, "The Politics of John Dos Passos," *Antioch Review* 10, no. 1 (1950): 23.
20. John Trombold, "Songs as Revolutionary Culture in John Dos Passos' *U.S.A.* and Other Early Works," *Journal of Modern Literature* 19, no. 2 (1995): 289–316. See also David Sanders, "The 'Anarchism' of John Dos Passos," *South Atlantic Quarterly* 60 (1961): 44–55.
21. Michael Denning, *The Cultural Front: The Laboring of American Culture in the Twentieth Century* (London: Verso, 1997), 186–88; Seth Moglen, *Mourning Modernity: Literary Modernism and the Injuries of American Capitalism* (Stanford, Calif.: Stanford University Press, 2007), 110, quoting John Dos Passos, "To Edmund Wilson," December 23, 1934.
22. Dos Passos, "To Edmund Wilson," 110
23. Melvyn Dubofsky, *We Shall Be All: A History of the Industrial Workers of the World* (1969), ed. Joseph A. McCartin (Champaign: University of Illinois Press, 2000), 168.
24. For an example of the way the life of a Wobbly radical coexisted with the life of the hobo, see Henry E. McGuckin, *Memoirs of a Wobbly* (Chicago: Kerr, 1987).
25. William Z. Foster, *Pages from a Worker's Life* (New York: International, 1939), 109.
26. Joyce L. Kornbluh, ed., *Rebel Voices: An I.W.W. Anthology* (Ann Arbor: University of Michigan Press, 1964), 169.
27. Frank Tobias Higbie, *Indispensable Outcasts: Hobo Workers and Community in the American Midwest, 1880–1930* (Urbana: University of Illinois Press, 2003), 136.
28. Higbie, *Indispensable Outcasts*, 138, quoting W. I. Fischer, *Solidarity*, November 8, 1913.
29. Dubofsky, *We Shall Be All*, 183.
30. McGuckin, *Memoirs of a Wobbly*, 70. This number is somewhat suspect. At the end of the year the AWO officially claimed to have a minimum of three thousand members; by late 1916 the number shot to over twenty thousand. Records were hard to keep and not all who claimed membership paid their dues. Dubofsky, *We Shall Be All*, 184.
31. McGuckin, *Memoirs of a Wobbly*, 71.
32. Ibid., 72.
33. Higbie, *Indispensable Outcasts*, 153.
34. For details on the "yegg" lifestyle, see Jack Black, *You Can't Win* (1923; Oakland, Calif.: AK, 2001). Numerous autobiographies speak to the sadistic nature of some bulls. For a fictional retelling of a hobo's trouble with a sadistic bull, see *Emperor of the North*, directed by Robert Aldrich (Los Angeles: Twentieth Century Fox, 1973; DVD, 2006), where Shack (Ernest Borgnine) tries to kill hobo "A-No. 1" (Lee Marvin), attempting to ride his train.

35. McGuckin, *Memoirs of a Wobbly*, 70.
36. Paul S. Taylor, *Adrift on the Land* (New York: Public Affairs Committee, 1940), 5–6.
37. Anderson, *Hobo*, 20.
38. Ted Grossardt, "Harvest(ing) Hoboes: The Production of Labor Organization through the Wheat Harvest," *Agricultural History* 70, no. 2 (1996): 286–87.
39. For a listing of some of the different organizations associated with hobos, see Anderson, *Hobo*, 230–49.
40. Lynne Marie Adrian, "Organizing the Rootless: American Hobo Subculture, 1893–1932" (PhD diss., University of Iowa, 1984), 74, 79.
41. Adrian, "Organizing the Rootless," 92–93, quoting editorial, *Hobo News*, July 1919. The relationship between militant Wobblies and editors of the *Hobo News* was contentious. As Wobbly leaders were arrested and expelled and IWW offices closed down after 1918, many former Wobblies found their way into writing for the *Hobo News*. The result was a more radical tone to the papers in both its articles and editorials until infighting and changes of leadership (at one point How was removed from the paper) led to the demise of the paper.
42. For criticism of how the Salvation Army treated hobos, see Edwin A. Brown, *Broke: The Man without the Dime* (London: Browne and Howell, 1913).
43. Roger A. Bruns, *The Damndest Radical: The Life and World of Ben Reitman, Chicago's Celebrated Social Reformer, Hobo King, and Whorehouse Physician* (Champaign: University of Illinois Press), 1–2.
44. Frank O. Beck, *Hobohemia: Emma Goldman, Lucy Parsons, Ben Reitman and Other Agitators and Outsiders in 1920s / 30s Chicago* (1956; new ed., Chicago: Kerr, 2000), 75.
45. Bruns, *Damndest Radical*, 177.
46. Adrian, "Organizing the Rootless," 127.
47. Foster, *Pages from a Worker's Life*, 108.
48. Higbie, *Indispensable Outcasts*, 153.
49. Adrian, "Organizing the Rootless," 136.
50. Bronson Batchelor, "The Hotel de Gink," *Independent*, January 25, 1915, 128.
51. After a series of violent confrontations in Washington State, where Wobblies were protesting U.S. involvement in World War I in 1918, 101 members of the radical union were charged with treason. The trial lasted five months, resulting in all 101 defendants being found guilty and given long sentences. This marked the beginning of the end for the IWW.
52. Misogyny runs deep in many hobo narratives. Dos Passos's depiction of Maisie is troubling but fits within most literary depictions of the hobo. See Floyd Dell's 1926 short story, "Halleluiah, I'm a Bum," in which Jasper, who becomes a migrant worker and joins the IWW, finds his biggest obstacle in life is not capitalism but avoiding marriage and mortgage payments. *Love in Greenwich Village* (New York: Doran, 1926), 153–90.
53. Dos Passos, *42nd Parallel*, 88.
54. Ibid., 89.
55. Christine Photinos, "Villainous Vagrants, Hard-Travelin' Hoboes, and Sisters of the Road: The Figure of the Tramp in American Literature, 1873–1939" (PhD diss., University of California, San Diego, 2000), 119.
56. Frederick Feied, *No Pie in the Sky: The Hobo as American Cultural Hero in the Works of Jack London, John Dos Passos, and Jack Kerouac* (New York: Citadel, 1964), 43–55.

57. Denning, *Cultural Front*, 186; Photinos, "Villainous Vagrants," 148; Dos Passos, *42nd Parallel*, 28.
58. Again, misogyny is rampant throughout these novels. For a detailed discussion of the troubling gendered relations in Dos Passos's *U.S.A.*, see Janet Galligani Casey, *Dos Passos and the Ideology of the Feminine* (Cambridge: Cambridge University Press, 1998), 131–76.
59. Dos Passos, *42nd Parallel*, 85.
60. Ibid., 254.
61. Barbara Foley, *Radical Representations: Politics and Form in U.S. Proletarian Fiction, 1929–1941* (Durham, N.C.: Duke University Press, 1993), 403–4; Nanney, *John Dos Passos Revisited*, 180; Cowley, "John Dos Passos," 34.
62. Moglen, *Mourning Modernity*, 223.
63. Ibid., 221.
64. Dos Passos, *42nd Parallel*, 73.
65. Moglen, *Mourning Modernity*, 223.
66. Dos Passos, *The Big Money*, 372.
67. Ibid.
68. John Dos Passos, "The Pit and the Pendulum," *New Masses* 1 (August 1926): 10–11, 30, in *John Dos Passos: The Major Nonfictional Prose*, ed. Donald Pizer (Detroit: Wayne State University Press, 1988), 89.
69. Thomas Strychacz, *Modernism, Mass Culture, and Professionalism* (Cambridge: Cambridge University Press, 1993), 119.
70. Ibid.

## 5. THE INTERRACIAL BOXCAR

1. Dan T. Carter, *Scottsboro: A Tragedy of the American South* (Baton Rouge: Louisiana State University, 1969), 4.
2. Ibid., 142.
3. *The Scottsboro Boys*, music by John Kander, lyrics by Fred Ebb, and book by David Thompson, Broadway, October 10, 2010.
4. Carter, *Scottsboro*, 31–46.
5. Flee Dustbowl for California," *Business Week*, July 3, 1937, 36.
6. Paul Garon and Gene Tomko, *What's the Use of Walking If There's a Freight Train Going Your Way? Black Hoboes and Their Songs* (Chicago: Kerr, 2006), 4.
7. Woody Guthrie, *Bound for Glory* (1943; New York: Penguin, 2010), 19.
8. Mark Wyman, *Hoboes: Bindlestiffs, Fruit Tramps, and the Harvesting of the West* (New York: Hill and Wang, 2011), 82–99, is a particularly insightful example of how governmental policy favored certain ethnic and racial communities.
9. Errol Lincoln Uys, *Riding the Rails: Teenagers on the Move during the Great Depression* (New York: TV Books, 2000), 31–32, quoting Herman J. P. Schubert, *Twenty-Thousand Transients: A One Year's Sample of Those That Apply for Aid in a Northern City* (Buffalo: Emergency Relief Bureau, 1935).
10. For an informative examination of the gender dynamics of youth while on the road, see Thomas Minehan, *Boy and Girl Tramps in America* (New York: Farrar and Rinehart, 1934).
11. Carter, *Scottsboro*, 13–14, 209, 223–29. Immediately prior to being pulled off the

train in Paint Rock, Price and Bates were in a jungle with other hobos. While the presiding judge refused to allow this testimony into the official record, it does show the intimate connection between Bates and Price with the hobo subculture.

12. James A. Miller, *Remembering Scottsboro: The Legacy of an Infamous Trial* (Princeton, N.J.: Princeton University Press, 2009), 15.
13. Carter, *Scottsboro*, 82.
14. Alfred Maund, *The Big Boxcar* (1957), ed. Alan Wald (Champaign: University of Illinois Press, 1998).
15. Jesse Steiner and Roy M. Brown, *The North Carolina Chain Gang: A Study of County Convict Road Work* (Chapel Hill: University of North Carolina Press, 1927), 134.
16. Uys, *Riding the Rails*, 14, 32, quoting Grace Abbot, chief of the Children's Bureau, Washington, D.C., *Statement on Relief for Unemployed Transients*, Hearings before a Subcommittee of the Committee on Manufacturers on S. 5121, U.S. Senate, 72nd Cong., 2nd sess. (Washington: Government Printing Office, 1933), 23–35.
17. Walter Wilson, *Forced Labor in the United States* (New York: International, 1933), 34–38, 55.
18. Uys, *Riding the Rails*, 13–14, 23, quoting Abbot, *Statement on Relief*, 23–35. "Class One" was designated for railroad corporations that had an operating revenue of more than $1 million.
19. Kingsley Davis, *Youth in the Depression* (Chicago: University of Chicago Press, 1935), 9.
20. Lowell Ames Norris, "America's Homeless Army," *Scribner's Magazine*, May 1933, 316–18.
21. Frank Freidel, *Franklin D. Roosevelt: Launching the New Deal* (New York: Little, Brown, 1973), 255–66. While it did not actually meet this need, when Roosevelt proposed the CCC camps to Congress on March 21, 1933, he stipulated that the camps would feed, clothe, and eventually place back to their homes 250,000 American boys.
22. *Putyovka v zhizn / Road to Life*, directed by Nikolai Ekk (Moscow: Mezhrabpom-film, 1931).
23. Kay Boyle, *Collected Poems of Kay Boyle* (1964; repr., Port Townsend, Wash.: Copper Canyon, 1991), 69–70.
24. Josephine Herbst, "Lynching in the Quiet Manner" (*New Masses*, July 1931), in *Negro: An Anthology*, ed. Nancy Cunard (New York: Continuum, 2002), 175.
25. Walter T. Howard, *Black Communists Speak on Scottsboro: A Documentary History* (Philadelphia: Temple University Press, 2008), 35, quoting B. D. Amis, "Dear Editor," *Liberator*, April 21, 1931, Fond 515, files of the Communist Party of the United States, Comintern Archives (microfilm copies available at the Library of Congress).
26. Robin D. G. Kelley, *Hammer and Hoe: Alabama Communists during the Great Depression* (Chapel Hill: University of North Carolina Press, 1990), 93.
27. Carter, *Scottsboro*, 137, quoting Anna Damen, "Letter," *Nation* 139 (1934): 674.
28. William J. Maxwell, *New Negro, Old Left: African-American Writings and Communism between the Wars* (New York: Columbia University Press, 1999), 133.
29. Howard, *Black Communists Speak*, 37, quoting William L. Patterson, "Judge Lynch Goes to Court," *Labor Defender*, May 1931.
30. J. Miller, *Remembering Scottsboro*, 17; the ACLU report he quotes is Hollace Ransdall, "Report on the Scottsboro, Ala. Case," May 27, 1931.

31. Howard, *Black Communists Speak*, 68, quoting Eugene Gordon, "A Call to Millions," *Labor Defender*, June 1932.
32. Carter, *Scottsboro*, 51.
33. Michael Davis, "Forced to Tramp: The Perspective of the Labor Press, 1870–1900," in *Walking to Work: Tramps in America, 1790 1935*, ed. Eric H. Monkkonen (Lincoln: University of Nebraska Press, 1984), 163, quoting editorial, *John Swinton's Paper*, March 26, 1885.
34. Caren Kaplan, *Questions of Travel: Postmodern Discourses of Displacement* (Durham, N.C.: Duke University Press, 2000), 155.
35. *Heroes for Sale*, directed by William A. Wellman (Burbank, Calif.: Warner Brothers Studio, 1933), DVD; *My Man Godfrey*, directed by Gregory La Cara (Universal City, Calif.: Universal Studios, 1936), DVD; *Riding the Rails: Teenagers on the Move in the Great Depression*, directed by Lexy Lovell (New York: Out of the Blue Productions, 1997), DVD.
36. Chris Robé, *Left of Hollywood: Cinema, Modernism, and the Emergence of U.S. Radical Film Culture* (Austin: University of Texas Press, 2010), 176.
37. *Wild Boys of the Road*, directed by William Wellman Jr. (Burbank, Calif.: Warner Brothers Studio, 1933), DVD.
38. Scott Eyman "Wild Bill William Wellman Interview and Filmography," *Focus on Film* 29 (1978): n.p.; Frank Thompson, "William Wellman: Movies Like the Man—Rugged, Sentimental, Two-Fisted," *American Film* 15, no. 1 (1989): 99.
39. For a comprehensive history of the studio during this decade, see Nick Roddick, *A New Deal in Entertainment: Warner Brothers in the 1930s* (London: British Film Institute, 1983).
40. *The Vagabond Trail*, directed by William A. Wellman (Los Angeles: Fox Film Corporation, 1924).
41. *Beggars of Life*, directed by William A. Wellman (Los Angeles: Paramount Pictures, 1928).
42. This type of interracial relationship is present in another of Jim Tully's books, *The Bruiser* (1936; Kent, Ohio: Kent State University Press, 2010), which has an interracial homosocial relationship between two hobos that bonds the men throughout their lives.
43. Wellman, however, denied any knowledge of the *Bezprizorni* or Ekk's film *Road to Life*. See Paul Buhle, *Radical Hollywood: The Untold Story behind America's Favourite Movies* (London: New Press, 2002), 212.
44. William Wellman Jr., *Forbidden Hollywood Collection*, vol. 3, *Wild Boys of the Road*, director's commentary (1933; Burbank Calif.: TCM Archives, 2009), DVD.
45. Joanne Hall, "Sisters of the Road? The Construction of Female Hobo Identity in the Autobiographies of Ethel Lynn, Barbara Starke and 'Box-car' Bertha Thompson," *Women's Studies* 39, no. 3 (2010): 227.
46. Nelson Algren, *Somebody in Boots* (1935; repr., New York: Thunder Mouth, 1987), 82–85.
47. Ibid., 87, 93–94.
48. Richard H. Pells, *Radical Visions and American Dreams: Culture and Social Thought in the Depression Years* (New York: Harper, 1973), 225.
49. James E. Goodman, *Stories of Scottsboro* (New York: Pantheon Books, 1995), 222.

50. Files Crenshaw and Kenneth A. Miller, *Scottsboro: The Firebrand of Communism* (Montgomery, Ala.: Brown Printing, 1936), 59, 297.
51. The *New York Times*'s review of *Wild Boys of the Road* states, "By endowing it with a happy ending, the producers have robbed it of its value as a social challenge." F.S.N. [Frank S. Nugent], "The Screen: America's Juvenile Hobos," *New York Times*, September 22, 1933.
52. Christine Photinos, "The Figure of the Tramp in Gilded Age Success Narratives," *Journal of Popular Culture* 40, no. 6 (2007): 1003.
53. F.S.N., "America's Juvenile Hobos."
54. Clarence Lee quoted in Uys, *Riding the Rails*, 134.
55. Garon and Tomko, *What's the Use*, 66; Paul Oliver, *Conversations with the Blues* (Cambridge: University of Cambridge Press, 1997), 75; Henry Miller, *On the Fringe: The Dispossessed in America* (Lanham: Lexington, 1991), 152.
56. See Garon and Tomko, *What's the Use*, 115–36.
57. Harry Haywood quoted in Howard, *Black Communists Speak*, 84.
58. Harry Haywood, *Black Bolshevik: Autobiography of an African-American Communist* (Chicago: Liberation, 1978).

## 6. THE SPIRITUAL BOXCAR

1. Jack Kerouac, *The Dharma Bums* (1958; New York: Penguin, 1971), 97.
2. Jack Kerouac, *On the Road* (1957; New York: Penguin, 1994), 105. Unless otherwise noted, all citations refer to this edition.
3. Gerald Nicosia, *Memory Babe: A Critical Biography of Jack Kerouac* (Berkeley: University of California Press, 1994), 247.
4. Kerouac, *On the Road*, 119.
5. Ibid., 173.
6. Jack Kerouac, *The Scripture of the Golden Eternity* (1960; San Francisco: City Lights, 2001), 30.
7. Nicosia, *Memory Babe*, 298.
8. Kerouac, *On the Road*, 140, 307, 91.
9. Ibid., 18.
10. Nicosia, *Memory Babe*, 77, 233.
11. Jack Kerouac, *Lonesome Traveler* (1960; repr., New York: Grove, 1994), 176–77.
12. Kerouac, *On the Road*, 307.
13. Kerouac, *Lonesome Traveler*, 173.
14. Kerouac's letters often recount his hoboing adventures. See Nicosia, *Memory Babe*, 457, 500, for an analysis of two hobo trips.
15. Kerouac, *On the Road*, 41.
16. Kerouac, *Lonesome Traveler*, 173.
17. See Jack Kerouac, *Visions of Cody* (1957; New York: Penguin, 1993), 101–11, and Kerouac, *Pic* (1971), in *Satori in Paris and Pic* (1985; repr., New York: Grove, 1994), 218–36. Kerouac also wrote about the figure in detail in his unpublished journal found in the Berg Archive, November 1, 1947, Winter 1946–48, New York (Ozone Park), New York Public Library.
18. Kerouac, *On the Road*, 104–5.

19. Ibid., 55.
20. John Clellon Holmes quoted in Ann Charters and Samuel Charters, *Brother-Souls: John Clellon Holmes, Jack Kerouac, and the Beat Generation* (Jackson: University Press of Mississippi, 2010).
21. Nicosia, *Memory Babe,* 298.
22. For a discussion of the significance of Kerouac's Franco-American roots, see Joyce Johnson, *The Voice Is All: The Lonely Victory of Jack Kerouac* (New York: Viking, 2012), 3–27. For a discussion of Kerouac's shamanistic writing style, see Thomas R. Bierowski, *Kerouac in Ecstasy: Shamanic Expressions in the Writings* (Jefferson, N.C.: McFarland, 2011).
23. Jack Kerouac, journal entry, November 1, 1947.
24. Norma Walrath Goldstein, "Kerouac's *On the Road*," *Explicator* 50, no. 1 (1991): 61.
25. Elspeth Probyn, "The Spatial Imperative of Subjectivity," in *Handbook of Cultural Geography,* ed. Kay Anderson, Mona Domosh, Steve Pile, and Nigel Thrift (London: Sage, 2003), 290.
26. Nicosia, *Memory Babe,* 189.
27. Kerouac, *On the Road,* 15.
28. Nicosia, *Memory Babe,* 189; Jeffrey Andrew Weinstock, "Lostness (Blair Witch)," in *Nothing That Is: Millennial Cinema and the Blair Witch Controversies,* ed. Sarah L. Higley and Jeffrey Andrew Weinstock (Detroit: Wayne State University Press, 2004), 237.
29. Nicosia, *Memory Babe,* 201.
30. Kerouac, *On the Road,* 106.
31. Gilles Deleuze and Claire Parnet, *Dialogues,* trans. Hugh Tomlinson and Barbara Habberjam (New York: Columbia University Press, 1977), 36–37.
32. Nicosia, *Memory Babe,* 359.
33. Kerouac, *On the Road,* 107.
34. Kerouac, *Lonesome Traveler,* 182, 174.
35. Nicosia, *Memory Babe,* 51, 421; Kerouac, *Lonesome Traveler,* 183.
36. Nicosia, *Memory Babe,* 585.
37. Kerouac, *Visions of Cody,* 38.
38. For information on the Duluoz Legend, see James T. Jones, *Jack Kerouac's Duluoz Legend: The Mythic Form of an Autobiographical Fiction* (Carbondale: Southern Illinois University Press, 1999).
39. Kerouac, *On the Road,* 23–28.
40. Jack Kerouac, "Letter to Neal Cassady, Jan. 10, 1951," in Jack Kerouac, *Kerouac: Selected Letters,* vol. 1, *1940–1956,* ed. Ann Charters (New York: Penguin, 1996), 307.
41. Nicosia, *Memory Babe,* 105.
42. Bob Gilmore, *Harry Partch: A Biography* (New Haven, Conn.: Yale University Press, 1998), 152–55.
43. The story, originally titled "Wine in the Railroad Earth," can be found in Kerouac, *Lonesome Traveler,* 37–84.
44. Gilmore, *Harry Partch,* 154. Partch's "Bitter Music" journal, not published until 1991, is a more straightforward interpretation in which he recounts his attempts to find "American music" in hobo jungles. His recordings of the hobos that he gets to know intimately—he sleeps with them; works with them; laughs, fights, and drinks with them—is a fascinating insight into both Partch and the hobo subculture.

Partch, "Bitter Music," in *Bitter Music: Collected Journals, Essays, Introductions, and Librettos*, ed. Thomas McGeary (Champaign: University of Illinois Press, 1991), 1–132.

45. Nicosia, *Memory Babe*, 664.
46. Gilmore, *Harry Partch*, 154, 153.
47. Ibid., 152.
48. Jason Spangler, "We're on a Road to Nowhere: Steinbeck, Kerouac and the Legacy of the Great Depression," *Studies in the Novel* 40, no. 3 (2008): 312–14.
49. Ibid., 322
50. Mary Paniccia Carden, "Adventures in Auto-Eroticism: Economies of Traveling Masculinity in Autobiographical Texts by Jack Kerouac and Neal Cassady," *Journeys* 7, no. 1 (2006): 1, 9.
51. Kerouac, *On the Road*, 8. For a discussion of the Beats and their male protest against white-collar work and suburbanized family life, see Barbara Ehrenreich, *The Hearts of Men: American Dreams and the Flight from Commitment* (New York: Anchor, 1987), 52–68.
52. Jack Kerouac, *On the Road: The Original Scroll* (New York: Penguin Classics, 2008), 109.
53. Kerouac, *On the Road*, 302.
54. Justin Thomas Trudeau, "Specters in the Rear-View: Haunting Whiteness in Jack Kerouac's *On the Road*," *Text and Performance Quarterly* 31, no. 2 (2011): 156.
55. Jack Kerouac, *Big Sur* (1962; New York: Penguin, 1992), iv.
56. Deborah Frehem, *Ghost Stories of St. Petersburg, Clearwater and Pinellas County: Takes from a Haunted Peninsula* (Charleston: Haunted Press, 2007), 82–83.

## AFTERWORD: THE END OF BOXCAR POLITICS

1. Mark Wyman, *Hoboes: Bindlestiffs, Fruit Tramps, and the Harvesting of the West* (New York: Hill and Wang, 2011), 271, 257–76.
2. Wyman, *Hoboes*, 261, quoting Fred Cummings, House Committee on Immigration and Naturalization, *Seasonal Agricultural Laborers from Mexico*, 1926.
3. Jack Kerouac, *Lonesome Traveler* (1960; repr., New York: Grove, 1994), 181.
4. For a history of the publication saga of *On the Road*, see Adam Gussow, "Bohemia Revisited: Malcolm Cowley, Jack Kerouac and *On the Road*," *Georgia Review* 38, no. 2 (1984): 298–311.
5. Paul S. Boyer, *Promises to Keep: The United States since World War II* (New York: Houghton Mifflin, 1999), 106.
6. John Alfred Heitmann, *The Automobile in American Life* (New York: McFarland, 2009), 134–35.
7. Cotton Seiler, *Republic of Drivers: A Cultural History of Automobility in America* (Chicago: University of Chicago Press, 2008), 10.
8. Jane Stern, *Auto Ads* (New York: Random House, 1978), 27.
9. Phil Patton, *The Open Road: A Celebration of the American Highway* (New York: Simon and Schuster, 1987), 13.
10. Jeff T. Brouws, Bernd Polster, and Phil Patton, *Highway: America's Endless Dream* (New York: Stewart, Tabori, and Chang, 1997), 32.
11. See John A. Jakle and Keith A. Sculle, *Fast Food: Roadside Restaurants in the Automobile*

*Age* (Baltimore: Johns Hopkins University Press, 2004); see Richard W. Longstreth, *City Center to Regional Mall: Architecture, the Automobile and Retailing in Los Angeles, 1920–1950* (Cambridge: MIT Press, 1998); Jane Holtz Kay, *Asphalt Nation: How the Automobile Took Over America and How We Can Take It Back* (Berkeley: University of California Press, 1997), 221–47; Brouws, Polster, and Patton, *Highway*, 32; and Jack Kerouac, *On the Road* (1957; New York: Penguin, 1994), 100. For a discussion of the way Dean embraces America's standardization, see Roger N. Casey, *Textual Vehicles* (New York: Garland Science, 1997), 112.

12. George M. Humphrey quoted in Seiler, *Republic of Drivers*, 100.
13. Michael J. Berger, *The Automobile in American History and Culture: A Reference Guide* (Westport, Conn.: Greenwood, 2001), 143.
14. Stephen B. Goddard, *Getting There: The Epic Struggle between Road and Rail in the American Century* (Chicago: University of Chicago Press, 1996), 49, 57.
15. Blaine A. Brownell, "A Symbol of Modernity: Attitudes toward the Automobile in Southern Cities in the 1920s," *American Quarterly* 24, no. 1 (1972): 43.
16. James J. Flink, *The Automobile Age* (Cambridge: MIT Press, 1990), 73–112.
17. Goddard, *Getting There*, 155.
18. Car production came to a grinding halt when the United States became involved in World War II and the auto industry became part of the government mobilization effort. Car companies, responsible for producing one-fifth of the U.S. military supplies, however, saw large profits during these war years. See Robert Sickels, *1940s* (Westport, Conn.: Greenwood, 2004), 206–7.
19. Quoted in Goddard, *Getting There*, 138.
20. Rudolph Daniels, *Trains across the Continent: North American Railroad History* (Bloomington: Indiana University Press, 2001), 163. From 1945 to 1960 rail freight declined almost 30 percent, and by the 1970s railroads carried only about 40 percent of the nation's freight. It was not any better for the workers themselves: immediately after World War II, railways employed about 1,400,000 workers. By the late 1950s the numbers decreased to 780,000.
21. Brouws, Polster, and Patton, *Highway*, 43.
22. Edith Wharton, *A Motor Flight through France* (New York: Scribner's Sons, 1908), 1.
23. Thomas MacDonald quoted in Goddard, *Getting There*, 109, 103.
24. See Wyman, *Hoboes*, 257–76.
25. Fredrick Mills quoted in Gregory R. Woirol, *In the Floating Army: F. C. Mills on Itinerant Life in California* (Urbana: University of Illinois Press, 1992), 83.
26. Wyman, *Hoboes*, 259.
27. Frank Tobias Higbie, *Indispensable Outcasts: Hobo Workers and Community in the American Midwest, 1880–1930* (Urbana: University of Illinois Press, 2003).
28. Ibid., 212, 206.
29. Wyman, *Hoboes*, 258.
30. Ben Benson, "Hobo Benson's Story: Hoboes of America," *Hobo News*, February 1937.
31. Dale Maharidge, *The Last Great American Hobo* (New York: Prima, 1993); Jacqueline Schmidt, *Done and Been: Steel Rail Chronicles of American Hobos* (Bloomington: Indiana University Press, 1996); Ted Conover, *Rolling Nowhere: Riding the Rails with America's Hoboes* (1984; New York: Vintage, 2001), xix; Cliff (Oats) Williams, *One More Train to Ride: The Underground World of Modern American Hoboes*

(Bloomington: Indiana University Press, 2003); William T. Vollman, *Riding toward Everywhere* (New York: HarperCollins, 2008).

32. Eddy Joe Cotton, *Hobo: A Young Man's Thoughts on Trains and Tramping in America* (New York: Harmony Books, 2002), 72.
33. In *Rolling Nowhere*, Conover, an accomplished journalist, questions the rhetoric of the older hobos whom he talks to and is skeptical of the way the hobo subculture remembers itself. He also meets nonwhite train hoppers, leading him to wonder about their relationship to the hobo subculture.
34. Since the 1980s, there have been other examinations of train riders who do not fit the hobo stereotype; unlike Eddy Joe Cotton, though, there is not a link between these riders and a hobo history. See Ted Conover, *Coyotes: A Journey across Borders with America's Illegal Migrants* (Minneapolis: Tandem Library Press, 1987); Sonia Nazario, *Enrique's Journey* (New York: Random House, 2007); Cary Fukunaga, *Sin Nombre* (Universal City, Calif.: Universal Studios, 2009), DVD; Rebecca Cammisa, *Which Way Home?* (New York: Docurama Films, 2010), DVD.
35. See Jean Paul Rodrique, *The Geography of Transport Systems* (New York: Routledge, 2009).
36. Jessica Hahn, *Transient Ways* (San Francisco: Passing Thru, 2002); Sascha DuBrul, *Carnival of Chaos: On the Road with the Nomadic Festival* (New York: Autonomedia, 1996; Michael Brody, *A Period of Juvenile Prosperity* (San Francisco: Twin Palm, 2013); Daniel Skaggs, *Freeload* (Missoula, Mont.: Highway Goat Productions, 2013); Steve Kilar, "Couple Found Dead in Florida Coal Pile Enjoyed Riding Freight Trains," *Baltimore Sun*, December 16, 2011.
37. Douglas Harper, *Good Company: A Tramp Life* (Chicago: University of Chicago Press, 1982), 192–96.
38. Wyman, *Hoboes*, 273.

# INDEX

JOHN LENNON received a PhD from Lehigh University and is an assistant professor of English at the University of South Florida.